flow

flow

Women's Counternarratives from Rivers, Rock, and Sky

Edited by Denisa Krásná and Alena Rainsberry

RMB

First Edition

For information on purchasing bulk quantities of this book, or to obtain media excerpts or invite the author to speak at an event, please visit rmbooks.com and select the "Contact" tab.

RMB | Rocky Mountain Books Ltd.
rmbooks.com
@rm_books
facebook.com/rmbooks

Cataloguing data available from Library and Archives Canada
ISBN 9781771607063 (paperback)
ISBN 9781771607070 (electronic)

Front cover: In her hometown of Tlayacapan, México, Brenda Gómez Ortiz highlines in front of the mountain Zihuapapalotl, which means "Butterfly Women" in Náhuatl. Photo by Kari Altuzar.

Frontispiece: A celebration of female athletes in Cheakamus Canyon, British Columbia. Alena Rainsberry, Brenda Gómez Ortiz, and Denisa Krásná simultaneously showcase whitewater kayaking, rock climbing, and highlining. Photo by Kate Candace Burke.

If an image is not credited, the credit is unknown.

Printed and bound in Malaysia

We acknowledge the financial support of the Government of Canada through the Canada Book Fund and the Canada Council for the Arts, and of the province of British Columbia through the British Columbia Arts Council and the Book Publishing Tax Credit.

To the fearless women who navigate the currents of adventure,
challenge the status quo, and redefine boundaries with each daring pursuit.
Your courage, resilience, and unwavering spirit inspire us all to seek our own flow.
This book is dedicated to you.

CONTENTS

Kavitha Mohan climbing in Badami, India.
Photo by Denisa Krásná.

FOREWORD

Learning to Tell Other Kinds of Outdoor Stories

I have been talked over, discredited, and not seen.
Despite my experience and skill, I am often overlooked as a person of value in the outdoors.

—Sydney Pham

As I wrote in *False Summit: Gender in Mountaineering Nonfiction*, the stories we have to tell about the outdoors and about ourselves matter. Who gets to tell stories and what kinds of stories are thought to be the right ones have influenced ideas about the environment, the meaning of risk and extreme sports in our lives, and even what kinds of lives we have been allowed to imagine for ourselves. Stories make things possible for those who listen to them. If stories of adventure only have one kind of narrative, for instance the idea of the Sherpa "Tharkey" (modeled on the real sherpa, Ang Tharkay) as helpful to white adventurers but not as committed to success as the white hero Tintin in the comic *Tintin in Tibet*, you might imagine that the only true adventurers are neocolonial white men and boys, and only the stories they have to tell are the ones we need to hear. If we think the only stories about outdoor sports that count are about a very narrow idea of what adventure is, our understanding of ourselves and the wilderness itself will become very narrow too.

If we change what we think success in the outdoors means and pay attention to the factors that lead to an outdoor life, there is so much more we can learn about and enjoy. Many of the writers in this book have had to surmount obstacles far greater than the summit of a peak or a successful session on a slackline. They have had to "prove" themselves as worthy of being included in the worlds of adventure sports before they could even begin to do what they love. So much of the lure of the outdoors involves the possibility that, when we are in nature, the restrictions of culture, including racism, sexism, and poverty, fall away. But the truth of being outdoors is that cultural norms come with us and can form a weight as heavy as that extra water you are carrying in your backpack, just in case. That weight keeps people thought to have the "wrong" bodies for adventure, including women, members of the BIPOC community, members of the 2SLGBTQIA+ community, and disabled people, away from even thinking they could try life outdoors and thrive there. Limited stories of masculine, neocolonial heroism continue to be powerful in the outdoor sports communities because it is assumed that ideas about conquering obstacles are the most important, and that time in the wilderness has to be an account of mastery

Naina Adhikari in front of the Minus Rapids on the Zambezi river in Zambia. Photo by Benny Marr.

over it and over others. Such assumptions do two things: they belittle and even exclude all the other ways of being outside, and they legitimate only those who make themselves fit the mold of white, masculine heroism, because that is the only heroism on offer. Everyone else just can't cut it. And that is what people who are thought to have the wrong bodies for adventure carry with them into the wilderness, weighing down every step they take as they try to imagine how to belong.

The stories in *Flow* lighten that cultural weight. Here you will find an account of "flow" not just as the heightened state of existence, when all problems fall away and someone is "one" with the activity. This kind of flow suspends culture, and the world falls away. But as Dorothea Hamilton points out in her essay "Like a Regular Mom, Just Cooler," flow is actually cultural and has a politics because of all the work it requires to get to that state. "The truth is," she says, "in order to find these flow moments in outdoor sports, you need a lot of practice." Practice takes time, expertise, and collaboration with other people. It takes a level of sacrifice that is not always possible for people who experience barriers to participation. That is why flow, and other heightened states of consciousness talked about in so many accounts of mountain climbing, rock climbing, surfing, kayaking, highlining, and other outdoor sports, is often associated with elite men who achieve it. It is less associated with women, who remain bound to the concerns of this world, with child care that can't always be arranged or jobs that can't be quit. Cooks in base camp and mountain porters are never expected to experience flow either, because they are supposed to look after those who do.

So what if we start to tell stories about flow that are also about the flow of our lives into the wilderness as a way to name the barriers to participation and to change what a good outdoor story is supposed to be about? It matters that Darcy Gaechter details "a long history of being told I can't do things because I'm too little, too short, not strong enough, or just because I'm a woman" in the world of kayaking, and puts dealing with sexism on the same level as navigating difficult whitewater. Stories in *Flow* about how to actually become a highliner or an elite rock climber when, as a woman, or a queer or BIPOC person, there are no obvious ways to be mentored, trained, and taken seriously by others in the sport show how important it is to understand what it takes to even arrive at the scene of an activity and participate in its culture.

In that arrival, at the launch point, the crag, the place where the line is rigged, at a place in life where they know and love what they do, the writers of these essays recount the moments of joy, achievement, and community that come after hard work and sacrifice. "I came to believe I deserved to be in these spaces," Sydney Pham writes of her career as a rock climber. Pham's belief in herself and in her own story marks the beginning of other ways to tell stories of the outdoors that change who belongs in the wilderness and what stories of the wilderness we should be ready to encounter.

—Julie Rak

Professor at the Department of English and Film Studies,
University of Alberta

ACKNOWLEDGEMENTS

First, we want to acknowledge Don Gorman, our editor Kirsten Craven, our proofreader Peter Enman, and the entire Rocky Mountain Books publishing team. Thank you for trusting in *Flow* and giving us the opportunity to bring this project to life.

Next, we want to extend our most heartfelt gratitude to the authors of *Flow* for believing in us and bringing their stories to light. You are inspirations to women everywhere by boldly being your most authentic, adventurous selves.

We want to acknowledge our mothers, Markéta Krásná and Sharon Rainsberry, for raising us to be strong women and encouraging us to pursue wild, beautiful lives on our own terms. Thank you for the gift of life, and for being our first and most unwavering cheerleaders.

I, Denisa, also want to thank my dad and my best friend in one person, Jiří Krásný, for inspiring me to embrace a life of nonconformity, rebellion, adventure, and happiness, urging me to follow my own vision rather than succumb to societal expectations.

I, Alena, want to express gratitude for my sisters, Alyssa Vecht and Elisa Reverman. Navigating girlhood growing pains and adolescent awkwardness with you was a privilege. I ceaselessly take inspiration from watching you both build and embody unapologetic lives.

We want to thank our friends and outdoor communities. Nothing is worth doing without adventure buddies to share in the joy and help you learn from your mistakes. Thank you for the camaraderie, acceptance, support, and many beautiful memories.

Lastly, we are thankful for our mentors along the way. We want to extend a special thank you to the women who have taught us in the roller-coaster journey of life. And to the women we both have and have not had the privilege of meeting who have blazed the path of adventure before us – thank you for showing everyone what is possible as living examples of women pursuing their wildest lives.

Marianna Tarczyńska taking a rest in a knee brace while sending "Muerte Subita" in Cuyuja, Ecuador. Photo by Elisa Toledo.

INTRODUCTION

Sowing the Seeds of Empowerment

It was the end of April 2022, five in the morning, when we set out for a long drive from Squamish, British Columbia, down to Mariposa, California, more than a thousand miles away. Listening to a classic Fleetwood Mac album, we turned onto Interstate 5 in the direction of Portland. Belting out the lyrics to "Go Your Own Way," we were already wide awake and excited for our next adventures in the Yosemite Valley, the climbing mecca and the birthplace of slacklining. It was also to become the birthplace of this book, whose first seeds we sowed in Canada in the past few weeks.

We traveled to Yosemite to cat-sit for a friend. It was the ideal excuse to live near the valley for a month. A cat and Yosemite? It didn't take long to convince us. Balancing work in the mornings and climbing in the afternoons became our routine. But since we arrived on Friday, we decided to spend our first day in the park with a proper challenge. The Half Dome. We hiked, climbed, feared, cried (well, almost), ran, and had fun. There was only one major disadvantage to climbing the Dome before the start of the season: a more challenging descent. Instead of the relatively comfortable wooden stairs installed there for hikers during the summer season, we had to make our way down the dramatic backslope of the Dome on two heavy steel cables, using prusiks for safety. All in all, it took us 23 hours to get back to our temporary home where Tulip, the cat, was awaiting us.

Anna Hanuš Kuchařová in Malta. Photo by Dan Černoch

This adventure left us slightly shaken for the next few days. Both physically and mentally. But at the same time we were feeling more energetic than ever. Although we had been on many adventures together before, there was something special about this intense climb. We both felt it and kept discussing it over tea and pancakes on the terrace during our work breaks. Soon, we came to the conclusion that, while we both value our male adventure buddies, this experience was different because we had to rely fully on each other, and there was no illusion of safety that we often attach to our male buddies. There were some intense moments on the Dome when we might have defaulted to letting our male buddies take the lead, but since they weren't there, we felt more responsible for each other. And more courageous too. More empowered.

This experience sparked our search for women who shared similar sentiments. Despite discovering a handful of inspirational books by well-established women climbers, we felt a void – a lack of stories from a broader spectrum of voices. Where were the stories from non-white women? From queer women? From those hailing from beyond the United States? We found one book that addresses the same concerns we were raising:

False Summit: Gender in Mountaineering Nonfiction by Canadian scholar, writer, and climber Julie Rak.

False Summit explores how gender, power, and representation intersect in climbing. Focusing on mountaineering nonfiction, Julie highlights how literature shapes a predominantly masculine identity in climbing, perpetuating gender disparities. She exposes the cultural construct of a "traditional mountaineering body," contributing to the marginalization of climbers who don't fit the hypermasculine mold. The heroic male climber, celebrated for physical strength and a fearless attitude, has defined climbing in a way that sidelines those who don't conform to this stereotype. Julie uses the metaphor of the "false summit" to vividly portray the challenges faced by climbers not recognized as legitimate based on societal norms. Similar to reaching what seems like a mountain peak, only to find it is a deceptive ridge obscuring the actual summit, the metaphor symbolizes the struggles of climbers who diverge from traditional ideals as perpetuated by outdoor narratives. Women, disabled individuals, and non-white climbers achieve remarkable feats, but their accomplishments often go unnoticed due to ingrained gender, ableist, or racial biases.

Furthermore, *False Summit* emphasizes that writing about climbing is integral, not peripheral, to the activity itself. Julie contends that these narratives are not mere accounts of adventures but crucial contributions to our collective understanding of climbing, identity, and humanity's connection with nature. These stories, far from being just personal anecdotes, function as essential cultural artifacts offering a window into the essence of what defines a "successful" mountaineer and an adventurer more generally. Julie advocates for more diverse, inclusive, and truthful outdoor counternarratives that challenge and expand upon entrenched norms. As she aptly declares, "It is time for other stories of achievement to matter as well."[1]

We couldn't agree more with Julie, whose words resonated with us. We want to read more stories from women adventurers. We also crave narratives that go beyond the conventional tales of reaching summits or conquering projects. While those achievements are significant, for many people they are not the main motivations for pursuing outdoor activities. We yearn for stories that illuminate the diverse facets of adventures, capturing the essence of our experiences beyond the pinnacle moments.

Back in Canada, it had dawned on us that our two main sports – whitewater kayaking and highlining – lack representation. In Yosemite, Julie's book reminded us yet again of the persistent lack of diverse stories within adventure sports and the urgent need for more authentic representation. A surge of energy fueled by the joy and empowerment from our Half Dome adventure inspired the convergence of these two ideas, leading to the concept for this book. We wasted no time, and by the end of the week we started approaching potential authors with our book proposal. Approaching the project with the urgency and responsibility akin to our climb up Half Dome, our profound hope is that this book imparts the same sense of empowerment to both our authors and readers that we experienced after our exhilarating climb.

Faith Dickey in the Fruit Bowl in Moab, Utah. Photo by Max Haimowitz.

Planting Diversity in Adventure Sports

The resulting book is a life writing collection of personal stories from female whitewater kayakers, climbers/mountaineers, and highliners from across the world. In other words, it is a collective effort by women who love spending time outdoors to make visible the often-underrepresented female experiences in adventure sports. The pages resonate with their genuine passion for their sports, creating a narrative that captures the essence of their adventures. While *Flow* aims to encapsulate the collective, shared experiences of these extraordinary women, it also presents a wide variety of personal stories from a diverse group of authors from different backgrounds who share their reflections on their journeys in the world of adventure sports. These stories provide an intimate and authentic look into the challenges and triumphs that women face in these white-male-dominated fields, and how they navigate the intersection of their identities within the context of the sports they love.

Flow includes contributions from a wide range of perspectives. From rising, ambitious intermediates to pioneers and world-class athletes. From countries across the world, all walks of life, races and ethnicities, ages, sexual identities and orientations, and from new athletes to women who have been rocking it in their sport for decades. As such, the book provides a platform for women whose voices have been historically silenced and whose perspectives continue to be vastly underrepresented. These include perspectives of racially minoritized women, queer women, women who are mothers, and retired women, as well as narratives from women from minority, non-English-speaking countries whose stories are rarely heard because of linguistic discrimination. The voices in this book present novel ways of connecting with the sport and the outdoors, the environment, and the community. By highlighting the sports' many intersections and establishing commonalities between the diverse female experiences in their communities, the book posits adventure sports as a potential site for the new wave of feminism through which women can both contest gender stereotypes and reaffirm their femininity.

Though *Flow* primarily focuses on the female experience, the authors take an intersectional approach in their analysis of the roles of gender, race, class, and sexuality in the social construction of adventure sports, as well as in their consideration of disparities in access to the outdoors. The main purpose of this book is to emphasize diverse ways of practicing adventure sports to challenge and help change the current white-male-dominated narrative that has long narrowly defined what constitutes success and further perpetuates inequality in these sports and beyond. Some of the stories in this book reflect on the ongoing gender disparity in these sports and identify the continuing patterns that keep the status quo intact. Other stories celebrate adventure sports for their nonconformity and liberating nature and highlight their potential to foster transcultural alliances and connections across difference and motivate a more conscious living with nature, in a balanced, sustainable way.

Flow is the first to draw connections between these three seemingly unrelated outdoor sports. And as you read through the stories you will encounter more connections than differences. Often classified as outdoor, "extreme" adventure, or lifestyle sports, whitewater kayaking, climbing/mountaineering, and highlining all require a high level of physical fitness, strength, and endurance, both physical and mental. They all inspire a strong connection to nature and involve navigating challenging terrain, such as rushing rapids or steep rock faces, often in remote and challenging locations. They all require a certain level of technical skill and knowledge of equipment and safety techniques. Additionally, they require balance, humility, surrender, respect, vulnerability, confidence, and trust. The value placed on aesthetics, particularly the beauty of the "line," is also common to all three sports. While competitive disciplines exist in each, competitions are not the most common variation of each sport. Rather, they each promote cooperation, community values, sustainable lifestyle, and connection with the environment. They also show how success should be personal, fluid, and constantly redefined.

While providing a safe base to return to, the three adventure sports covered in *Flow* serve as a means to discuss more universal topics that are relevant to a wide range of outdoor activities, as well as society in the broadest sense. For example, authors describe how their sports facilitate deeper connection with nature and provide means for both personal and societal change. In addition, the authors discuss the influence of their sports on their identity. They reflect on how much their sports define who they are and how they see themselves versus how others see them. They consider the impact of their sports on their resilience, determination, passion, discipline, bravery, and other personal qualities.

As many of the stories will show, these adventure sports require that their practitioners learn how to work with and through fear. The authors consider the balance between community and competition in their sports and assess their relationship to risk and danger by recounting how they grapple with fear and other mental challenges. While fear is often shown as gendered, it is a universal emotion experienced by people of all cultures, ages, and backgrounds, and can thus create a sense of shared vulnerability and connection.

Through their experiences, the book's authors offer us an array of counternarratives that challenge conventional wisdom and inspire us to see the world in new and different ways. Despite their diverse backgrounds and life paths, these women have a lot in common. Disturbingly, their accounts show that (gender) discrimination, inequality, misrepresentation, and exclusion still exist in the world of adventure sports. However, their stories also offer hope and show how the "extremeness" of these sports can both be weaponized and used to promote freedom and equality. *Flow* shows how adventure sports can become the new site for international transcultural feminism that bridges differences. The women in this book may come from very diverse backgrounds, but they all share their passion for pushing their limits and embracing the unknown.

Flow

The word "flow" in the book's title has multiple literal and symbolic meanings, which are characteristic of all three sports. Most importantly, it refers to the flow state, or being in the flow, a state of mind in which one is fully engaged in an activity and

Mueller

lost in the present moment. Adventure sports often serve as a means to enter the flow state that others strive to achieve through practices like meditation. Time, too, takes on a different cadence within the immersive activities of adventure sports. When we are fully engrossed in an activity, the conventional passage of time often transforms, creating a space where moments stretch, compress, and take on a unique rhythm. This temporal flow adds another layer to the richness of the experiences shared within the book.

Additionally, the term "flow" symbolizes the fluidity and interconnectedness inherent in these sports, where movement and momentum become integral components of the overall experience. The rhythmic harmony of the activities mirrors the seamless mental state of being in flow, creating a synergy between physical engagement and mental absorption. But flow extends beyond the elemental and physical aspects; it encapsulates the broader concept of moving with or against flow. The significance of flow in its myriad manifestations, whether in the gentle current of a river, the subtle movement of air, or the dynamic motion of physical activity, underscores the essence of this book.

The narrative in this book also flows organically, and the organization of chapters into three parts – Rivers, Rock, and Sky – mirrors the natural landscape. This intentional structure enhances the thematic unity of the collection while offering readers a metaphorical journey through various terrains. Each part also contains a short introduction to the sport covered, providing context and insight into the sports explored in the book, making the exploration of outdoor adventures more accessible and enjoyable for all readers. These introductions serve as navigational guides that ensure readers, whether familiar or new to these outdoor activities, can fully immerse themselves in the flow of the collection, appreciating the nuances of each adventure sport. The glossary also serves as a valuable companion, enhancing the reader's understanding and engagement with the specific terminology associated with the sports depicted. It becomes a bridge between the seasoned adventurer and the curious novice, fostering a shared language that bridges the gap between experiences and understanding.

Embedded within these narratives are overarching themes that resonate across disciplines and backgrounds. Fear, flow, time, representation, community, control, connection, determination, vulnerability, pressure, injuries, spirituality, and personal growth, among others, all emerge as powerful forces shaping the experiences of adventure athletes. Whether confronting their deepest fears, finding solace in the flow, or forging lifelong connections within their community, these athletes reveal the profound impact of adventure sports on their lives and identities.

Ultimately, the stories captured within the pages of *Flow* exemplify the breadth of human experience and the transformative power of adventure sports to inspire, challenge, and unite individuals throughout the world. We believe this book will touch many hearts and inspire its readers to pursue their own passions and dreams, to break down barriers, and to live life to the fullest.

Faith Dickey, the first professional female highliner.
Photo by Max Haimowitz.

PART I: RIVERS

Whitewater Kayaking

Whitewater kayaking is a discipline of kayaking practiced in rivers where the landscape has enough change in gradient for the water to form features as it moves downstream. As water flows down mountains and through valleys, it passes over rocks and uneven ground, which creates turbulence – rapids. The agitation of water in rapids causes the water to mix with the surrounding air, and it is the aerated water – whitewater – that kayakers are drawn to. In essence, whitewater kayaking involves navigating through rapids and the natural features of a river in a kayak using a paddle for steering and power. Rapids can vary in difficulty from small waves to enormous features. Navigating, or running, rapids requires significant planning and skill, as well as immense mental fortitude.

Although imperfect and often debated in the kayaking community, the standard system used to describe whitewater is a I–V scale. As the number increases, so does the difficulty and associated danger. Class I is used to describe moving flatwater. New kayakers

Maddie Kimmel throws her paddle on Salto Blanco del Sur Waterfall in Chile. Photo by Logan Smith.

often practice on beginner-friendly class II rapids to master basic skills. Class III rapids require more skill and technique to navigate. Increasing in size and consequences, class IV rapids involve even more advanced skills. Class V rapids demand expert techniques and capability to paddle, and mistakes can be extremely dangerous.

Millennia before inland rivers were explored by whitewater kayak, the Indigenous Inuit and Aleut Peoples of the Arctic created the world's first known kayaks for hunting and traveling in icy waterways. Crafted from skins stretched over a frame of whalebones or wood, these first kayaks laid the foundation for the modern sea kayak. Designed for traveling on lakes and oceans, sea kayaks are 14–20 feet (4–6 m) in length and are often made from lightweight fiberglass. Whitewater kayaks have deviated even further from their Artic roots. They are much shorter – usually 7–10 feet (2–3 m) long – allowing paddlers greater maneuverability in a dynamic river environment, and are made from tough plastic to allow for impact against rocks.

Advances in whitewater kayaking were spurred by early innovations and interest in whitewater rafting, which started to become commercially available in the 1940s on the Salmon River in Idaho. Rafting allowed people to experience wild rivers in unprecedented ways and increased in popularity over the decades. In tandem, innovators were improving the technology of whitewater kayaks and safety equipment like helmets and personal flotation devices (PFDs), allowing for steeper and bigger rivers to be run in the 1970s and 1980s.

Today, whitewater kayakers seek rivers to paddle all over the world and enjoy many different styles of river. Two of the main categories of rivers are "big water" and "creeking." Big water paddling involves large volumes of water, usually in wide rivers, with large waves and huge holes. "Holes" are a hydraulic feature characterized by water flowing back upstream after passing over a depression or boulder. This backflow creates turbulence that can be powerful enough to flip a kayaker and is one of the most common features to be navigated around in a river. Creeking is typically used to describe narrower, steeper, lower-volume rivers or creeks. Technical moves are required to navigate around rocks and over steep drops. One key technique is a "boof" stroke. Taking a boof stroke, or "boofing," is a special paddle stroke a kayaker uses at the top of a drop or feature to propel a kayaker over it to avoid getting caught in the turbulence below.

Perhaps the most dramatic discipline of kayaking is running waterfalls. Many kayakers are drawn to the allure of free fall and the beautiful lines of waterfalls all over the world. Extreme precision is required as falling from such heights can be dangerous. When a kayaker goes over the edge, or lip, of a waterfall, the impact of the landing can put immense force on the body.

The most established whitewater competition is slalom racing. Slalom is a competitive style of racing where participants are timed while navigating downstream and upstream gates in whitewater. First appearing in the Olympics in 1932 under the greater category of canoe slalom, the first slalom races took place on flatwater. As the sport evolved, canals were constructed to create artificial riverways, allowing slalom moves to be practiced on whitewater.

Freestyle kayaking, or playboating, is the art of performing tricks in standing waves, either in the river or in an artificial whitewater playpark. Playboating is typically practiced in a short, or "slicey" (lower-volume), playboat, allowing for greater maneuverability. Competitions are held for kayakers to perform combinations of surfing, flips, and spins for points. For some kayakers, playboating is not confined to playparks, and they take playboating techniques to the river. Downriver freestyle blends freestyle moves with river running, bringing impressive tricks to new heights, including flips and arial rolls over waterfalls.

Whitewater kayaking requires commitment to become proficient and to learn proper safety techniques. The steep learning curve can be a deterrent for many as it often involves capsizing, or flipping, in the river many times before a beginner paddler gains enough practice to stay upright. A key part of whitewater kayaking is the "roll" – when a kayaker accidentally flips upside down, they must flip back upright in the water without exiting the kayak. By using a sweeping motion of the paddle, it's possible to leverage the boat to rotate and roll upright. Learning to roll is a critical part of the learning process in order for the kayaker to avoid a "swim" after each flip.

When someone flips upside down and cannot roll back up, they must swim, or wet-exit, the kayak. This involves pulling a handle on the sprayskirt that is worn around the waist and wraps around the cockpit of the kayak, keeping the inside of the boat from filling with water. When a kayaker pulls the sprayskirt, they can separate themselves from the kayak. Swimming can be dangerous, especially in higher-class rapids, because the person is often exposed to rocks and water features as they go through rapids without a boat. A "swimmer" must get to the side of the river, often involving a rescue by a fellow kayaker. Swimming is an unavoidable part of the learning process for beginners, but as kayakers progress they aim to minimize swimming as consequences increase and rescue efforts involve more risk.

Safety is a key component of kayaking. Mistakes on the river can quickly turn into a dangerous situation, and kayakers must pivot to handle sudden rescue efforts. A standard piece of gear to carry on the river is a throw bag, a rope attached to a small bag. Holding one side of the rope and throwing the bag at the swimmer allows them to be pulled to shore. The dependence on each other for safety creates a social dynamic where kayakers tend to paddle with people they deeply trust. Members of a crew often feel strongly bonded to the others, knowing their friends will mobilize to action in a rescue situation.

For many kayakers, time on the river is not just a sport; it's a lifestyle. A large part of river life takes place at the "put-ins" and "take-outs," the beginnings and endings of a stretch of river. River access points at parking lots and highway pullouts can be filled with lounging paddlers. When they aren't pushing their limits in whitewater, kayakers like to sit back and chill out, reinforcing community bonding off the water as well as on it. This "what's the rush?" mindset reflects the relaxed nature of river life that kayakers embrace. Inspired by the noise of car keys jangling in someone's hand, parking lot "jangle" is a staple of kayaking culture.

The social aspect of kayaking culture also manifests in kayaking festivals and races organized around the world. Following seasonal river flows, kayakers gather to test their racing skills and participate in festive community events on rivers revered for the quality and difficulty of their whitewater.

In recent years, there has been a growing movement of events organized for women, BIPOC kayakers, and new paddlers. Groups like Diversify Whitewater are dedicated to promoting equity and access to the whitewater world. There has also been growth in the number of events organized to celebrate the accomplishments of female kayakers, highlighting experts pushing the extreme limits of the sport, as well as rising stars who are starting to make big waves in the community. *Flow* aims to contribute to the movement by increasing the representation of kayakers who are helping to refresh the narratives told of the whitewater world.

pyranha
ROYALE

CHAPTER 1

Eddying Out for Injuries: Reflections from the Bench

By Maddie Kimmel

Should I run it or portage? It was another Saturday lap on the Little White Salmon River in Washington, one of the most classic class V runs in North America. It's a kayaker's paradise; the water is bright blue and green moss decorates the almost endless boulder gardens and waterfalls. Running the Little White is like a dance in the way that you count your strokes from Getting Busy, the first rapid, all the way to the fish ladders at the end. The squad and I had regrouped right above Spirit, a 30-foot (9-m) waterfall toward the end of the run.

I've run Spirit countless times before and the uncertainty wasn't coming from a place of insecurity in my abilities. As addicting as the feeling of soaring off the lip feels, the landing on Spirit tends to be higher impact than other waterfalls of similar heights. It's also the third to last significant rapid on the Little White, and after an otherwise good lap, it is tempting to portage to avoid taking the high-impact hit from the landing and having to immediately deal with the following mess that is Chaos. Chaos isn't a particularly tall drop, but it has a swirly entrance and a canyoned-in landing. If you mess it up, the only way to get out is by getting roped out by your friends to be pulled to shore. In the end, I decided to run Spirit instead of portaging because, at the moment, it sounded like the most fun option!

I left the eddy and charged to the horizon line. Planting my right blade, I soared through the air and my kayak skipped out and away from the waterfall after a surprisingly soft landing. Chaos was next. I peeled into the current, following the tightrope-like eddy line bordering the swirly water above Chaos. As I made the turn around the corner, one of my friends was in the eddy right above the easier left line I usually take. No big deal, I'd just take the main line. As I went to take a left sweep stroke to line up to the drop, it felt like my arm got stuck in the mud and it went limp in front of me. Oh, fuck – my shoulder is out of its socket right above this recirculating hole. Whatever was about to unfold, I knew a dislocated shoulder was just the beginning.

I went over backwards and the stern of my kayak smacked a rock. I don't know if I even tried to roll, and I don't remember

Kayaking the Little White Salmon River in Washington. Photo by Jackie Kimmel.

pulling my sprayskirt to swim. Separated from my boat, I eventually resurfaced from the water. Luckily, one of my friends had portaged Spirit and was right at Chaos with a rope. The throw bag smacked me in the face and I held onto it with everything I had. When I finally made it back to shore, my friends Owen and Toad helped me climb the boulders to get onto shore. They got me ready to put my shoulder back in. As they lifted my arm, I screamed as I felt my shoulder click back into place.

I've missed out on the invincibility of youth. My peers are able to send hard and run big drops while not doing one minute of PT (physical therapy) and surviving on a diet of Mindy Mart corndogs. At 19, I should be in the prime of my body-abusing years! However, it seems just about once a year I find myself in the ER with a new life-altering injury. Over the past four years, I've spent at least a quarter of that time off the water due to injuries. These days I feel like a teenage geriatric with my abundant collection of PT equipment and mandatory pre-paddle warm-ups. Is this what it's like to turn 30? Damn, getting older really does suck.

I'm stuck in an injury Groundhog Day. Or maybe a game of whack-a-mole is a better description, because as soon as I am able to get back onto my feet and in my boat after one injury, another one comes hurtling my way. The last time I had an unbroken body was when I was 15. Though not long ago, it feels like another life. I long for those youthful days with a body free of scars that doesn't constantly crack.

As is surprisingly common with kayakers, I hurt myself for the first time off the water. And, no, it was not mountain biking. Rather, I crashed while riding motos in Moab. I was on fall break from World Class Kayak Academy, a high school where students travel the world, go kayaking, and receive an accredited education along the way. It was the fall of 2020, and the COVID pandemic was still in full swing. Instead of me going home, where I'd be spending more time in quarantine with my parents, my school friend Ryder invited me to come hang out with him. The plan was to kick it in Boulder, Colorado, and then head to Moab, Utah, for the weekend to go dirt biking. Ryder is a true free spirit, and I've yet to find someone with more infectious stoke. He's a connoisseur of psychedelic/classic rock and claims the only way to really listen to Pink Floyd is by listening to the entire album in song order. I also know he's been busted surreptitiously listening to Christina Aguilera, so I take his music opinions with a grain of salt.

I didn't make it 24 hours in Moab before injuring myself. As we were heading downhill on a trail to the dunes, I couldn't find the foot break. I was told to not touch the hand break at all costs because that risks flipping the bike. So I clung on to the clutch, hoping I could just coast the rest of the way down the hill.

"Coasting" would be a generous word to describe what unfolded. Gravity just caused me to accelerate and gain speed. Having no sense of control, I couldn't stay on the trail and was launched off the bike. On the landing, I smashed into a boulder and barrel-rolled the rest of the way down the hill. My side took the entirety of the impact, which knocked out the structure of the socket in my pelvis that holds in the femur. However, this was unbeknownst to all of us at the time, myself included. I knew something was off, but I was still high on the adrenaline and was initially very coherent. All we knew was that I couldn't stand up on my own. As my friends lifted me, my hip just slid out of its socket, causing my whole leg to unnaturally give out and fall to the side.

I was watching it all go down from a third-person perspective. It was one of those "I didn't even know that was possible" feelings. Seriously, I didn't even know a hip was a joint you could dislocate until then. I legitimately felt like someone punched me hard enough in the gut to knock me outside my own body. Hips are not like shoulders that can just be popped back in by your friends on a riverbank. I had to get airlifted from the emergency room in Grand Junction to Denver because they didn't have the proper anesthetics to reset it.

Getting from the trail to the first hospital in Grand Junction was an endeavor in its own right, requiring a four-by-four ride back to camp and then a long truck ride on bumpy dirt roads to town. Throughout it all, the only pain meds I had were a few Ibuprofen tablets, which I didn't receive until we returned to our campsite at least an hour after the accident.

On the seemingly endless truck ride out of the desert, the second-worst thing that could happen happened – I had to pee. With my hip fully out of its socket, I crawled out of the back seat, put my dislocated leg off to the side, squatted on one leg, and pissed on the side of the road. By the way, I had fantastic aim and managed to not get a drop of piss on myself. I crawled back into the truck and we kept chugging along to the ER. I don't think I'll do anything nearly as hardcore as that ever again.

Dreaming of more days like this on the river. Photo by Kalob Grady.

Twelve hours later, I made it to the Children's Hospital in Denver. After having two surgeries and spending a week in the hospital, I left as a titanium woman with seven screws, four plates, an orthopedic spring, and one nine-inch (23-cm) scar on my side. Luckily, my mom was already on her way to pick me up in Colorado in the RV, and my dad was close behind her on a last-minute plane ticket. So, sponsored by a Valium prescription, we made the journey home to Maryland in style.

Life as I knew it was flipped on its side. I went from spending the majority of my time outside to the confines of the living room chair and my parents' bedroom (it was the only bedroom in our house that didn't require going up or down stairs). The new home decor was safety handles and guardrails. I couldn't do anything by myself. I had to constantly yell, "Dad!" "Mom!" "Jackie!" "I need ____," to my parents and younger sister. The ground had never felt farther away – if I dropped something, it just stayed there because I couldn't bend over to pick it up.

Insomnia set in, making not just the days but also the nights an endless battle against my body. Without physical activity, I couldn't fall asleep. I had this ache to move, but I was stuck in a full hip brace. When I could fall asleep, I had nightmares where either my leg went limp each time I tried to take a step, or I was going into surgery again. I purposely saved my crying for the nights as my family slept because it was the only time I had any sense of aloneness. I was deeply ashamed I couldn't be the strong person I thought everyone expected me to be. I didn't want my family to know I was mentally struggling. I had already dragged them through so much, so I didn't want to burden them with my worries on top of everything else.

Devoid of kayaking, my 15-year-old self entered a full-on identity crisis. Whitewater kayaking is my passion. It empowers me to be strong, independent, and capable. My entire life was centered on the sport; it's what I did with my family and all of my friends. And, hell, I even went to a kayaking high school! Kayaking was more than just a hobby – it was part of my identity. Without it, I felt like a part of me had died. I mourned for the person I used to be and resented the weaker person I had become.

It certainly didn't help that I had a raging case of FOMO and was back to doing online school while all of my friends were in-person and paddling cool rivers all over the southeast USA and Ecuador. As much as online school sucked during the pandemic, at least we had all been in it together. This time, however, I was alone and missing out. I couldn't open my phone without being reminded of all of the things I was missing out on.

Those early few weeks felt like the longest year of my life. Despite channeling all of my misplaced energy into reading the mega stack of books my friends sent me, embroidering virtually everything in sight, and assembling a 6,000-piece Hogwarts LEGO set, I felt like I was stuck in time. My parents and little sister were so excited to have me home. I couldn't match their enthusiasm because home in a hip brace was the last place I wanted to be.

The turning point in my recovery came when I was able to start PT. It was the best because I got to leave the house, see someone with a different last name than mine, and actually start to move! It was the first time I had an actual recovery plan where someone told me both that recovery was possible and how to get there. I don't know what magic existed on the third floor of that PT office building, or the secret powers my physical therapist, Jen, possessed, but I wasn't only walking again, I was taking my first strokes on the river just eight weeks post-surgery! That's when the engines fired and time finally picked up. I saw the light at the end of the tunnel and knew I could get through this.

I find that, in recovery, it's the last 10 percent that gets you. My perspective dilates in the last stretch because that's where I get a little taste of a comeback, but it hasn't happened quite yet. Even as I returned to World Class Kayak Academy for school and was the closest to being fully recovered that I'd ever been, I couldn't have felt further from being back. Long hikes to the put-in kept some rivers off limits for me, and freestyle still caused a sharp pain in my side. I envied my friends who were running the rivers I had dreamed of while I struggled to carry my boat. It felt like being held hostage by my own body.

My desire to be back to my full ability overshadowed my appreciation for how far I had come. Even though I had achieved my goal of returning to school and was actually paddling harder whitewater than before my injury, I was unable to appreciate how remarkably quick my recovery time frame had been. I was and still am an impatient person. Of all the people I struggle to be patient with, I am the most impatient with myself. In this situation there was no outside blame to be placed because my recovery was solely in my hands. As a result, what I thought was a form of self-accountability was actually a harsh and self-deprecating dialogue with myself. *C'mon, Madz, you should be recovered by now. You're not weak. Get over yourself. Stop feeling sorry for yourself, and why can't you just move on? You're never going to get back to where you were.*

Eventually, the school year came to an end. Somehow I convinced my parents to set me loose on the west coast for the summer. I didn't have a car or a driver's license. The plan was to loosely kick it with my best friend Naomi in White Salmon, Washington, and then head with her to Banks, Idaho, for the North Fork Championship (NFC). The whole paddling community made a yearly pilgrimage to this event, and people came from all over the world to compete and paddle the big water style North Fork of the Payette. There were two main parts to the NFC: a qualifier held on S-turn, a class IV cruisy section, and a finals, which was a slalom course held on Jacob's Ladder (Jake's), the largest and most consequential rapid on the North Fork. One of the most impressive aspects of this event was the sheer caliber of the women's category, where only the top five contenders progressed to the finals.

After four weeks of kayaking, jangling, and driving way too fast on backroads, Naomi and I, along with our friends Jesse and Rain, piled into the Subaru and made our way to S-turn. At the pre-race meeting, Naomi and I purposely picked bib numbers 38 and 40 so we would be racing as close as we could to each other. In the end, we never knew what happened to bib number 39 and I raced with Naomi right on my tail. Though there was a 30-second time interval between us, and we received our own times, Naomi and I were in it together.

Racing on the North Fork Payette in Idaho. Photo by Hayley Stuart.

Later that evening, the initial awards ceremony announced the qualifier results and who would be moving on to the finals. The women were announced first. When I heard the announcer call, "At 16 years old..." I knew I had qualified. Standing on stage with a coveted black jersey in hand, I was filled with a rainbow's worth of emotions. I knew I had raced well, but qualifying was not what I expected. As soon as I stepped off that stage I started bawling, first from being overjoyed at placing fifth, and then from fear of thinking about racing Jake's. I ran into two of my closest friends and mentors, Cole and Kalob. Hoping to dispel my fears, they promised to help me run Jake's.

Though only the top five were announced, when the rest of the results were released, we discovered Naomi had also finished in the top ten, coming in hot at seventh place! Unfortunately, Naomi and Rain had to head back to the Columbia River Gorge because Rain had his high school graduation the next day, and we weren't able to celebrate together. I don't think it was a coincidence that Naomi and I both put down some of our best results together. Even in situations like a competition where there is only one winner, there is still room for collective success. The fact we supported each other and genuinely wanted the other to succeed, just as much as we wanted ourselves to succeed, made it all the more rewarding. I have yet to recreate that same feeling of togetherness that Naomi and I had at the NFC in a competition setting.

The next day I went with Kalob to scout Jake's and I was speechless. The water appeared to be randomly exploding over rocks, and eddies surged unrelentingly. It was by far the largest piece of whitewater I'd ever considered running. Starting from the top, Kalob broke down each move for me from Rodeo Hole through Taffy Puller and the end at Witch's Tit. Kalob then gave me some space to make my decision. I sat on the boulder on the riverbank, evaluating my options. I saw the line. I was intimidated, but I knew I had the desire and skills to run it. I just couldn't help but feel small compared to this colossal piece of whitewater. I was overwhelmed with nervousness.

As I walked back to Kalob's truck to get my gear, Sage Donnelly, one of the best kayakers in the sport, found me. Something about her, maybe it was stoke or just that she believed in me, caused my nerves to dissolve. And when Sage offered to let me follow her and run Jake's together, I was suddenly excited to run it. I laced up my shoes, put on the black jersey and, with a cleared mind, made my way downstream with Sage. My line was flawless: every stroke exactly what I envisioned it to be. At the bottom, I was bubbling with so much excitement that I hiked back to the top and ran it again!

Then came the hard question: Was I ready, *really* ready, to race Jake's? Running Jake's and slalom racing, where you have to complete slalom gates through the biggest features, are two very different beasts. As I walked back to the car after my second lap, I knew the answer. I was a 16-year-old kid just beginning to dip her toes into class V and was not confident enough in my skills at the time to start going for gates. If I did decide to race, I feared it would be solely because others expected me to, not because I had the genuine desire. So I gave up my spot in the finals to the next woman who was eligible and willing to race Jake's: Anna Wagner.

Honestly, I didn't really care all that much to not be racing in the final because I had accomplished so much more than I originally set out to do. Besides, the NFC wasn't going anywhere. So I walked away proud, confident, and happy to cheer for Anna on the sidelines. She had been getting in multiple practice laps on Jake's, and I was excited to see her crush the finals. I made racing Jake's my goal for the next year and dedicated the entirety of my year to training to compete in the finals.

Unfortunately, not everything goes to plan. The following year, I came down with a gnarly case of COVID the day before the NFC. Instead of racing, I was in Boise, Idaho, fighting the hotel front desk clerk to let me check into a room under the age of 21 with a fever and brain fog so severe I could barely read the side of the NyQuil bottle. Over 30 combined practice laps on S-turn and Jake's in the days leading up to the NFC were for nothing. My mom had to fly out to help me get back on my feet. We supported my friends on the livestream, but it stung. This wasn't how things were supposed to go! I did the responsible thing last year by giving up my spot and had spent the entire year properly preparing for this race. I did all the "right" things. It was a practical joke taken too far to be benched once again, despite finally feeling ready. I was angry. I was bitter. All my hard work felt like it was for nothing.

The following year, the NFC was canceled indefinitely. I will never get the chance to slide off the legendary start ramp. My dad says sometimes life gives you lemons, but I say sometimes it gives you COVID. Just because you give something your all doesn't mean it's going to go the way you hoped it would.

However, before I knew what disappointments the next year

would hold, I left my first (and only) NFC on top of the world. I wasn't just where I was before my injury. I was even better! My results at the NFC were proof. I had been chasing this carrot on a stick in front of me for so long, desperately trying to get back, and I had made my comeback. I finally felt like I had autonomy over my body again. Everything finally felt like it was possible again. The injured part of my life was officially over, and it would all just be a small blip on the long journey of life like everyone told me it would be.

The harsh reality is that one decent race result didn't change a thing. As I continued to paddle into the fall, it became apparent this injury was not something I could give my all into overcoming in the short term and just move on from. Because I couldn't get closure from this injury, my hip became a ball and chain attached to my right leg. The situation was a complete catch-22. I was technically recovered and was even better at kayaking than I was before. But the battle to get my body back wasn't over yet. My brain could not process how I was able to do great things but still be simultaneously hurting.

A day doesn't go by where I don't experience some form of discomfort in my hip. Sitting is my arch nemesis and kayaking is a sport spent almost exclusively on your ass. It's actually worse than sitting normally because the shape of the boat's cockpit forces my hips into an awkward position that aggravates my injured hip even more. Regardless of the amount of PT that I do, my right leg falls asleep virtually every time I go kayaking.

There are no days off from injuries. They are a constant from the minute I wake up in the morning to night, when they steep into my dreams. It is incredibly draining to have something in the back of your mind all the time. I can't just let go of it either because I'm constantly doing this wellness math in the back of my head. *When are we going kayaking? Because I need enough time to warm up and I don't want to hold everyone up. When are the water levels going to be the worst so I won't feel guilty about taking a rest day? Is today going to be a long day? Because I need to make sure I bring the kayak that hurts me the least. How long am I sitting down to study? Because if it's for a long time I need to find a tall tabletop so I'm not sitting the whole time.* It adds another level of anxiety onto everything I do and ultimately makes it almost impossible to just be present in what is in front of me. I exist in the future, thinking several days in advance, trying to maximize the quality and time I can spend on the water while also minimizing pain. This impossible balancing act is a total buzzkill because there is no such thing as spontaneity, which is one of the best parts of being young and alive!

When you're at the beginning of an injury, it's okay to be having a hard time. But after a year or two, you start to sound like a broken record. Maybe I just haven't found the right words to encapsulate the experience without sounding like I'm throwing a pity party for myself, or I just can't get my friends to understand what's going on. When you're young and the majority of your friends are in their physical prime, having a chronic injury is really isolating.

Despite the pain and the shortcomings, I still had big goals I wanted to achieve. It would just look a little bit differently than I imagined, and entail extra rest days and continued physical therapy. One of those goals was to learn how to Cobra Flip, a downriver freestyle trick invented by Aniol Serrasolses where you do an aerial roll off of the bow of the boat as you go off a waterfall.

My first attempt was unsuccessful. I was so excited to be upside down that I forgot to look for the light on the other side to complete the motion. I ended up landing completely upside down off the 20-foot (6-m) waterfall. Undeterred and understanding how to fix it, I hiked back up to try again.

Visualizing the move, I put in at the top. I knew exactly what I needed to do. Spotting the lip, I came in with speed. I lined my bow up with the lip, put my head down, and looked for the sky on the other side. My boat cleanly snapped around me, and the motion was exactly what I envisioned it to be.

Instead of cheering on the landing, I couldn't make a sound from having the wind knocked out of me. I managed to land with my spine stacked in the small pocket of water at the bottom that was unaerated. The speed and rotation of the trick increased the impact of the 20-foot free fall. It was as if my upper back had been exposed to absolute zero, causing my muscles to instantaneously freeze, halting all movement. It's never a good sign when you can't carry your own kayak out of the river, let alone need help walking to the car. I couldn't even take my own gear off. My grand victory lap for the Cobra was the commencement of the injury sequel.

I didn't want anyone to know I'd hurt myself. Outside of those who were there, my parents and two of my closest friends, no one else knew the whole story. To me, the most important parts of my kayaking are the "how" and the "why," more so than the achievements themselves. It isn't just what you do but also how you do it. After all, that is the core reason I gave up my spot to race Jake's at the NFC – because I wanted to ensure I was racing for the right reasons. I worried that, by sharing I'd hurt my back, other people would assume I had just recklessly thrown myself off this waterfall. I was terrified others would think I was sketchy.

Deep down, I started to question myself: *Was I sketchy? Did I go about this in the wrong way?* Maybe I did violate my own values. I didn't know whether to be proud or ashamed. Even though I cleanly landed it, hurting my back made me feel undeserving of it all.

The problem is that all everyone else saw was a ten-second clip of the Cobra Flip. From the outside, you could only see the "what" piece of the goal. I didn't just fail to tell the whole story of hurting my back. I also left untold the two years of thought and preparation that led up to sticking my Cobra Flip.

Before running Jake's, and even shattering my hip, I had the Cobra in the back of my mind. In fact, it goes back to the summer of 2020 when I was paddling with Clay in Rock Island, Tennessee. Clay is the kayaking equivalent of Tony Hawk, one of the few OGs still getting after it. The dam wasn't releasing much water that day and Clay suggested we practice Cobra Flips off a tiny two-foot (half-meter) wave. He coached me through the basic movement and we practiced over and over again. I left Rock Island fully obsessed with the Cobra. I screen recorded Instagram videos of Dane Jackson and Aniol Serrasolses, the best men in the sport doing Cobra Flips. I slowed these clips down, played them back, and compared them to other clips taken from different angles. Even though I wasn't anywhere near a waterfall where I could attempt it, I brought the Cobra Flip to class II just like at Rock Island. I practiced on such tiny waves I might as well have been practicing on flatwater. I visualized the trick before I went to sleep at night, envisioning it from my own perspective and imagining how I'd execute it.

When I broke my hip, I was so focused on being able to go kayaking again that I temporarily tabled the Cobra, along with all other kayaking-related goals. However, after I recovered, it all ended up coming together. I wasn't just physically in place to attempt one but also paddling the Upper Palguín River in Chile, the very river where the trick was invented! It made it even more appealing to attempt one. I had already overcome so much to even be able to walk to a waterfall for scouting a location. I had this cool opportunity to bring this goal full circle from pre-injury to post. Instead of having a special and rewarding moment, I left the experience adding to my list of body ailments. My back has never quite felt the same since that landing and still affects me today.

It made it so much worse that I was getting clout for it. In that year's Whitewater Awards, my Cobra Flip ended up winning Downriver Freestyle Trick of the Year. I felt like a fraud because I wasn't just neglecting to be honest with what really happened, but I personally felt like I had left the Cobra Flip somewhat incomplete. Hurting my back wasn't the way I wanted to accomplish it.

Simultaneously, I also felt trapped by the fact I was the first woman to land a Cobra Flip. I was acutely aware the Cobra was something bigger than my own personal endeavors. So few women even attempt downriver freestyle tricks. If I told people I hurt myself, what sort of message would I be sending? I thought hurting myself in the process was more detrimental to women's progress in kayaking than completing it was progressive. As the token woman to land one, I felt like I had this pressure to be a good role model. The last thing I wanted to do was to fulfill a stereotype that women fall short. I wondered if I should have left the Cobra to one of the older, more experienced women like Nouria Newman, Anna Wagner, or Sage Donnelly. Surely, they would've done it without breaking themselves and feeling like a disappointment to all of women's kayaking in the process.

Even with all my inner turmoil around the trick, I had already been dealing with my hip for the past year and I was NOT going to let another injury get in the way of doing what I loved. Even with continued PT, kayaking hurt so much already, so what was a little bit more? And the Chilean X-ray showed I didn't technically break any bones in my back, so I was FINE. I knew how to take it and I just needed to stop being overdramatic about it all.

I took it easy for the next couple of weeks and just got right back to it. I had a referral to get an MRI and see a spine specialist, but I never booked the appointment. Instead of starting the process of getting a real diagnosis, I nicked my dad's portable TENS machine and did more yoga to get relief from the pain. Everyday after kayaking, I used the TENS to send electric pulses into my back, trying to release the tightness. I ignored how my arms would fall asleep in the mornings and the tingling sensations

Cobra Flip on the Upper Palguín River in Chile. Photo by Kalob Grady.

in my back. Something was definitely wrong, but I didn't want to know, nor did I want anyone else to. If this was the price of being able to paddle at the level I wanted to, I said ring me up and bring it on.

And this plan of ignoring the pain worked really well. The following year I had the best year of kayaking in my life. I wasn't just running the Little White for the first time but was starting to run it at higher flows, and came in fourth place at the Little White Race in 2023. Even though I didn't race at the NFC the second time around, I was training on Jake's before the event and had the skills and confidence before I caught COVID. I won the Great Falls Race on my home river in Maryland, the Potomac River. I even ran the Middle Fuy in Chile, where the entrance is a 50-foot (15-m) waterfall. Even though I had a perfect line, I spent the following day in the fetal position from the back pain. I saw the pain as just the price of being able to do what I loved. No pain, no gain, right?

Kayaking is what I love the most in this world, but it also is what physically hurts me the most. Now it's been so long since kayaking hasn't hurt that I actually can't remember a time when kayaking doesn't come with a side effect of physical pain. Every time I go kayaking, I'm simultaneously stoked to be on the water but also always looking around the next corner for the take-out where I can get out of my boat and catch a break. It was easy to continue to paddle hard and ignore my body initially because even when I did the things I was "supposed" to do, I still hurt. I felt like I had come to a crossroads where I could either quit kayaking or push through the pain to do what I loved. So I just kept going at the pace I was at because I thought it would make me happy. After all, I was still kayaking.

I existed in a weird place where I was rewarding myself for continuing to ignore my body. It made achieving goals even more fulfilling because I was not only overcoming everything to reach the finish line, I was also showing my body that it didn't get to make the rules. If I just worked hard enough and was mentally tough enough, I thought I could push through any level of physical pain. My body might not have been invincible, but I thought with enough persistence I could make my mind invincible. And then it all fell apart. When I thought I had it figured out, I found myself freezing on the riverbank of the Little White with my shoulder newly reset, watching one of my friends clip himself to a rope and jump into Chaos to retrieve my kayak.

Shoulder injuries are one of the few injuries where it is actually worse to be young. The statistic surgeons told me is that about 80–85 percent of people who dislocate their shoulders under the age of 20 and don't get surgery end up re-dislocating their shoulders. So if you can't buy yourself a beer in the United States, you better be doing preventative PT and taking care of your shoulders! As an 18-year-old kayaker who was at a much higher risk for shoulder injuries than the average person, surgery felt like the best way to go about things in the long term. I was headed back to the operating table.

After an insurance wild goose chase and the longest four months of my life, I was finally able to get shoulder surgery back home on the east coast. I found myself back in my favorite place: my parents' living room chair. If my mom would let me have my

way, I'd haul that chair to the driveway, drench the damn thing in kerosene, and throw a match at it. Through each injury, I've been told these experiences will make me stronger. But over the past four years, I just seem to become even more broken as time goes on. Instead of overcoming one injury and then moving on to the next, my hip, back, and shoulder injuries stacked on top of each other.

At six and a half months out of shoulder surgery, two years post-back injury, and four years post-hip surgery, I have never felt worse. Some days all I can manage is getting out of bed and paddling my local class II section. It's like there is a sash of pain from my left shoulder to my right hip. Moving feels impossible, and I just want to lie flat. I do my usual "fix my body" checklist: stretching, foam roller, lacrosse ball, electric pulses with the TENS machine, self-cupping, and lying on the Shakti bed of nails. It doesn't always help.

Emotionally, I'm exhausted from having my body kick the shit out of me everyday. It's like I'm in need of a long nap. But then I'll go take one and as soon as I wake up I feel like I need another. Four years deep in the injury world, and I really feel like I should be better at this by now. In the past, I used to daydream about kayaking and all the places I was going to explore when I recovered. It was a tool to motivate myself to get better and ultimately give me hope for the future. But now the thought of going on a kayaking trip, or even just running class IV again, isn't motivating, it's anxiety inducing.

It is really hard to have fun when during and after kayaking

Stern squirting in a slicey kayak. Photo by James McCloud.

you're in a world of hurt. Each person possesses their own pain tolerances and employs individual methods to balance their passion with enduring discomfort. If I'm not persevering through it and giving it my absolute all, then I'm either being weak or I just don't love kayaking enough. I feel like I've now reached a point where my passion for the sport alone is not enough to overcome the pain.

On top of it, because I've made a remarkable recovery in the past, I feel like I have this obligation to pull it off again. I feel that, if I can't pull it off the same eight-month rally from couch to top-five-race-result time line, I'm falling short. Or worse, it's a sign I'm not working hard enough, not strong enough, and, ultimately, that I am not enough.

The Little White Salmon Race is coming up again and there is no way I'll be ready to race. I really want to be there to see everyone and support my friends. But I'm also dreading seeing everyone because I know I'm going to be bombarded with questions about my recovery. I can't give both a positive and honest answer. I know it comes from a place of love where my friends want to know how I'm doing, but to me these interactions become constant reminders of how I'm not doing well, as if the daily physical pain is not enough of a reminder.

All of this catalyzes into this feedback loop: I'm physically hurting when I go kayaking, then I become frustrated because I'm not as far along in my recovery as I should be, and, finally, I'm criticizing myself in all the things I could have done better. I just find myself spiraling as I go around and around this self-deprecation loop. There is so much anxiety around kayaking right now that I'd rather save myself from the physical pain and the emotional toll and not go at all.

All I really want right now when I wake up in the morning is to not be in pain. I want to be able to fall asleep without having to position myself in an awkward sprawl, with my right leg bent out to the side and my left shoulder extended in the opposite direction, because it's the only position that relieves the constant tightness so I can relax and fall asleep. I want to actually feel good in my own body. I haven't had that feeling in almost half a decade.

Something is different on my third trip to the bench. Before, I was a girl discovering just how much I was capable of and how far this body of mine will take me. But now I sit here as a young woman, and there's been some redecorating. I'm not a doctor, or a physical therapist, nor do I have any real medical training, but what I do know for sure is that our bodies are systems. Though all of my injuries happened from accidents, I think my failure to fully address my hip and back physiologically likely put me at a higher risk of a shoulder dislocation. I prevented myself from effectively healing any of my injuries by ignoring my body, burying my feelings, and rashly trying to move on.

I've been obsessed with "getting back" for years now. But would I really want to go back to the 15-year-old version of myself? Definitely not! That version of me couldn't have achieved a tenth of the things I've accomplished. I was a naive and immature kid who knew nothing about the world. I like to think I'm a cooler, wiser, and more well rounded person now.

I think we should rename "comebacks" for athletes because we never return to the place we once were. Whether we leave these experiences better for it or having to face more challenges, injuries are an ever-evolving process. Recovery is not a destination we reach but an ongoing journey. Just because times are hard, it doesn't mean they always will be. I think my body was trying to tell me something all along. I just couldn't be bothered to listen. It took breaking myself three times to realize I can't keep pitting my body and my brain against each other. Healing cannot be forced into fruition. If I ever want to get better, the self-hatred had to stop.

If there's anything I've learned over the past four years it's that I'm surrounded by an amazing community of people who have my back. I really am my own harshest critic. Nothing is harder and, quite frankly, sadder than being your own bully. It's time to take the foot off the gas pedal, take a step back, and accept where I'm at. I don't have any big kayaking goals on the horizon. In fact, I'm currently anti-goal. I'm most interested in what is going on in my mind and heart, and chasing what makes me happy. If that entails running class V again, great. If it includes spending some time off the water, that is equally okay too.

Although everything I've seen in the movies tells me time travel is a bad idea, given the opportunity to hit the reset button and do it all over, I wouldn't change a thing. I'd still go to Moab and shatter my hip, do that Cobra Flip and hurt my back, and still run Spirit that day in April and dislocate my shoulder. I am so grateful for all of the pain, anger, and hard times, because it led me right here to the now. I don't think I have it all figured out, but my journey is only just beginning. My chapter of injuries was simply the prologue to the rest of my life. I do believe the best is yet to be written.

NRS
SEALS

CHAPTER 2

Waters of Change: Flowing on the Currents of Empowerment

By Naina Adhikari

The River Beckons

As a young girl growing up in the serene hills of Nainital, a small town in the foothills of the Indian Himalaya, the only waves I knew were the gentle ripples of Naini Lake. Deeply inspired by my Uncle Eddy, I started kayaking at 13 years old. Little did I know the unpredictable currents would soon take me far from familiar lakeshores. It was the Ganga River that beckoned, a powerful force that would shape not only the course of my paddling but also my journey of self-discovery.

Venturing from an all-girls convent school into the world of whitewater kayaking was as unusual as it could get. The river became my playground, and my kayak my vessel of transformation. But the challenge extended beyond the roaring rapids; it was convincing my parents, especially my mother, to let their teenage daughter navigate a world dominated by men. They were afraid of sending me 186 miles (300 km) away from home to practice a sport they didn't understand. In India, families are overprotective of their girls and want them to grow up in a safe environment. So it took my family a lot of courage to let me go.

Ten years later, I understand my family's initial hesitations. The journey wasn't just about learning to paddle hard rapids. It was about overcoming societal norms and my own limitations. From a shy teenager thrust into an unfamiliar sport, I emerged as a bold, independent woman. I learned to navigate not only the turbulent waters of the Ganga but also the complex currents of human interactions.

From the Ganga to the Futaleufú

A decade after I started kayaking, my journey took me to foreign waters, with Chile becoming the backdrop for my first

Under the historic bridge Lakshman Jhula in Rishikesh, India. Photo by Naina Adhikari.

international kayaking expedition. Two American kayakers became my pillars of support, guiding me through the exhilarating rapids of the Futaleufú River. Flying out of my country for the first time and kayaking abroad helped me become mentally stronger and also helped my family build confidence seeing me out in the world. At first, it took a little convincing to get my parents to understand the whole Chile idea because it was a strange land I was heading to, but in the end it was all agreed upon and they sent me off with blessings and luck. After following incredible women down the massive rapids of the Futaleufú, I came back to my home country changed forever.

The opportunity was first set in motion when, in a rare instance for me, I wrote to this amazing kayaker Brooke Hess, who I came across on Instagram years ago. While I was super hesitant to write to her initially, it turned out to be one of the best decisions I ever made. She responded to me and, after learning about my story, interviewed me for a magazine and suggested we kayak together. A few months later, after my interview was published in NRS's (Northwest River Supplies') blog *Duct Tape Diaries* and the magazine *Kayak Session*, she wrote to me again saying she was going to travel to Chile with her friend Hailey from Alaska and that she would love for me to join them. She was an incredibly inspiring kayaker to me, and while the invitation to join the trip was nothing short of an honor, the chances of me flying out of my country were low.

As much as I wanted to join, I knew I was in no position to fund my trip. But like they say, if you want something hard

Kayaking the big water of Chile with Brooke and Hailey. Photo by Bhupendra Singh Adhikari.

In the middle of the Mundaca rapid on the Futaleufú River in Chile. Photo by Bhupendra Singh Adhikari.

enough, you find ways to get there. Brooke acted as a catalyst and suggested we pitch the idea of writing to NRS about it to help get me a sponsorship. We went ahead with it and it worked. I was headed to a different side of the world, to paddle with women from completely different cultures and backgrounds that I hadn't even met before. I was excited, but I was scared to take a huge leap of faith to undertake something of this magnitude. But even at such a young age, I knew this was my moment.

My visa application process felt like a nightmare, and I wasn't sure it was going to happen. Three months into working through the visa documents, my visa got rejected. I didn't give up. I applied again and, finally, it all fell into place. I acquired my visa to Chile thanks to the generous help and support from NRS, Phoebe, Nancy, and Mariann.

When I arrived in Futaleufú, I had no clue what lay ahead. I was doubting my kayaking skills and underestimating myself. The anticipation kept building until I saw Brooke and Hailey running toward me in their Crocs, beaming and screaming with joy. It was at that moment I knew I was going to be okay. The warmth of their welcome I received that first day immediately put me at ease in the new, foreign land. The days that followed only got better, as I was in the company of two badass women with whom I was going to paddle on one of the most beautiful rivers in the world.

The first day on the Futaleufú, I didn't feel extremely comfortable, intimidated by all the world-famous kayakers around me. But Brooke and Hailey introduced me to the Futa in a way that made me feel comfortable. We started with the El Macal section to White Mile and then progressed to the more difficult Bridge to Bridge section. Kayaking on the Futa was a dream.

Growing up in India, I didn't get to witness senior female kayakers, and this experience made me realize why it's so important. Not disregarding the fact I had a great male mentor to look up to, and I owe a lot to his guidance. When I was in Chile, I shed happy tears because I'd never been led down any rapid by such incredible women. I can still recall how madly Brooke was cheering for me, and the most beautiful smile Hailey had on her face after seeing me get through the Mundaca rapid. I could feel it, their happiness for my success. There were many times when Brooke was leading me and I was super motivated to try rapids that were out of my comfort zone and to paddle better and harder than ever before. There were some days when I felt like I was crushing it, and there were days when I felt like I was losing control over my boat. Again, Brooke and Hailey assured me it's okay to feel that way; that it's okay to not always paddle in rhythm. When I felt weak in my strokes, it was very motivating to see the warm, illuminating smile on Hailey's face as she told me I was good enough.

Another highlight was paddling with Benny Marr, the coolest legend ever. It was nothing short of a dream when Benny parked his duo kayak right across from me at the put-in and asked me to paddle with him. Kayaking with him was a beautiful and powerful experience. I'd grown up watching him in videos, and getting to be on the river with him halfway across the world made me believe in dreams and greater powers. He's an amazing kayaker and an incredible human being.

Kayaking is not solely about the thrill – it's all things empowering as well. It brings people from different origins, cultures, and backgrounds to unite on the river and share the sheer joy of being in it. Coming from a community of almost no women kayakers to eventually paddling with the women of Chicas al Agua was one highlight of many. Chicas al Agua is a program in Chile where young girls are given free kayak workshops, environmental lessons, and several more enriching sessions. We were humbled to be a part of it and lead these beautiful young *chicas* down the river in their home section. What an empowering feeling it is to support each other, to look out for each other, to cheer and to love and to grow together. When women support each other, great things happen, and paddling on the Futa with all these wonderful kayakers was an indescribable feeling for me.

By the end of the trip, I was leading my friends down the biggest rapids on the Bridge to Bridge section. It's not just kayaking skills I took back but a plethora of learning, love, support, and strength I'll carry for the rest of my life going forward. I have so much gratitude for the people I paddled with in Chile, and I left feeling inspired to move forward with greater courage and skills, and to make my country and fellow kayakers proud.

Shadows on Foreign Shores

Coming from India, a land rich in culture and diversity, to a country in South America was quite exciting. The cultural difference was significant, but I soaked in every moment. While there were many positive moments of the trip, there were also experiences that greatly affected me.

Because I am from India, I have a dark complexion, and while I have never felt even a tad bit less because of it, there was an encounter on the riverbank where a white kayaker credited my kayaking skills to my skin color. It was disheartening to be judged based on my complexion rather than my skills. This wasn't my first encounter with racism, but the sting felt sharper on international soil.

A worse event occurred on my journey back home from Chile. I arrived in Santiago, where I would fly out the next day. Denied check-in at the Airbnb I had booked, I found myself stranded late at night on the unfamiliar city streets. Desperate to find a safe place to spend the night, I called a taxi to take me to a hotel. Instead, the taxi driver drove me to a brothel. Although I managed to physically escape, the emotional scars of that harrowing night linger.

Through these bitter experiences, I began discussing with others how race, gender, color, and creed are often subjects of discrimination. It was clear that creating biases based on these identifiers does nothing but bring the sport, and everyone involved, down. I proudly carry the cultural banner of Indian heritage, my identity becoming my source of strength. The challenges, the triumphs, and the moments of vulnerability all shaped me into the person I am today. The river, with its unpredictable currents, mirrors life's journey – a relentless pursuit that molds us, tests our mettle, and ultimately reveals our inner strength.

Navigating the Rapids Alone

As I continued to push myself in the world of whitewater kayaking, the reality of being the only female paddler in my country began to sink in. In a sport dominated by men, I stood out like a sore thumb, a lone figure amid a sea of masculinity. While my passion for kayaking fueled my journey, the emotional weight of being the odd one out was heavy on my shoulders.

In a male-dominated environment, unwanted attention became a constant companion. What started as innocent camaraderie with my male counterparts, who once called me their sister, soon changed. The dynamic shifted to where they viewed me through a different lens.

The challenges extended beyond the riverbanks, infiltrating the sanctity of my personal space. Drunken men would bang on my door at night, leaving me feeling anxious and exposed. Yet, in my naiveté, I never shared these struggles with anyone, fearing I would be held responsible for the unwanted attention.

The thought of burdening my parents with these hardships was unbearable. I couldn't consider the idea of being forced to give up kayaking, the very thing that brought me solace amid the chaos. So I kept silent, shouldering the weight of my struggles alone.

What broke my heart the most was the absence of anyone to stand up for me in these moments of vulnerability that continue to this day. The kayaking community, for all its camaraderie on the river, felt like a lonely place when faced with the harsh realities of being a female paddler. It was this void, this sense of isolation, that drove me to seek out a river family of my own.

Ganga Girls

It was with that taste of the all-women's expedition in Chile that I understood the power of how female mentorship can bolster another's morale and self-esteem. I wanted to create this culture of solidarity and kinship – of having the other's back physically, emotionally, and psychologically – in India. It was time to take the energy and the spirit of Chicas al Agua and build something special on my home river.

And thus, Ganga Girls was born. More than just a platform for female paddlers to come together, I envisioned it to be a beacon of support and solidarity in a world that often felt indifferent to our struggles. Through the formation of Ganga Girls, I found strength in numbers of like-minded women who shared my passion for kayaking and inherently understood our unique challenges. Nearly a decade after I started my own whitewater journey, there was finally a community of women kayakers in India.

In April 2023, eight of us, women and girls, set off from Rishikesh as the first all-female whitewater expedition crew on the Ganga River and in India. We started our journey at the confluence of the Bhagirathi and Alakananda rivers. For most of them, this was their first multi-day kayaking expedition. In fact, I myself had never done any kind of expedition on the Ganga, despite it being my home river. This trip was special for each of us.

Jackson
NRS

It would also be one of my first times stepping into the role of mentor. As part of an all-woman instructor crew, we had a mission to instruct, guide, and empower the girls on and off the river.

Day one of the expedition was all about introductions: to the river, to each other, and to camping. The first section of the river was mellow, giving us plenty of opportunity to practice rolling in a predictable environment and to get to know one another. At camp, we worked on throwing rescue bags and showed the girls how to pitch a tent. Over dinner, we shared our personal stories and bonded over both our similarities and our differing backgrounds.

Motivation and energy were high when the sun rose on the second morning. Everyone was focused and eager to get on the river. The women were excited to test their skills on the whitewater, which would be more challenging that day. After another successful day on the water, practice continued again at camp – from swimming to rolling and throw bagging. That evening, we all hiked to a beautiful waterfall.

The group had some anticipation and nerves about the next day – it would be the most challenging section of whitewater. Throughout the evening we discussed what the rapids would be like, how to read the water, how to choose a line, how to assess the risk of a swim, and the personal decision-making process of whether to run a rapid to portage it. I listened mostly; it was such a moment of pride to hear them all talk so proficiently about these things. That they not only had their own perspectives and opinions but felt confident enough to voice them proved we were doing something right – and important.

Me with the Ganga Girls on our first expedition.

Aside from the paddling discussions, we also had a session on menstruation hygiene and the principle of "leave no trace" while out in the wilderness. There were reflection sessions where the girls shared their feelings about our time together on the river and the importance of teamwork.

On the third day, each of the girls navigated the big rapids successfully. Guiding them through each rapid reminded me of my time in Chile and how the patience and encouragement from the amazing women I paddled with had reassured me that I had the necessary skills. And now I was able to pass on that encouragement to the Ganga Girls.

Organizing an expedition like this and being an expedition leader was new to me and well out of my comfort zone. But there is no change without discomfort. As much as good planning and organizational skills are important for an expedition, it is equally important to be flexible and be able to roll with the punches when unexpected events occur. I learned how even a simple smile and some words of encouragement can push your crew through physical exhaustion to finish strong as a team.

There is immense power when a group of people with similar interests gets together to work toward a shared goal. They say the strength of a community is measured by the selfless actions of each individual member toward the well-being of the whole. And the entire crew of Ganga Girls lived up to just that.

The year 2024 marked not only the second expedition of the

A special moment before starting our expedition at the Koteshwar Dam on the Bhagirathi River. Photo by Aryan Panwar.

Beena, one of the Ganga Girls, leading me down a rapid. Photo by Aryan Panwar.

Ganga Girls but also the birth of Nari Nauka, India's inaugural all-female guide course. I helped organize the expedition, and helped usher in the first batch of female Indian certified guides. This was made possible with the help of Jeremy, Elisha, Julie, and the local outfitter Red Chilli Adventure.

The creation of Ganga Girls and Nari Nauka has been a silver lining in the storm of my own kayaking journey. It's a reminder that, even in the loneliest of times, there is hope – hope for change, hope for solidarity, and hope for a future where no paddler, regardless of gender, has to navigate the rapids alone.

Empowering and Healing

The Ganga River has been more than just a playground. It's been a source of healing and strength. In its mighty currents, I've found solace, surrendering myself to the flow and emerging stronger than ever. Kayaking has been more than a sport. It's been a transformative experience – a journey of self-discovery and empowerment. It's a feeling I wish to share with others, particularly underprivileged girls who have faced unimaginable hardships in their young lives. Because the condition of women is so bad in my country, with crime rates against women being so high, it is important for me to do something since I myself have also experienced so much in my day-to-day life. I believe that every girl, regardless of her background or circumstances, deserves the opportunity to embark on this journey, to feel the rush of the river beneath her kayak and the wind in her hair.

Watching the girls practice rolling on the river. Photo by Aryan Panwar.

My mission extends beyond just empowering underprivileged girls; it also encompasses supporting the warriors of human trafficking – those brave souls who have escaped the clutches of exploitation and are rebuilding their lives from the ground up. Their stories of resilience and survival are a testament to the indomitable human spirit, and it is an honor to stand by their side as they reclaim their freedom and dignity. But my desire to help underprivileged girls goes beyond just providing them with a new adventure. It's about giving them a chance to reclaim their power, to rewrite their stories, and to realize their full potential.

My journey as a kayaker is not just about paddling hard rapids or winning races. It's about using my passion and privilege to make a positive impact in the world. And through empowering underprivileged girls and supporting survivors of human trafficking, I hope to create a ripple effect of change – one paddle stroke at a time.

The Potential of India's Rivers

India, with its vast natural resources and diverse landscapes, is truly a land of unparalleled beauty. Among its many treasures, the rivers stand out as lifelines, weaving their way through the fabric of the nation and sustaining millions of lives along their banks. As a kayaker, I've had the privilege of exploring the untamed beauty of Indian rivers, and each expedition fills me with a sense of awe and wonder.

From the roaring rapids of the Ganga to the serene backwaters of Kerala, the versatility of Indian rivers is truly remarkable. It's a testament to the diversity of nature that adorns our land, and I feel an immense sense of pride knowing I belong to a country blessed with such abundance.

As an Indian, I am deeply rooted in my culture and heritage, and I carry this pride with me wherever I go. But more than just a source of personal pride, I see kayaking as a potential avenue to showcase the beauty of India to the world. If given the recognition and attention it deserves, kayaking has the power to put India on the map as a powerful force within the world of adventure sports.

But beyond the realm of sport, kayaking can serve as a poignant reminder of the importance of preserving our rivers. In recent years, India's rivers have come under increasing threat from pollution, encroachment, and unsustainable development. By promoting kayaking as a sport, we not only create a platform for athletes to excel on the international stage but also draw attention to the plight of our rivers.

These rivers, which have sustained us for centuries, are the lifeblood of our nation. They nourish our lands, provide livelihoods to millions, and serve as a source of inspiration and spirituality for countless communities. Yet they are often overlooked and neglected in the rush for progress.

Through kayaking, we can reignite the connection between people and rivers, reminding us of the vital role they play in our lives. It's a call to action, a plea to safeguard these precious resources for future generations. And as a proud Indian kayaker, it is my hope that, someday, I can play a part in making my country proud – not just on the podium but in the preservation of our rivers, the very soul of our nation.

Setbacks and Growth

There was a big gap from when I started paddling to when I continued as a regular kayaker. This long hiatus made me restless, prompting me to travel across India to hone my kayaking skills. From the big waters of the Indus and Zanskar to the monsoon creeking in Kerala, I knew I had found my way to happiness. I also paddled quite a lot around my home river, the Ganga, which is surrounded by Himalayan rivers like the Mandakini. It is one of my favorite creeks in India, but unfortunately now dry due to a dam. Then there were the Alakananda, Pindar, and Bhagirathi rivers. These were the waters that surrounded me, and I got to paddle them under the guidance of Shalab Uncle.

Everything was going smoothly until my brutal road accident on the Leh-Manali highway in Ladakh. Despite painful injuries to my head and shoulders, and bruises all over my body, falling from my motorbike broke me emotionally and mentally more than it did physically. The accident turned into a crime in the eyes of many, with people becoming very insensitive toward me and victim-blaming me by inquiring why I was riding my bike at night. In their eyes, I became a bad example for other girls. One of my friends even tried to physically attack me, and my seniors excused it by saying, "He is frustrated and hasn't earned money due to COVID, so all the anger is coming out on you." Is that any excuse to be violent with anyone? I haven't found the strength

Pushing my own limits on the Zambezi River, in Zambia, Africa. Photo by Kent Christensen.

to be fully vocal about these reactions, but maybe one day I will. The insensitivity and judgment left my soul crushed.

I almost quit paddling. I didn't feel okay being around the same people who had broken my trust. While I believe I maintain a thick skin when it comes to outside noise, the trauma of having to listen to people talk so insensitively about me and the entire incident was very difficult to handle. It was exactly then that I got the chance to go to Chile with Brooke Hess. I believe there is a certain power that plans things for you in unexpected ways, and that was my time to shine. I was unsurprised by the lack of support from many of my own people – how could a girl go to Chile and paddle the Futa before the male kayakers? But I knew I was on the right track because I sensed others could no longer discredit me. I would not stop my journey as a serious kayaker.

After my Futa trip, I represented India at the Canoe Slalom World Championships in Augsburg, Germany. After that, I returned to India to continue competing in international festivals like Malabar, Meghalaya, and the National Games, making the podium many times. I was rallying with my boat across India and the world for kayaking and races until I found myself on one of my dream rivers: the Zambezi, in Zambia, Africa. I paddled there for a month under the guidance of Benny Marr. It was a life-changing experience. As much as my skills improved under his mentorship, the bond I formed with him was unmatched. I found myself with the biggest cheerleader, friend, mentor, and idol. Sometimes you need the right people to push you and instill confidence, and that's what Benny did for me. There was a time when I was struggling to paddle again due to emotional setbacks, and now I had reached a point where I couldn't imagine myself not paddling. This is a journey of self-belief. Later, I got the opportunity to paddle on some European gems like the Verzasca and Vorderrhein in Switzerland, the Soča in Slovenia, and the Egua and Mastallone in Italy. I also got to compete in World Cups in Prague and Germany. I was soaking in every single moment as a learning experience.

As I look forward to the future, my aspirations in kayaking and beyond continue to grow. The experiences I have had on rivers around the world have fueled my passion and driven me to push my limits further. My journey is far from over, and I am excited about the possibilities that lie ahead.

CHAPTER 3

Defying Expectations and Finding Strength in Adversity

By Darcy Gaechter

It is not about winning. It is not about losing. It's about showing up and being seen...and if you are going to show up and be seen there is only one guarantee, and that is, you will get your ass kicked.

—Brené Brown

Kayaking has given me the courage to live with uncertainty. This has meant coming to understand there isn't much about my life I can control and figuring out a way to live in harmony with this fact. All my hope for success and all my fear of failure rest on the sturdy shoulders of uncertainty. Knowing this, and having the guts to go for it anyways, has been helped along by my kayaking career. The acts of launching my kayak into unknown waters and untethering my life from the metaphorical safe shores of "the normal" to see what is beyond the horizon have become inextricably interwoven. Kayaking, through its multifaceted challenges, has given me the resilience to face the rest of life. Pouring so much of my time and energy into this sport has helped me manage fear, build connections, and reinforce my grit and determination.

Kayaking, through trial and error, has also helped me figure out what matters in life. For years (decades really) I thought it was the accomplishments that mattered, and I single-mindedly ignored the truly important stuff in life – the human connections, the conversations on the porch, the small moments of contentment – in my misguided quest to do more. I'm the fourth woman to kayak the Grand Canyon of the Stikine River in northern British Columbia. I'm the first woman to kayak the Amazon River from source to sea. I've written my name in the Book of Legends on the Bashkaus River in Siberia. I kayaked the Middle Kings in California, and so on. The fact is, very few people care about any of this. What they care about much more is how I am treating them in the moment. Am I being kind? Am I listening? Am I giving space for what they need? I don't regret most of this as it helped me learn more about what there is to appreciate in life. It just took me a long time to shift my focus. I still enjoy making goals in all realms of my life. I still like to try

Trusting my own skills and experience. Photo by Matt Power.

On the Cosanga River in Ecuador. Photo by Jason Blevins.

to do unexpected and astonishing things. But I've learned a lot about the way I think about my goals and how I approach them. Everything involved in the quest for extraordinary, and who you surround yourself with along the way, is so much more important than the arrival there.

But kayaking wasn't always the center of my focus from which I drew other life lessons. Trying to break into the realm of class V kayaking brought me plenty of judgment and negative feedback from strangers. The emotional costs of entry were high. When I sat down to write this chapter, what immediately came to mind were the multitude of challenges involved in being a woman in a "man's sport." A detailed list of all the painful ways people judged me for being a woman and being small started forming in my mind and I got angry. I relived all those moments that made me feel unimportant, less than, that shook my confidence, and made me mad at the world.

I prodded myself to keep thinking, and the second thing that came to my mind was the many small acts of kindness people showed me along the way. These moments were tiny, insignificant-seeming at the time. I bet the people doing them often didn't even realize what they were doing (as I'm sure the people saying the negative things didn't put much thought into it either), but they were extremely meaningful for me. Thinking about these things made me happy and hopeful.

I want this chapter to lean toward the happy, but discussing the infuriating deserves some space as well. I dedicated half this chapter to relaying the negative aspects of what it was like for me to be a woman in kayaking at a time when there were very few women in the sport. This part dwells on the not-so-nice aspect of human nature. The second half celebrates the awesomeness of people. I want to point out moments that kept me going in this sport as a reminder to myself to keep on working hard to pass this same good energy on to the next generation.

Proving the World Wrong

I have a long history of being told I can't do things because I'm too little, too short, not strong enough, or just because I'm a woman. I also have a long history of turning this feedback into fuel for my fire that drives me to prove all these people wrong. I never intended for pain and anger to be the driving forces in my life, but so often it seems like they are. The drive to prove my worth has been strong for as long as I can remember.

My parents gave me a skateboard for my eighth birthday and, as I brought it outside to ride it, the neighbor boy came out and told me "girls can't skateboard."

I played volleyball in high school and, although I was short, I could jump high. I could also read the block well and hit the ball to the empty spaces on the opposing team's court. I got excited, but then the head coach told me I was too short to bother trying to play in college.

This sort of commentary continued when I started whitewater kayaking, especially as I got good at it. I have countless memories of being at the put-ins for class V rivers, meeting other kayakers who were getting ready to go, and then inevitably hearing something like, "Are you sure you are good enough to do this run?"

A kayaker came up to me at the put-in on a river in Canada and the first words he ever spoke to me were, "I'll make sure to bring my rope today. I bet you're gonna need it." This was a particularly brazen comment. Most people weren't so upfront about their cruelty, posing their doubts as questions rather than outright deriding comments, and I remember how mad this guy made me. Later that day, I ended up throwing my rope to the guy who said this. I saved him after he got trapped in a sticky hole and swam. The look on his face as I pulled him to shore and hauled him up onto dry land was priceless. I hate to admit it because it drags me down to his level, but it was extremely satisfying.

Another time, I was talking with a group of kayakers while Don was running shuttle for the Moose River in New York. Don and I had just finished running the Bottom Moose, the most difficult stretch of the Moose River. This other group had run the easier Lower Moose and then had driven down to the take-out of the Bottom Moose to meet their friends. Most of us were having a fine time chatting about non-kayaking-related topics. Then a man came up to me and asked, "Did *you* just run the Bottom Moose?"

"Yes," I answered.

"But did you run Magilla?" he countered.

The Bottom Moose is rated class V, but it's not a particularly hard type of class V owing to the giant pools above and below each rapid. Magilla is the biggest and most intimidating rapid/falls on the run and it's right at the take-out, so many kayakers opt to take out above it rather than running it.

"Yes," I repeated, "I did run Magilla."

Then he looked me up and down and said, "Well, if you can do it, I can do it."

He then proceeded to give me a long-winded explanation of why he hadn't yet run Bottom Moose, but now that he'd confirmed I'd run it, he surely would go and run it as well.

He was a complete stranger.

We'd never met before and he knew nothing about me. For all he knew, I was the best kayaker in the world (although, of course, he assumed I was not).

I even got this from a non-kayaking woman once. There was an organized release of water from one of the dams on the Snake River in Idaho. This release would provide water for the Milner section. All kayakers had to register with this woman, a representative of the power company, before entering the mile-long class V section. As I registered, she asked me, "Are you sure you want to do this? There are some big rapids down there and you are so little!"

I didn't blame this woman. I understood I didn't look like the kayakers she was used to registering for this class V section. Still, it wasn't what I wanted to hear right before putting on a difficult section of river.

I was usually with Don Beveridge – my partner in life, business, kayaking, everything – and I never heard anyone ask him these sorts of questions. It's easy to think, *Ah, just ignore these people; they don't know what they are talking about!* And I agree, but their persistent messages, meant to keep me small and to keep me feeling inadequate, eventually took a toll on the way I

Running the Moose River in New York state. Photo by Don Beveridge.

thought about myself. It's important to point out that all of the comments on the riverside came from strangers who knew absolutely nothing about me; who had never met me before. What's inexplicable from my point of view is that even if I were thinking these things (and I did make my own judgments about other people), I would never walk up to a stranger and say any of this to them. I still don't know what compels people to share their judgments about me to my face, without even first asking my name.

It's well accepted among social scientists that we harshly judge others because we feel inadequate. Brené Brown is a research professor in the field of social work. She has spent the last two decades studying courage, vulnerability, shame, and empathy. Here is what she has to say about why we judge other people: "Research tells us that we judge people in areas where we're vulnerable to shame, especially picking folks who are doing worse than we're doing. If I feel good about my parenting, I have no interest in judging other people's choices. If I feel good about my body, I don't go around making fun of other people's weight or appearance. We're hard on each other because we're using each other as a launching pad out of our own perceived shaming deficiency."[2]

Logically, I can see this in the people who voiced their judgments of me. And I, too, am guilty of judging other people. When the man from the Moose River started talking to me, just as he decided I wasn't a very good kayaker by looking at me on dry land, I also deemed him not to be a very good kayaker by looking at him on dry land. He looked like he was in his mid-50s and looked out of shape. As his hurtful comments unfolded, I found myself thinking, *Yeah, good luck to you buddy. You aren't exactly the model of fitness over there.*

I defended my own criticism of him by saying I was just doing it because he did it to me first. But judging is judging, whatever the justification. It's hard to escape. Our brains are constantly judging people and situations in order to simplify them and fit them into some reality that makes sense to us. It's our brain's way of trying to protect us – what is dangerous, what is not.

When I find myself judging other people, I try to stop and ask myself, *How much does this have to do with me, and how much does it have to do with them?* The answer, almost always, is that it has to do with me. Then I try to file my judgment away and allow myself to be proven wrong by gathering more information about the person or thing I am judging. I rarely, if ever, feel the need to voice my judgments in front of the person I am judging.

Even if all these people hadn't marched up to me to share their opinions about my belonging on hard rivers, I probably would have had many of these ideas (doubts) in my head anyway from things I'd seen or read. When I was getting into the sport of kayaking, every kayaking movie and magazine featured either only men, or 99 percent men. I had always been a bit of a tomboy, so fashioning myself as "one of the guys" came more easily to me when I imagined myself as a good kayaker. Still, the media made clear there was an accepted profile of who was a badass kayaker and who wasn't. In its framing, I was not a badass kayaker. The representation in the media sent a clear message that women don't belong in the top echelons of this sport. It has gotten somewhat better over the last decade, but the representation gap is still striking.

I read an article in a kayaking magazine about kayaking difficult big water when I was about three years into my kayaking career. There was a paragraph dedicated to the notion that women are ill-suited to paddling hard, higher-volume whitewater because they simply aren't strong enough to match the force of a big, powerful river. I can clearly see the ridiculousness of this article now. I have a lot of class V big water experience and I know NO ONE is strong enough to overpower 20,000 cubic feet per second (566 cubic meters per second) compressed through a canyon creating crazy hydraulics, boils, and seams. I'm not saying that strength plays no role in the sport of kayaking, but it's rarely the deciding factor between a good line and a bad line. One's ability to read the water and work with the river seems far more important in my experience. It's all about finesse, figuring out where the water wants you to go and trying to match your will to the river's. But in my early 20s I was more impressionable, and I still thought that if something was printed in a magazine, there must be some truth to it.

Don and I spent the summer of 2003 in Alaska working as raft guides on Six-Mile Creek near the resort town of Girdwood. We started looking into some kayaking opportunities as the summer work was slowing down. I'd grown up in my kayaking life hearing stories of Walt Blackadar's harrowing first descent of Devil's Canyon on the Susitna River and I wanted to go and see the place for myself. Don wanted to go too, but we couldn't rally the other strong kayakers in Girdwood. Don and I decided we would go, just the two of us. I started researching the logistics, and I talked to Gerry Moffat, who had done the river before. Most people had either put in at the road bridge and paddled 100 miles (160 km) of flatwater to reach the canyon or flown into a lake and then bushwhacked their way through the alders down to the river. The hike requires kayakers to traverse perfect grizzly bear habitat. Gerry told me his pilot had landed the floatplane on the river when he went. No pilots were offering that service, but I started asking around. I found a floatplane with a pilot who said he'd never landed on the river before, but when I wondered aloud if it were possible, he enthusiastically shouted, "I'm willing to give it a try!" into the phone.

We met the pilot early in the morning. He weighed us and our kayaks stuffed full of overnight gear, then we took off into a hazy morning. The smoke from nearby wildfires was so thick that the pilot worried about being able to see his landing. We identified the lake where most pilots landed and that would serve as our plan B. Our pilot descended lower to scope out the river. We circled the river miles upstream from the first hard rapid. The river looked flat from high above, but we could see two-foot-tall (half-meter) rolling waves as we descended further. They weren't breaking but were tall enough to give the pilot some pause. Imagining us nosediving into the river and the plane sinking, I said, "We don't mind hiking from the lake if this looks too dangerous."

Instead of taking my comment as the out it was intended to be, I think the pilot took it as a challenge. He silently circled around again, flew lower, and then touched the plane down on the river. He landed facing upstream and we bounced through the rolling waves until he beached the plane on a gravel bar on river right. We all quickly jumped out of the plane and unloaded our kayaks.

We started paddling and had a relaxing seven miles (11 km) of class II before entering the canyon. We could hear the ominous roar before we could see the first spray from the whitewater. The rapid at the entrance to Devil's Canyon is massive. It's called Devil's Creek and it's hard to scout. We climbed the river left bank and were hiking around in the alders (making as much noise as possible to try to scare away the bears) and trying to get glimpses of the enormous rapid through the thick brush. There was a huge hole in the main channel. From a few hundred feet up on the bank, it looked as big as a house. River features always look much smaller when you are scouting from up high. I didn't even want to imagine how big the hydraulic would be if I messed up and found myself inside of it. We both agreed we needed to stay far away from that feature. The problem was that every route that allowed us to avoid the biggest hole required us to deal with numerous lesser holes, many of which fed into the monster hole. No line looked good.

"What have I gotten myself into?" I wondered aloud.

My big, lofty plans always seemed great from the comfort of dry land, with logistics and images of grand adventures swirling around in my head. More than once I'd regretted where my planning had landed me, and this was one of those times.

We trudged around the forest for close to an hour trying to get as many vantage points as we could to find a solution to this puzzle. We finally found a line we were reasonably comfortable with – at least we thought we were from our scout far away. I didn't love it, but it was the most appealing of our options. It was huge, but the line was good.

Work with the water, use the laterals, don't fight the current, tap into the water that's going where you need to go, keep forward, and paddle hard!

That's what I told myself as I sealed my sprayskirt and prepared to launch. We decided we would run the right channel for the entrance – the best way to ensure we'd miss the gigantic hole – so we had to start the rapid with a big ferry out to the opposite side of the river. From there, we'd have to turn and punch a series of breaking wave holes to get back to the middle of the river where the two channels rejoined. After that, we'd have to prepare ourselves to get shot through the next rapid called The Nozzle, a constriction where the river goes from hundreds of feet wide to less than 100 feet (30 m) wide. The full power of the river gets squeezed through this point of bedrock and creates a massive breaking wave-hole, the energy of which then discharges in a chaotic mess of waves and hideously big whirlpools.

That miserable magazine article jumped straight to the forefront of my mind as soon as I shoved off from land and started ferrying out to the far side of the river.

Damn, this water is powerful and I'm not even to the hard part yet, I thought to myself. *What am I doing here? Women can't paddle big water! The article said so!*

Then an immediate reawakening to reality: *That article is total crap. You can do this! Get focused.*

I managed to get my mental state back to a positive one in time to enter the crux of the rapid. No doubt those thoughts

The first woman to kayak the Amazon River from source to sea. Photo by Matt Power.

had more to do with my own fear in the moment than with the industry commentary on women, but the point is if that article hadn't been written (and published), I wouldn't have thought about it at this inopportune time.

The rest of the trip went well. Don and I both had good lines and we felt proud and exhilarated when we finished the last rapid. I had, once again, proved that small women could paddle hard whitewater. More than anything I was proving this to myself, because none of the detractors were around to witness or appreciate my accomplishment.

In 2013 I became the first woman to kayak the Amazon River from source to sea. Our team of three – David Midgley, Don Beveridge, and I – became the first team to do the entire river in kayaks. I had the silly idea that kayaking the entire Amazon would finally be the thing that proved my worth as a kayaker to the world. I fantasized about coming home and, all of a sudden, having people recognize my various accomplishments as a kayaker, rather than them glancing at me and immediately discounting me as someone capable of adventuring and kayaking feats. It was a nice delusion.

Society didn't let me live in my fantasyland for long. Once my book *Amazon Woman* came out, I was giving a talk at a bookstore in Edwards, Colorado. A man from the audience walked up to me as I was standing at the lectern preparing to get started and asked, "Are you the presenter? Because you don't look big enough to kayak the Amazon."

Hmm, I thought, as feelings of annoyance and shattered hope washed over me. I tried hard not to let my face betray my true emotions, somehow feeling the stupid notion that I shouldn't be rude to this guy who was being so rude to me.

I stared at him blankly for a few moments, then said, "Well sir, it turns out you don't have to be that big to kayak the Amazon."

That was the end of both my conversation with him and my silly hope about the world taking me seriously. It would be back to business as usual with me out there with the chip on my shoulder, trying to prove my worth to the world.

I'm pretty good at turning the negative energy I get from these strangers into something useful for my own purposes. It's become my survival strategy. I feel lucky that, instead of saying, "Yeah, you're right, I shouldn't try this," I've always forged ahead with what I wanted to do. My detractors-be-damned attitude seemed to be something innate in me. Without it, I would have never achieved any of my goals.

It does something to your psyche, however, when you are constantly hearing this kind of feedback from the world. Confidence can be a fragile and fluid thing in kayaking. This is true in all sports and all facets of life, but I think to an even higher degree in whitewater kayaking. It's a typical cycle for kayakers to slowly build up their confidence through more training and more successful days on the river. Eventually, we start to feel confident, maybe even a little cocky, and that's when it happens: a major beatdown, a bad swim, or some other harrowing mistake on the river. These experiences inevitably knock us back down to pre-confidence, putting us in a position where we question both ourselves and our dedication to the sport. Then we have to take a step back and slowly rebuild that confident – but not overly confident – state. So, even if I arrived at the river feeling good about my belonging there, a stranger's comments did have a way of making me question myself.

Am I getting overly confident?

Are they right?

Don't be an idiot. They don't know you or anything about you or your kayaking skills.

I got this.

But what if they are right?

This is the sort of mental gymnastics that often ensues after a thoughtless quip from a stranger on the riverside.

Managing fear on the river above a big rapid and managing what to do with other peoples' judgments of me require the same sort of mental toughness. I often spend too much time wrestling with the difficult tension between my own belief in myself, the real dangers I'm about to face, and the reality as perceived by these strangers. Breathing deeply to allow myself a few uninterrupted seconds to think is always my starting point. Momentarily blocking out the rest of the world and doing a deep check into how I am feeling in the instant. Then, deciding to trust myself to make the best decision based on my years of experience and training, plus my thoughts and feelings at that moment, is what always gets me through. Learning to trust myself was a long process fraught with struggle, but a progression that was helped along by the good in people as often as it was impeded by the bad in people.

The Value of Kindness: Finding Courage, Purpose, and Community in Uncertain Waters

> *Kindness is more than deeds. It is an attitude, an expression, a look, a touch. It is anything that lifts another person.*
>
> —C. Neil Strait

Our brains are hardwired to imprint instances of embarrassment, anger, or failure more thoroughly on our memories than other experiences. It's a protection mechanism for the future – don't mess up like that again! But small acts of people being nice, or kind, can also make a deep impression. In a world that often made me feel like I didn't belong, and could never belong no matter how hard I worked just simply because of my gender and stature, there were a few moments of seemingly insignificant kindness that made all the difference for me.

These instances came from both women and men, which I think is important. Support can come from many different sources – we just have to find the right fountains.

These gifts of kindheartedness came in different forms: a high five and "nice line" after I ran a rapid; an encouraging word; an invitation to go kayaking; another small gesture that showed someone believed in me. I'm talking about small acts of thoughtfulness that might seem insignificant but can mean the world to someone.

Hilda, the head volleyball coach at Skidmore College in Saratoga Springs, New York, found me during my senior year of high school. She saw my potential and convinced me to come play volleyball at Skidmore. I thrived as an outside hitter there under her leadership. Once I finally had someone who believed in me, and who helped me reach my potential, I felt unstoppable. I won Player of the Year and All Conference. It only took the right person believing in me for me to realize what I could accomplish.

The first act of kindness in my kayaking career came from a woman I worked with at the rafting company. At the urging of my middle school track coach, Brad, I got a job at the local rafting company when I graduated from high school. I was 18 and all my fellow guides were in their mid-20s or early 30s. They were my heroes and I looked up to them. Most of them went kayaking after work, so I decided I needed to learn how to kayak. When a fellow guide heard I was interested in kayaking, she decided to lend me all her gear for the summer. She confided in me that she'd had a bad experience on the river. She wasn't ready to quit the sport and sell her kayaking gear, but she wanted to take a break and would be happy if I used her gear, all of it – kayak, paddle, helmet, sprayskirt, dry top – for the summer so I could learn how to kayak. Not only was this generous – I never could have afforded to buy all that gear myself – it was also the loving shove toward the river that I needed. Her act said, "Go for it! You can be a kayaker!"

The next implicit act that got me on my way was that these god-like raft guides who I looked up to let me go kayaking with them. They were all much better than I was, but they let me join them on their after-work trips. I sucked at kayaking. I swam. I floundered. I hated the fact I was so terrible at it and felt deeply embarrassed when they all had to wait for me to swim my gear to shore, empty out my kayak, and get going once again. But that humiliation came from me. The other kayakers didn't heckle me or act impatient or tell me I was bad at kayaking. They surfed and played while they waited for me and then invited me to go with them again the next time they went.

My kayaking career had an inglorious beginning. I've never had any formal instruction and have mostly learned by watching other people and trying to copy what they were doing. I didn't know how to roll for my first year of kayaking. That meant that every single time I tipped over, I had to swim free of my kayak, swim all my gear to shore, empty out my swamped kayak and relaunch. All of this took energy, both physical and mental. It also meant my progression was slow. While others were surfing waves, I just sat in the eddy and waited. I didn't want to try surfing because I knew it meant I would tip over and swim. After a summer of this, I was fed up and decided I needed to figure out how to roll. A few of the guys had spent some time with me in eddies trying to explain the basics, so I at least had a starting point. In the fall, after my first summer of kayaking, I went to visit a friend in Phoenix, Arizona. She lived in a condominium complex that had a pool. She also worked from 7 a.m. until noon, so I spent five hours per day in her pool for a week.

People would have wondered why I was trying to drown myself if there had been witnesses to my struggle. I spent a lot of time upside down in my kayak, desperately wrenching my head and arms to the surface of the water and dog-paddling my way to the side of the pool to grab on and save myself. There was a lot of swimming, cursing, frustration, and anger. But by the end of that week not only could I roll on both sides but I could hand roll on both sides as well. And this was what really made my kayaking learning curve take off.

After I learned to roll, Brad – the track coach who recognized my athletic ability and had originally encouraged me to get a job at the rafting company – invited me to go down the Grand Canyon with him. Brad was always one of my best supporters and encouragers, and his invitation was an unspoken validation of my worth as a kayaker and team member. It meant the world to me.

By then, I was good at rolling but not much else. I still didn't really know how to use the water to my advantage, and I didn't know how to brace, so I pretty much tipped over in every rapid. But, hey, I could roll! I was excited, but nervous, to kayak the Grand Canyon. It was a big group of the "cool rafters," plus me. These people were my heroes, but I wasn't comfortable around them. I was still the young one who didn't know much about the river, the world, or life, and I didn't exactly feel like I fit in. I showed up with my Wave Sport XXX, ready to keep my head down, work hard at camp, and kayak the Grand Canyon.

The best kayaker in the group was a guy named Gary. He wasn't a raft guide, so I didn't know him. He was a ski patroller (which was also very cool in my worldview), and he was a good and bold kayaker. We met at the put-in and, for some reason, he never doubted me, although there was plenty to doubt back then. He would paddle over to me every now and then to tell me a line, or more often to point out what looked to me like the most massive wave or hole I'd ever seen in my life and tell me he was going to go surf it.

"You should try too," he would urge me.

Compared to my skills now, I still sucked at kayaking on that Grand Canyon trip. But Gary noticed I could roll and that I wanted to learn and get better. His encouragement was exactly what I needed to keep my progression going. I didn't go into many of the holes he pointed out on that trip – they still seemed too intimidating to me. But the ones I did go into were thrilling and adrenaline-producing, leaving me with a fast-beating heart and huge smile on my face afterwards as Gary paddled over to high-five me with an equally big smile on his face. That Gary believed in me and my kayaking enough to encourage me to play in these monster holes was a huge confidence booster and yet another message that said, "You can be a kayaker, so keep trying!"

In addition to the Grand Canyon trip, I also went to Nepal in my second year of kayaking. The Nepal trip changed my view of life and sealed my love for the sport. Realizing my kayak could take me to remote places I could never have imagined, and would offer a path to encounter people with completely different cultures in far-away mountain villages, was one of the most exciting revelations I've had about kayaking. I knew with blazing clarity what I wanted out of the sport after that trip to Nepal. Despite this insight, the first trip to Nepal was extremely hard for me. I went with a friend who was a much better kayaker and nearly every river we did was too hard for me and scary. After a few years had passed, and I had become a much better kayaker, I wanted to go back to Nepal. I wanted to re-run the rivers we'd done before but feel comfortable this time. And I wanted to go alone.

I booked six weeks of time off from work and a ticket to Kathmandu. In the months that followed, the Maoist Insurgency, which people also called Nepal's Civil War, got worse and started making the news on a regular basis. Many of the rivers I wanted to paddle were in conflict-riddled valleys. I felt for the people I had met there just a few years earlier and thought about how easily and quickly their lives had been turned upside down. I kept in touch with some of them via mail, but the letters slowed and then stopped altogether. I started to think that traveling alone in Nepal might not be the smartest thing to do. I was discussing this with a friend when he suggested, "Why don't you come to Ecuador with us? We have a kayaking trip planned there in January."

I had to get out my globe – yep, that's how I did it back then – to figure out where Ecuador was. Then I changed my ticket from Kathmandu to Quito. I had no way of knowing it then, but that decision set my life on the trajectory that enabled all of my notable kayaking achievements. These friends had booked a trip with Small World Adventures (SWA) for one week. I still had my six weeks of time off and I planned for a longer stay in Ecuador. I flew down a week before the kayaking trip started and had adventures around Quito, learning I really couldn't speak Spanish at all and getting adrenaline rushes by trying to navigate the city's bus system, hostel world, and bar scene.

I met Don, Larry, and Melody when it was time for the week of kayaking with SWA. Even though I swam on the first day of the trip – much to my horror – Melody somehow recognized something in me. She saw that, despite my lapse in skill on day one, I was capable and competent, and she let me know she saw that by telling other guests in the group to watch and follow my lines as the week went on. When Don and Larry joined the trip midweek, they treated me the same way Melody did. I never felt doubted, looked down upon, or judged.

I still had four more weeks in Ecuador after the week of kayaking with SWA. I went back to the Andean Highlands to resume my busing and touring adventures, and Melody invited me to come back in two weeks to paddle with them on their week off. That led to a discussion that Melody was going back to school to get her PhD in entomology, and it resulted in Larry offering me a job for the following season.

I came back to SWA as an employee the next January, and Don and Larry taught me so much about kayaking, life, Ecuador, and business. They always did it in a way that placed me in their estimation as an equal, as a smart, capable person with value. I never felt they looked down on me as a lesser paddler than them (which I was), or as a naive kid (which I was). They welcomed me into their fold as an equal and it was the greatest gift they could have given me.

The reconciling of the negative and positive forces in our lives is a constant dance we must learn to navigate gracefully. We will all live with persistent tension. Choosing how much brain space to allow each aspect of our lives to occupy is the challenge. Kayaking has been good training for this. My job at the top of a huge rapid, if I want to run the rapid, is to not let fear overtake my thinking processes. I need to assess the rapid as objectively as possible: What are the hazards? Where does the water want me to go? How likely am I to end up in one of the hazards versus in the safe parts of the rapid? How hard are the moves involved in a successful run of this rapid? How am I feeling right now? Consciously deciding what factors and influences on the river (and in life) to listen to is an important but difficult skill to practice. I won't say master, because I don't think any of us ever really master it, but we can always keep working on it.

I won't let myself run the rapid if my heart is racing uncontrollably. I try to calm myself down by taking a few moments to breathe deeply and figure out why I want to run the rapid, and how good I feel about the line. If my heart keeps beating faster than I want it to, it's time to pick up my kayak and walk around the rapid. As discouraging as that can sometimes be, I'll always prefer the dissatisfaction of walking a rapid to the disappointment in myself after having a lapse in judgment that may lead me to run the rapid and have a bad line. Recognizing when fear has taken over rational decision making is one of the hardest parts of kayaking. Paradoxically, if you aren't thinking rationally, it's hard to recognize these things. But learning this skill is crucial to a successful kayaking career.

In life, too, learning which fears, thoughts, and emotions to give space to, which to respect, and which to ignore is crucial to a contented life. There will be detractors and negative people in all walks of life, not just in sports. My sport has undoubtedly helped me cope, even though it's also helped make me a target of these critics.

Being carried downstream on what can feel like an out-of-control current in a class V river is a good metaphor for life. Sometimes we feel like we are styling all the moves: surfing waves with ease, catching small eddies in the middle of a complex rapid, boofing over big holes and effortlessly skipping out of them. Sometimes all the pieces fall into place and we feel like we are unstoppable. Yet other times, often only moments before or after having that sense of invincibility, we feel completely out of control, like nothing we do works, no paddle stroke feels right or gets us back in the flow of the current. In both cases, we can't stop. We can't hit pause on the river; it's going to keep on flowing regardless of what we do. We also can't hit pause on life. When things aren't going our way, we can't shout to the director to change the script. We can't redirect our tragedies or misfortunes with a turn of our boat. In both cases we must face what's happening to us. The calmer we can make ourselves in both situations, the more time we'll have to call upon our experience and our resilience to deal with whatever obstacle is in front of us. Often that means mustering up the self-awareness to walk around a rapid or ask for help when your life feels like it's falling apart. Both actions, no doubt, take more courage than mindlessly plunging into a rapid you shouldn't run, or stubbornly facing hard life situations alone.

Remembering all of the small acts of kindness I received in my journey as a kayaker has served as a good lesson. There are so many big problems involved in any life, and it can feel overwhelming not knowing how to tackle them. Where do we begin when something seems so insurmountable? I remind myself to start small. Start with that one act of kindness. That one extending of a hand, an invitation, a compliment. You never know when your small act of kindness might be all it takes to counteract others' negativity and set someone's day, or life, on the path they've been hoping to find. If you can do that for someone else, you'll be one step closer to having the right tools to deal with whatever you are facing in your life.

Jackson

CHAPTER 4

Journeying Downstream: Building Inner Strength and Sisterhood on the River

By Jenny Vasquez

Kayaking has transformed how I live and see myself in this world. The experience of oneness with nature, myself, and the people around me cannot compare to anything else I have been a part of. A deep-rooted sense of self expands my perspective to what else there is to discover in this magical world. When reflecting on my experiences thus far in kayaking, each moment contributes to a larger part in my journey in many, many layers. At its core, kayaking is just something I love doing and is one layer of my life that has allowed me to get to know myself and those around me on an intimate level. My friends, who are my chosen family, have taught me to believe in myself, to question myself, and to navigate through everything in between. Gratitude does not even begin to describe how I feel for everyone who has contributed their time and thought in helping me become the kayaker I am today.

My whitewater journey began when I started working as a raft guide in 2021 on the French Broad River in North Carolina. Two months after being introduced to the river, I was guiding a group of friends in a raft during one of the most epic annual whitewater community events – Gauley Fest in West Virginia. The Gauley River was quite the step up from the class II and class III rapids I was just beginning to get acquainted with. I vividly remember the first time I saw kayakers going down the Upper Gauley River, at a rapid called Pillow, and thinking to myself in awe, *I want to do that one day*. My memory took a snapshot in slow motion. These tiny colored boats that were sometimes upright, but mostly upside down, absolutely amazed me. Most people would look at this for the first time and be completely turned off, but there was something about feeling the power of the river with such closeness that I immediately felt drawn to. The French Broad is where I had experienced my first true encounters with the physical and mental challenges of whitewater. That summer I quickly understood there was a high level of critical thinking that was necessary for safe decision making in whitewater. And that the further you progressed in the sport, and the more difficult the whitewater became, the more critical you needed to be with your decisions.

Surfing at the Pride Paddle Parade I co-organized with Ken Kullby in White Salmon, Washington. Photo By Kate Candace Burke.

Making an entrance into the eddy at the Skookumchuck Narrows, British Columbia, before getting my first ride of the day in. Photo by Leif Anderson.

I faced many challenges during my first season of raft guiding. I couldn't maneuver the raft the way I wanted to, and I had little instruction on what a raft trip should even look like. This made for a steep learning curve and resulted in a lot of self-doubt, especially because I started on a season with low water levels. This meant there were many rocks to get stuck on, and, trust me, I got stuck on every single one of them. During that first rafting season on the French Broad, there were multiple times when I felt extremely insecure and scared when taking a group of people down the river. Sometimes my guests would feel my nervous energy and other times they wouldn't have the slightest notion I was pretty much as clueless as they were about how the trip was going to go.

A masquerade of confidence is all I needed for a group of people to trust me with their lives. When I first started guiding, a successful day included the following: no one getting hurt, feeling trust from my fellow raft guides, and sticking the line on one of the more difficult rapids on the run. Since that first season a few years ago, my definition of success has drastically changed. It now includes having fun, using my skills to challenge myself, introducing people to the sport, listening to my body and feelings in my environment, and learning to trust myself. The lessons I learned while raft guiding served me well as I started to kayak. Thankfully, I caught the kayaking bug so strongly that nothing could keep me from learning. I was completely unaware that this sport would change the trajectory of my life.

Although kayaking has taken over the way I spend my time in whitewater now, I still use my roots in rafting to get people on the river who otherwise wouldn't be out there. No trip was more meaningful than when I introduced the people I love most to my newfound love for the whitewater world. I grew up in North Carolina. Of my parents' children, I am their only daughter, and I was the first to leave the house and go to college. My parents taught me to connect to our Colombian roots by cooking and caring for others and hosting social events and dance parties. In turn, I wanted to connect them to the outdoors. When I took my parents whitewater rafting for the first time, they had to trust me to take care of *them* on the river. Although I initially felt insecure about being their raft guide, I felt relief in knowing I had the help of my badass friends, Alena and Malorie. Their support allowed me to be able to create memories with my parents that will last a lifetime.

While it is a deeply intimate experience to share the beauty of the river with others, I acknowledge it is also a privilege. At their core, all outdoor sports have barriers to growing their communities. The proper safety gear can be expensive and is often a financial barrier before a beginner knows whether whitewater kayaking is a sport they want to pursue and financially invest in. This can be especially difficult in rural areas, but if there is a kayaking community present, it is more than likely there is spare gear lying around, waiting to be used by someone who wants to get into it. Fortunately, when I joined the rafting community I made friends with a tight knit group of kayakers in Boone, North Carolina, that generously lent me kayaking gear and taught me basic skills as I swam my way down our local class II rapids. I found other beginner kayakers and we ran sections together where there was room for error. In the beginning, I had pretty limited knowledge about making judgment calls of where to kayak and what the potential consequences could be. At times, it was definitely daunting and discouraging. I had the foundation set in terms of gear and buddies, but it was time to face a new challenge, one that was intangible: fear.

When I first started kayaking regularly, my fear presented itself in the form of a turning stomach to the point where I felt like I wanted to throw up, my heartbeat skyrocketing, my body trembling, and constant thoughts of *Should I be doing this?* racing through my mind. Although these occurrences have lessened in frequency, I still feel the physical manifestation of my fear in high-consequence situations. I have completely accepted this as a feeling I will need to become familiar with and make my friend.

In some way, accepting that this relationship with fear will never completely disappear helps in learning how to deal with it in a holistic manner.

How exactly do you make fear your friend? I used to think fear would just leave once I became as good as the pros I watched obsessively on YouTube, which was pretty naive and unrealistic. As I have continued to learn to understand it, I have found comfort in knowing I haven't been the only person to feel this way. This was especially true when I asked one of my housemates, an extremely skilled kayaker, "At what point will the fear stop?" He replied that it will never go away, and with reflection I realized the feelings I have labeled as fear are ones I needed to be most curious about in situations where they arise. The stomach grumbles, chest tightening, nausea, and inability to regulate my heart rate are all sensations that happen as a result of my dysregulation in breathing and thoughts. I started to label what was going on in my body and just allowed myself to breathe in the moment. It does not "cure" the feelings, but it certainly offers a moment of comfort when I'm going into new rapids that push my limits. My fear would lead me to doubt my abilities and feel insecure with crew dynamics. Simply put, it was fear of the unknown.

To search for coping mechanisms to deal with the intensity of my fear, I started to narrow down what it was stemming from. In the beginning, it was directly related to a few factors: I didn't have a roll, I had little experience and technique, I didn't feel like I knew what I was doing, and I felt impending shame after a swim. I definitely wallowed in all of it and it made for some pretty entertaining laps down the river and eventually some good stories. The ability to laugh at myself helped with my mental resilience, and I also gave myself space to sit with disappointment.

When I first began, my biggest barrier to pushing my limits on the river was my inability to roll. I would get so freaked out by the idea of being upside down because, as you can imagine, being upside down while the current mercilessly carries you downstream is disconcerting, to say the least. But I knew if I wanted to have fun kayaking I absolutely had to learn how to roll, so I started attending weekly roll lessons in my final year of college. I swam out of my kayak a lot in the pool. I remember how scared I would become before flipping over to practice. I desensitized myself to the unsettling sensation and learned how to orient myself by slowing down the process. Step one: think. Step two: think about setting up. Step three: do. Not so easy when your brain feels like it's all over the place. A friend told me that one day I wouldn't even have to think about it and I'd be upright. At the time I couldn't comprehend one word he was saying.

Once I had some semblance of what I was doing in a pool, I'd practice flipping myself on purpose in the river in friendly currents. Rolling in the river proved extremely difficult as now I was moving downstream instead of staying in one spot. Sometimes I would get it and sometimes I would swim. That's just how it goes, and having patience with myself was invaluable as I developed a reliable roll. Over time, I realized I had transformed the helplessness I felt while upside down into a powerful tool to calm myself and process what to do when I make a mistake in a rapid or find myself in a sticky situation on the river. These lessons translate effortlessly to navigating the difficulties of life.

Craving year-round access to a backyard playground of whitewater, in the summer of 2022 I moved to the Pacific Northwest, where I spent the summer in a slicey boat practicing tricks. I spent that entire summer obsessively learning how to stern squirt – dipping the tail end of the kayak into a seam of mixing currents that results in the boat going from horizontal to vertical. I understood the theory of the skill, but my execution was poor and I flipped often, resulting in a lot of roll practice. Unless I wanted to swim every time I tried to stern squirt, I had to trust that I could get myself back upright. After months of consistently practicing, I realized it was not the end of the world to be upside down. As my roll improved, a lasting confidence grew that would prove crucial in my journey.

While working on my roll helped tremendously in increasing confidence, fear began to shift for me. At this point in my journey, fear has become a completely different beast. Whereas before I could identify reasons to be scared, now I don't always have a way of pinpointing the cause. Perhaps it is Mother Nature telling me, "You better be freaked out because I can be scary," when the rivers are raging and full of water. The feeling of the deep rumbling of whitewater is unlike any other noise in the world. There was a time when my fear physically manifested the exact same way it had in the past. The feeling of nausea on an empty stomach and my mind racing was in a strange way comforting. I recognized and could name the feeling. I turned to my crew for support but also reminded myself that the ability to trust myself went beyond the comfort of another person telling me, "You can do this."

When I am feeling nervous, I sit with my feelings above the rapid and think to myself that, in spite of the fear, *I really can do this*. I'll even say it out loud: "I can do this." The key is to believe it. I'm not just trying to play a mind game – that never works. By truly believing in my thoughts and words, I perform better. It has been wonderful being able to formulate this consistent practice of believing in myself. Without kayaking, I wonder who I would be and how I would relate to myself during difficult moments.

Another very practical thing I do is kayak a section of river I know is entirely within my ability and just focus on the fun before trying more difficult whitewater the next day. By centering fun and practicing skills, I instill confidence in myself beforehand, filling up before a challenge. The question "Should I be doing this?" transforms into "How can I do this?" Practicing visualization for new and familiar rapids and imagining how it would feel to successfully run them has also allowed me to quite literally see how to run hard whitewater with confidence. I am sure that, as I develop as a kayaker, I will also develop the way I deal with fear and find different ways of approaching the feeling. For now, I am content that these coping mechanisms have allowed me to become the kayaker I currently am. Learning to deal with fear is one fruit of kayaking, and another is tapping into the flow state.

One evening, as summer transitioned to fall, I felt flow for the first time. I was in my newly purchased creek boat, still working out its quirks on the White Salmon River with Marlee, a fellow kayaker. Because we were short on daylight hours, we decided this would be a fast lap. Similar to a practice race lap down the river, we would take little breaks. As we started paddling, I remember going into a state of rhythm that started with my feet,

Finishing a solo lap in style on Maytag rapid in on the White Salmon river in Washington. Photo by Connor Hayes.

crawled up into my legs, and then into my hips, core, and arms until they were all dancing with one another. Everything was instinctual and thoughts about my position in the boat and where I needed to point my kayak were nonexistent. I just felt my body moving in sync with the boat – a direct extension of my body. I was completely aware of where I was placing my paddle and the way the edges of my boat in the water affected my direction. Mostly, it was a state of mind where I felt so comfortable in the flow of the river, in the flow of paddling, in the flow of the environment. I was filled with overwhelming feelings of happiness and gratitude for the life I am able to live and experience. With the subtle understanding that nothing is permanent, and yet there I was, completely present.

Journal entry:

I ran BZ Falls today to challenge how my mindfulness outside of kayaking is brought into it. The flow state was happening to me and I had no control over it, it wasn't until I spoke with a friend about my experience of running BZ Falls that I had realized that I had channeled flow state and was working with it to become ultra aware of my surroundings and run a clean line. The last time I had run this rapid was close to a year ago and I had walked around it consistently since. Nothing bad happened the last time I ran it, in fact, I felt really good at the bottom, but my brain was very jumbled and I didn't feel like I had experienced the rapid, I felt it was all luck since I totally blacked out and can't quite remember how it went since I was terrified at the top of it. I more so just let the rapid happen to me as opposed to feeling like I could break it down. I was also just flat out scared. The sound the rapid made, the way it looked wasn't clear to me so I opted to walk the line. For about a month prior to today, I had been considering running it and never felt quite ready for it. This morning I had mentioned to a friend – the coordinator of a local intentional paddle group – that I felt ready to run it. When we got to the eddy above, she asked me, "Do you want to run BZ?" I said, "yes." I got out to scout it, watched her run it and said to myself, "I can do this." I visualized where I wanted to be when I went over the lip and knew I had the skills to run it clean. Slowing everything down, my breath, my brain, my paddle strokes, time, it felt smooth. I had successfully entered through the top of the drop and it took little effort to put myself exactly where I wanted to be. It felt amazing.

The river has allowed me to enter a state of just being. In a world where we are constantly trying to control what we are doing, where we are going, what our next move is, the river has served as a place of refuge in allowing me to let everything go and just be connected with my surroundings. I have started lying back on my kayak so I am able to look up and see the sky and trees that surround the river. I am simply flowing with the natural pace of it. For those breaths and moments, I am completely immersed in my own world and the world around me, and am able to remind myself that I am exactly where I need to be at that very moment. There aren't many other activities in my life, if any at all, where I have felt so whole and alive. As I move through this world, I hold my awareness of my surroundings close to my heart. I do feel as though my spirit has taken this gift of kayaking and is using it as a vehicle to create an inner strength to face obstacles on and off the river. Through kayaking, I have felt my confidence grow to pursue hard things and take care of myself.

Although kayaking appears to be individual, it is very much a team sport. As often as possible, I choose to paddle with people I trust as fellow kayakers, as well as friends. *Do I feel comfortable with the people I am going down this river with? How do I feel around them? Do I know if this person will have my back if something happens to me?* It is so important to listen to any gut feelings, especially in difficult whitewater where consequences are high if someone makes a mistake. But when I'm with people I know will be there for me, I find I can easily tap into the right mental state in order to paddle my best and enjoy the beauty of the experience. By understanding how much of a difference kayaking with the right group can make, I remain intentional about who I spend my time with, both on and off the river.

This taps into the undeniable importance of group dynamics on the river. There is something special about the collective joy experienced within a crew. The feeling of connectedness is often unspoken in the moment but felt by the group as a whole. In some of the most challenging whitewater I have paddled, this group flow manifests in nonverbal communication, such as facial expressions or a single confidence-inducing nod or smile, or in paddling order, with stronger kayakers either taking the lead down a difficult rapid or following behind in a safety position. These seemingly small things make me feel deeply seen and supported by my paddling friends and contribute to a sense of safety and confidence that allows me to push myself in difficult rapids. In my early days of kayaking, I hadn't realized how much even a single person I didn't feel comfortable with in a group could affect my sense of security on the river, inviting fear into my mind and potentially inhibiting my ability to perform well. In a supportive group, it's easy to lean into the fun and encouragement, which I've found most often when paddling with women.

My relationship with my masculine and feminine side is rooted in my childhood and both sides have influenced the kayaker I am today. Growing up with two brothers, there were many times when I had to hide my true self in order to not show weakness in a masculine environment. There was very little space for expression and acceptance and, as I've grown into an adult, I've brought this acquired intensity with me. As I deal with my inner thoughts relating to fear and self-doubt on the river, it somehow feels natural for me to default to a very hardened and detached sense of self. I deem this my masculine side when kayaking because it requires me to enter this "tunnel vision" mentality. I tell myself, *I know you can do this*, even when I am not entirely sure of it. Especially when kayaking with an unfamiliar crew running hard whitewater, I find myself putting on this protective shell, this hardened masculine side. Drowning out any thoughts of doubt, my ego starts to do the internal, and sometimes external, talking. It's something I have become aware of and am working on. In those moments, I am completely relying on my skill to get through whatever is downstream and I find flow through total focus. There is a sense of having to make myself big in a way I associate with my culture in a psychological sense but also in

Playing in my local backyard run in White Salmon, Washington. Photo by Niq Baldwin.

the way I kayak. I am pretty small, so muscling my way through forces much bigger than me will not cut it, but tapping into the masculine mindset helps.

As I lean into that, I make sure I'm balancing it with all of the other characteristics that make me who I am, including my softer side. Connecting with other women in the kayaking community is invaluable; the ability to communicate openly and feel truly understood fosters deep and stable connections overall.

Not long ago, I was running some of the biggest whitewater I had ever run with a friend. The volume of the river was not the style of whitewater I was familiar with. That day, we were going to a flooded class III river, which would make a swim incredibly dangerous, because downed trees on the banks become a major hazard. We geared up and walked to the river and got to a point where we needed to cross shallow water to get to a spot where we could get into our kayaks. During the entire walk I was contemplating not putting on. My body didn't feel the strongest and I was totally in my head about what would happen if something went awry. With my friend, I knew I could be honest about how I felt. I told her I didn't think I needed to put on. Without hesitation, we started walking back toward the car. Then I asked for a pause, and she was patient. Completely comforted by the fact there was no judgment, just pure acceptance of the space I needed in that moment, I looked at the river and again at myself and decided I could overcome my fear. So we made our way back to the river.

So often it feels like an unspoken rule that one cannot express fear openly in a group, especially with men or unfamiliar people. I try to break this norm by openly expressing myself in whatever setting I am in. When kayaking with the women I've built strong friendships with, I feel empowered in my decision making. I am able to speak up for myself and have the space to say out loud that I am nervous or afraid. I'm able to reason through why I feel the way I do and feel supported to ultimately make my own decisions, without pressure or judgment. I am committed to speaking up for myself and voicing my fears, and have always found it to be worth it.

My chosen home is in a hub of amazing women that have exposed me to many different teaching and kayaking styles. One of the local kayakers, and one of the best in the world, Natalie Anderson, hosts a weekly intentional paddle group that is oriented toward mentoring women. Each week there is a new technique highlighted, discussed, and then practiced. Her gentle wisdom, inquiry, and drills have helped widen my awareness of how I kayak and significantly improved my technique. My friend Kallie Kurtz has been the best teacher for giving beta – information – about how to get down specific rapids or features. She has led me down many new and challenging runs, inspiring confidence in me with reliably good beta and lines. Another friend, Melissa Vaughn, constantly gives me strength and nuggets of wisdom. She continuously reminds me there is always more for me to learn and celebrates my successes on the river.

I am incredibly grateful for the guidance of these women, and many more, for the impact they have had on my ability to be a stronger, more courageous, and skilled kayaker. They are my sources of inspiration when I envision myself as a confident leader in whitewater. When I participated in an annual all-women paddling event at my local river, the organizer of the event asked who could be leaders for each group. I felt more than excited to raise my hand, knowing I was capable of stepping up to the task. It felt special to be able to show three strangers-turned-friends down a section of river that taught me all of the basic skills I utilize every time I get in my boat. It also allowed me to expand my typical social circle and meet new people of a variety of ages, some having never experienced the White Salmon River before.

Before everyone put on the river, there was open communication about apprehension or fear anyone was experiencing, and what the flow of the entire group of 45 women rafting would look like. This experience provided space for new people to come together, for others to step into leadership positions, and for all to enjoy the wonder of the White Salmon. It was all executed beautifully. The experience was unique because I can't imagine another space where I would have so eagerly volunteered to step into a leadership role for strangers. I felt confident and inspired afterwards, especially after seeing the huge smiles on the women's faces at the bottom of the last major drop on the river, called Husum Falls. It was also extremely gratifying to hear praise on the beta I gave them that day, and I felt comfortable enough to ask for any critique as well. As the currents of the river carried us to the end of the run, I realized that true leadership isn't just about giving the "right beta" – it's about fostering confidence and embracing the transformative power of sisterhood on and off the water.

Kayaking forces you to face dark parts of yourself. Because of this, it has felt easier to take instruction and be vulnerable with the women around me. I know they can inherently relate to where I'm coming from and help give me tools to deal with whatever challenges I'm facing. They are tuned in to the energies of the people around them in a way I don't notice as often when paddling with men. It is just the reality I have found to be true to me and I wonder if other women have felt this as well. Since I grew up with brothers, I had often felt disconnected from women because it felt difficult for me to relate to them, but I found my true community in the women of whitewater.

When I reflect on the impact kayaking has had on my life, I am in awe of its immensity. It isn't every time that I go on the river that I feel intense fear, go into a flow state, or paddle with a group of people I would consider my best friends, but I do feel privileged to have it as an outlet for creative expression and connection with nature and people. Experiencing fear and working through it makes kayaking worth it. Entering a flow state makes kayaking worth it. Going downstream with an all-time crew makes kayaking worth it.

The relationships I have built with my body, boat, and water will stay with me for the rest of my life, regardless of how it changes. I have incredible gratitude for the friendships I have cultivated and for the endless support I am able to give and receive in those relationships. In many ways, this is just the beginning of my journey, and I am incredibly excited to ride the highs and trust I will have the mental fortitude to overcome the lows. The river's lessons are far from over. I know that, through the rush of future thrills and coming challenges, I will have my kayaking community to learn from, and lean on.

pyranha
SINCE 1971

CHAPTER 5

Into the Current: Learning to Roll with the River Punches

By Alena Rainsberry

Middle Middle, Snoqualmie

Whatever happens, it will all be over in less than 30 seconds. I took long, audible breaths and tried to slow my racing heart. I was in an eddy above a rapid called House Rocks, named for the house-sized boulder positioned halfway down. Wanting it to be over and for the anxiety to end, I inhaled one more shaky breath. I shouted, "Okay!" to my companions and entered the current.

One year after plunging head first into the world of whitewater kayaking, I'd paddled the middle section of the middle fork of the Snoqualmie River – Middle Middle – many times. When traffic and daylight allowed, it was a quick drive to the river after work from Seattle, Washington. Pulling into the parking lot of the put-in used to make my palms slick with sweat because I swam in House Rocks rapid on my first ever descent of Middle Middle, tumbling down the rapid without my boat. But months of practicing had transformed the Snoqualmie from a nerve-racking training ground into a whitewater playground.

At the White Salmon Pride Parade on the river.
Photo by Kate Candace Burke.

That evening was different; the Snoqualmie River was flooded. Its water levels were three times higher than normal. The features of the river would be changed with the increased amount of water. The eddies would be washed out, significantly limiting options for slowing down or stopping. A swim would be long and uncomfortable. I steadied my resolve and slid my boat into the water.

We paddled the upper rapids on the flooded river and my heartbeat quickened as we approached House Rocks. The first part: aim down the middle and turn left. I entered the rapid and a huge wave crashed laterally into me, almost pushing me over. I stabbed my paddle into the water in a desperate attempt to stabilize myself. My kayak rocked from side to side, undecided whether or not to stay upright. Steadying the wobbles, I squinted, searching the next part of the rapid for the features I had become familiar with. But the high water level was obscuring the rocks I was used to aiming toward and the waves were in all the wrong places. I couldn't make sense of the chaos I was hurtling toward. The roar of the current faded to my periphery and the seconds stretched out. *This is it, my doom.* I looked toward the forest at the river's edge, the yellow evening light piercing through the trees. The sunbeams illuminated the mist hovering over the river and I crashed through the surging waves.

Everything was white, and then I was out, and upright. The other kayakers were waiting for me below the rapid. I joined them and Paul leaned over his boat and slapped me on the back in celebration. Gasping for the air I still couldn't believe I was breathing, my mind raced to catch up with my body. At the take-out, my legs trembled as I carried my boat from the river. Still wired, I drove home satisfied but shaky.

As I struggled to sleep that night, the image of yellow evening light over the river kept flashing in my mind. *What if you'd flipped in House Rocks?* But I hadn't flipped. What was so hard for my brain to understand about that? I should just go to sleep, because I was FINE. *But what about next time...*

I weighed my panicky feelings against how much excitement and joy I'd experienced in my year of kayaking. The thought of quitting to avoid risk eventually passed. I was determined to improve my skills and mindset. I wouldn't be paralyzed by fear again.

First Rolls

A chance encounter introduced me to the world of whitewater. I was hiking in the North Cascades mountain range in Washington with friends in early October. They had an invitation from co-workers for rafting the Skagit River the following day, not far from our hike. There was enough extra gear, so I'd been approved to tag along. After our hike, we camped on a dirt mountain road and woke up above thick rain clouds floating in the valley, purple in the early morning light. We drove down the mountain and met Paul, Adrienne, and Eric that Sunday morning at the river. They loaded us into a small raft and escorted us down the class III section like a small flotilla. The small, agile kayaks looked more fun than the raft as they zipped back and forth on the river, leading us through the rapids. I learned they were new to kayaking themselves, and I asked how hard it was to learn to roll. Their reply was, "Want to try?"

Two days later, I was in Seattle's Green Lake attempting to roll under their guidance. Two days after that, I got my first roll and then did ten in a row. The next day I drove two hours to buy my very own used kayak I found on Craigslist.

After the lake sessions, Paul and Eric took me to the closest river training run, a half-mile section below Snoqualmie Falls called Powerhouse. In the class II rapids, they drilled me on fundamental skills like entering and exiting eddies and ferrying across the water. When I caught the edge of my kayak the wrong way on the current, I flipped. The shock of the cold would immediately induce a brain freeze, and the current dragged me upside down over rocks in the shallow water. But I focused on what I'd practiced in the lake to stave off panic. *I'm SO calm.* Then I'd bring my paddle up and around, trying to reach the oxygen above the river's surface. If I couldn't roll up after multiple attempts, I had to swim. By the time I splashed to shore, disappointment and frustration replaced my panic. *Why couldn't I get it?* After each swim, Paul and Eric retrieved my kayak and dumped the water from it. I snapped my sprayskirt over the cockpit again and paddled back to the current. And the next week they would text in our group chat, "Powerhouse?"

Safe Space

The COVID pandemic was sweeping through the world, inducing uncertainty about the future and every aspect of daily life. Even leaving the house to buy groceries was tense as I joined the ranks of other mask-clad shoppers. My unease compounded as I stepped back into the house I rented with my partner at the time. Although we cared deeply for each other, we were coming to the painful conclusion that our differing priorities would inevitably cause our paths to diverge. Neither of us had the financial means to prematurely terminate the lease, or the heart to end our relationship, so we continued to live together through the early days of the pandemic.

As the fall turned to darker winter days, I felt myself shrink. I found it hard to embody my outgoing nature and had to force a semblance of a sense of humor. Through the widening rift between my partner and me, and the hundred other complications of the early days of the pandemic, I felt myself drowning mentally and emotionally. So, when I found the river, she became my escape.

It was easy to throw myself wholeheartedly into the learning process of kayaking. I focused on navigating the cold water, reading the river features, and practicing the techniques. There was a slew of new slang to learn and customs to acquire. With my personal life in turmoil, it was unexpectedly soothing to be forced to focus on very immediate, basic needs in the river. *Can I breathe? Am I warm? Do I have enough energy to keep going?* It forced my mind into the present, and through the distraction I found reprieve from dark moods and anxious thoughts.

Skykomish

It was a crisp, fall morning almost a year after I found the river. The heat of the summer had left and the leaves were just starting to quiver with the anticipation of seasonal change. I was itching to paddle. A friend and I were headed to the Skykomish River in Washington, a wide river with crystal-clear blue water that cuts through the striking, rocky peaks of the Cascade Mountains. He knew of some other people that would be at the river that day and we were going to meet up with them. I was nervous to kayak with new people but determined to paddle well.

We met the other kayakers at the put-in parking lot. All men. Tall, middle-aged guys who weren't very chatty. Half their size, with less than one-tenth of their experience, I was suddenly very cognizant of how short I was standing next to them. I also felt a growing unease that there wasn't space to mess up. That I should perform well to prove a five-foot-tall woman was meant to be there. *It's ok, you'll do fine. You won't swim. And you WON'T flip on the first rapid.*

We got in our boats and the cold spray from the first rapid splashed my face. As if my anxiety were directing a self-fulfilling prophecy, I flipped right on cue. I rolled up ungracefully at the

bottom of the rapid, my cheeks turning red despite the freezing water. The guys cast glances in my direction but didn't say anything and continued downriver.

I spent the rest of the run painfully conscious of each move. *Was that a good boof? Should I have caught that eddy?* I looked over at my friend, taking relaxed strokes and smiling in the lovely weather, unaware of the critique wreaking havoc in my mind. If he had flipped right away, would he have felt so self-conscious?

Or was I even being judged? I couldn't tell if I was making it all up, being sensitive, or overthinking everything. Maybe they didn't think anything of it, or had already forgotten, or hadn't paid attention in the first place. But why did I care what others thought of me? I was kayaking for myself, not for them, so what they were thinking shouldn't even matter. If they were, in fact, judging me, then their opinions should matter even less.

Through the flurry of thoughts, I focused on the warmth of the sunshine permeating my waterproof drysuit. Looking over the side of my kayak, I saw salmon through the glassy water. Their speckled backs camouflaged against the brown and gray of the river rocks, but the flexing motion of their bodies gave them away. Careful not to disturb them with my paddle strokes, I floated past. I imagined flipping just to see the surprise on their fish faces as I joined them underwater.

Paddling in front of Mount Index on the Skykomish River. Photo by AJ Frank.

Pushing myself to improve in big water on the Skykomish River. Photo by Will Baker.

Swim to Win

A few months later, a desire to combine my wanderlust and my newfound love for kayaking led me to the lush jungles of Ecuador. I filled my days with petting the local dogs, practicing my beginner Spanish, and eating ice cream in the equatorial sun. I became a habitué at the local kayak hostel, sharing the river with new friends as paddlers came and went. Over the months, I could feel myself getting smoother and more confident in my kayak as I navigated the technical boulder gardens of the jungle rivers.

One night over beers at the hostel, I was convinced to sign up for an upcoming slalom race. There was only one other woman who was signed up. Despite not liking the pressure of competing, and not caring about being faster than others, I put my name on the list. I wanted to increase the size of the women's division.

On the day of the race, I stood at the river's edge and studied the course. It started in a calm side channel before meeting up with the main body of the river. The first move was a ferry in strong current and big waves all the way to the other side of the river, right above two massive holes before the first gate. I saw a rock barely poking out of the whitewater above the ferry line. I decided I would use that as a marker to paddle toward before allowing the bow of my boat to be pushed downstream. But I didn't feel confident.

A race official held my boat until, "3, 2, 1, go!" I paddled the short, flat section until it flowed into the rushing current. I hesitated briefly, heart pounding, then entered the whitewater, my kayak angled upstream for the ferry move. The current pushed against my boat and after very little cross-river progress I was pushed sideways and dropped into the first hole. I pulled my sprayskirt and the water rushed around my legs and filled my boat as I swam, all within 30 seconds of my start time. I finished the course clinging to the back of the rescue kayaker's boat in front of the riverside spectators, but in my mind I was in the past, telling my hostel friends that, no, I would not be competing in the race, thank you very much.

I dragged myself and my boat, the latter delivered to me by another safety kayaker, out of the water. Disappointment consumed me. I pushed through the bushes and up the hill that led to the path back to the beginning of the course. I stopped at the top of the hill. I didn't want to watch the race alongside the rest of the crowd. I stayed near the end, watching every other paddler confidently swish through and around the gates. *Not even one more swimmer?*

My friend Nathan took his turn on the course. After his lap, he paused next to me on the hill, looking out at the water. "Hope you're not beating yourself up."

I stared mutely ahead. My throat tightened as I watched the next kayaker ace gate after gate. Nathan hoisted his boat higher on his shoulder and continued toward the other spectators.

I thought back to the elation of the previous day. Nathan, Sal – an extremely talented and charismatic paddler from the UK – and I had kayaked Chaco Canyon on the Quijos River. It was by far the hardest section of river I had ever run. The jungle canyon had been juicy with whitewater, its stunning basalt walls rising above us as we flowed down the river. Nathan and Sal had helped me scout and navigate the intimidating rapids. The exhilaration was visceral as we paddled down the final waves, shouting with joy. Just one day later, as I stood watching the race, the dismay I felt after my swim matched the intensity of the previous day's high. The emotional roller coaster of kayaking was as turbulent as the whitewater, and the extremes left me drained.

I would have been content to never do a slalom course again, but it was time for my second lap of the race. I slid into my boat and waited for the countdown. *Can't possibly be worse than the first time.* I paddled to the start of the ferry move, charged into the current, digging my paddle deep. I kept the marker rock in sight, managing a few more strokes than the first time, but still was pushed downriver and into the hole again. This time I did not flip. I stayed upright and surfed out the hole, using its power to push me to the opposite side of the river to the eddy with the first gate. I was so elated to make it past the first move and still be in my boat that I paused to take a breath and refocus. Sal was the judge for that gate and she smiled big at me. I only made two of the four gates, but I didn't care. I was happy at the end of the course.

As one of two women in the international women's category, I automatically qualified for finals. I groaned when I learned I had to go for a third time. In the finals, I paddled before my competitor. Even though I was faster than my second lap, I still missed half the gates. If the other racer made even three of the gates, she would win. After I finished my final lap, I stayed in an eddy just downstream of the final gate as she came down the course after me. At that moment, I caught myself hoping she would botch her ferries, or flip, or swim. Would winning affirm to me that, yes, I was skilled enough to be here? I had never watched someone paddle and *wanted* them to mess up. In the end, she also completed two of the four gates. But because she had spent extra time fighting for the third gate, my time was quicker.

Later that evening, the local restaurant was filled with laughing and chatting kayakers as we waited for the awards ceremony. The organizers presented me with the medal, but the "win" felt contrived, arbitrary. Considering my swim on the first lap, I wasn't sure I deserved it. I just couldn't bring myself to regard *faster* as a valid metric of my abilities. I preferred the celebration of the previous day after Chaco Canyon. While Nathan, Sal, and I had waited for our taxi, we'd jumped up and down to stay warm in the rain and debriefed the run. They knew how nervous I'd been before starting down the river. Their high fives and shouts of encouragement after each rapid boosted my confidence more than any medal.

Mining and Marching

The vibrant jungle city of Tena, Ecuador, where I'd been living for months, is oriented around a single long main street bisected by the confluence of the Tena and Pano rivers. On February 9, 2022, I joined hundreds of people gathered at the *malecón* (promenade) by the river. "*Napo es vida, no minería!*" (Napo is life, no mining!) The chanting grew stronger as more people congregated. Locals, Indigenous Peoples, and kayakers marched through the streets in Tena. Protesters filled the street from sidewalk to sidewalk. We marched through the streets and over the main bridge, eventually ending in front of a local government office, chanting while local leaders of the protest made speeches in Spanish through loudspeakers. It was an unprecedented turnout, the local café owner told me with proud tears in his eyes. Many people of Tena and the greater Napo valley had come together against the exploitation of the land. Kayakers, local and foreign, showed up to march as well, but it was the local organizers that gave speeches in front of the government office and have been fighting to protect their rivers and land.

Illegal mining has been problematic in the province of Napo for years. A local paddler pointed it out to me on my first day in Ecuador on the Jatunyacu River. Many of the surrounding rivers join the mighty Jatunyacu as tributaries to become the Napo River that flows into the Amazon and eventually empties into the Atlantic Ocean.

Even in my few months in Ecuador, the mining on the Jatunyacu had noticeably worsened. Every time we put our boats on the river, there were more machines, more diggers, and less riverbank. By the last time I paddled the river, many of the natural rapids were completely changed. The native banks and beaches of the river were transformed into piles of gravel.

Sarayu River

Before I returned to the US from Ecuador, Nathan mentioned he would be paddling in the Indian Himalayas the following fall, if anyone else was interested. Eight months and a 16-hour flight later, I joined him in New Delhi and we traveled north to the mountain town of Rishikesh. We were soon laughing in roller-coaster-sized waves in the big water of the Ganges.

A week later, we got an invitation to join an expedition to run the Sarayu River, a tributary of the Ganges in the corner between Nepal and Tibet. The Sarayu had previously been run very few times and the promise of crystal blue water cascading through valleys of the Himalayan foothills made joining an obvious choice. We met up with the rest of the crew and traveled for two days by Jeep through Himalayan pine forests and beautiful mountain towns. Looking over to Tibet, the views of the Himalayas towering over the valley between us took my breath away.

The expedition crew consisted of a colorful mix of local paddlers and other foreigners, ranging from some of the best kayakers in India to rafting newbies from Denmark. Our flotilla would include two rafts, one with passengers and one with gear, plus 11 kayaks. Nathan and I rounded out the group of 16 people. Fifteen men, and me.

I found out quickly this was not a trip that happened to have only guys; it was a guy's trip. Our first night as a group set the tone with whiskey drinking and beedi smoking. As a non-smoker with a low alcohol tolerance, I couldn't even pretend to participate and immediately felt the social gap.

Our journey started at the mountain city of Bageshwar at a Hindu temple dedicated to Lord Shiva. He is said to have harnessed the power of Ganga, the river goddess of the Ganges, in his dreadlocks. We greeted the *baba*, the custodian of the temple, before exploding our gear under the banyan tree to repack it in the rafts. Our group set off in high spirits, laughing in the sun. We didn't exactly know what to expect. No one in our group had run the Sarayu before, except the man guiding the raft with the

Camping with the guys on the banks of the Sarayu River in India. Photo by Alena Rainsberry.

Danish boys, which followed behind the kayakers. In single file, our procession of colorful plastic boats followed the cerulean waters through macaque-filled hillsides and quartzite canyons. I studied Nathan and the other kayakers in front of me, adjusting my line as we cruised through a series of class IV rapids. I was focused on the angle of my boofs and keeping my balance in the swirly water. But through the whitewater I could feel doubt stirring in my mind. *What if it gets harder? What if you mess up and swim?*

That night we camped close to another Shiva temple, perched on a hill next to the beach where we laid out our sleeping bags and cooked dinner. In the morning, before the rest of the crew woke up, I walked up the hill to wander the temple grounds. I was careful not to disturb the resident *baba* praying in one of the buildings. Sitting on one of the walls overlooking the river, I took some deep breaths, relishing the stillness of the morning. I mentally prepared myself for the physical and emotional energy needed to get through a day of unknown whitewater and socializing with the group. The persistent doubt was still buzzing in the back of my mind. I felt the weight of being the newest kayaker by years, or even decades, and the feeling of needing to prove myself as the only woman in the crew. I tried to take the responsibility from my shoulders and leave it on the stone wall at the temple that morning. There was no reason the next part of the river would not go well. After all, I had paddled just fine the day before. *You got this*, I whispered to myself. The social dynamic? I steeled my resolve to not let the smoking and drinking bother me and to focus on my experience and the gratitude I felt to be in such an unimaginably beautiful place.

The kayaking the next day was spectacular. At the top of each rapid, the unknown features obscured below the horizon line, I took a deep breath and hardened my resolve. When the roar of the upcoming rapid was loud enough for my apprehension to turn to fear, I would audibly reaffirm "You got this" so that my forced confidence was louder than my voice of doubt. In some of the rapids I threaded my way through the features, catching small variations in the current to quickly change direction and efficiently work my way down the best line. In others, I fought my way down, getting pummeled by the force of the water, obstinately rolling up after the river spat me out.

Even as the others relaxed and joked, I stayed focused as we paddled rapid after rapid, the Sarayu weaving in and out of canyons as it snaked its way through the mountains. We stopped at a small, sloped beach for camping that night, completely surrounded by dense jungle. The guys swapped boisterous stories and laughed, smoking beedies and hash and drinking whiskey around the campfire. I quietly stepped away from the group and climbed a house-sized boulder at the river's edge. My energy was drained, completely spent from concentrating on the whitewater. I had none left to socialize and found peace in my moment alone. From my boulder, I enjoyed being adjacent to the campfire festivities. We were still connected by being on this expedition together and in our shared love for the river. I looked away from the campfire beach toward the even smaller beach where I'd set up my sleeping spot. There hadn't been enough space to position my sleeping bag more than a few feet away from the leopard prints at the water's edge. As evening turned to dusk, I peered into the darkening jungle beyond our tiny riverside camp and wondered what the leopard thought about the sudden party at her drinking spot.

A week after we finished the expedition with the large group and the rafts, Nathan and I wanted to paddle the blue water and epic rapids of the Sarayu River again. Two more of his friends had just arrived from the UK – we would redo the Sarayu as a four-person kayak self-support trip.

We arrived in Bageshwar again late in the evening and slept under the temple's banyan tree. In the morning, as we shoved gear into our boats, I felt the all-too-familiar doubt creeping into my mind. It refused to dissipate in anticipation of redoing the challenging whitewater. In my dejection, I confided in Nathan, "I feel so much pressure to not mess up. I've already paddled it, I should be able to do it again."

He replied in his matter-of-fact way. "You're the only one putting that pressure on yourself." It was Nathan-speak for "It's okay, you got this. No pressure or judgment here."

I finished packing before the boys and sat at the river's edge in the morning sunshine, stretching my legs out over the bow of my kayak. I knew I'd soon have to assume the cramped paddling position for hours. Inspecting the striped pebbles on the shore, I searched for a Bageshwar souvenir as I waited for my friends to make their way down the temple steps and join me at the water.

Moonlight Magic

After returning from India in the fall, I was more determined than ever to improve my skills. I moved to White Salmon on the southern border of Washington state along the Columbia River Gorge, known simply as "the Gorge" to kayakers and other outdoor sports enthusiasts. A tributary of the Columbia, the White Salmon River is spring-fed and has enough water for paddling even in the driest summer months.

About a month into settling into my new home, I walked across the bridge overlooking Husum Falls on a blustery winter day. There was another woman on the bridge also looking at the falls. "Are you running it?" I asked. Jenny, I learned, was over a year into kayaking, just as excited as me, and even more driven to run big rivers. We decided right there on the bridge to be training buddies. Thus began "Wet Wednesdays," meeting up before daybreak in the freezing winter mornings to paddle before work. Pushing each other as we developed more advanced skills, we set our sights on new, bigger whitewater. As spring melt from the nearby mountains raised the rivers to heart-pounding levels, we tested our physical and mental strength on the Gorge's beautiful rivers.

At the beginning of summer, the full moon of June drew local kayakers to the nighttime magic of a moonlight paddle. The moon was just starting its circadian accession as over 20 kayakers and even a few rafters laughed and howled into the night from the velvety dark water. When we arrived at the take-out, my friend Kate pointed out that the moon was now fully overhead. We weren't ready for the magic to end. Kate, Jenny, and I drove back to the top and slid our boats into the water again, this time soaking up the mysterious hush of the night under the ethereal moonlight. We paused in an eddy in the middle of the run and Kate turned to me. "I'm so glad you moved here!" In the easiest section of the river, surrounded by friends I'd known for less than half a year, my tears of gratitude flowed into the nighttime water as we floated between the dark canyon walls.

Final Five, North Fork Payette

Later that summer, I stood with my friend Sage Ebel on the side of Idaho's Highway 55 scouting a rapid called Juicer. Massive waves and even bigger holes left little doubt as to the rapid's namesake. Swimming this would be a long, dangerous situation. Sage, a much more experienced kayaker, talked me through the line. Boof the flare rock at the top, skirt past a hole, drive back right and boof, boof, boof down the right side of the river. I took my time to study the water as I tried to memorize the line and imagine what it would be like in the middle of it before we hopped back in the car and drove to the top of the run.

The big water of North Fork of the Payette draws pro kayakers to Idaho each summer. The last five miles, the Final Five, are known as the easiest part of this infamous river. This section would be my introduction to big water class V, and even from the highway it looked enormous. Sage had led me down the first half of the run the previous day. Since I had done well, she was going to lead me down the entire Final Five, including the biggest rapids at the end – Juicer and Crunch.

It was a big step up for me, and I was thrilled to be with Sage. She gave me the beta I needed and didn't rush me while scouting. She didn't sugarcoat the difficulty of the river but let me know she was confident I could do it. I realized with delight that the confidence I felt in my skills wasn't forced; the voice of doubt and impending embarrassment was simply absent. I'd been kayaking hard all spring and felt ready for this challenge.

We paddled through the beginning section from the day before and took a break at the optional take-out before the last two big rapids. "Feeling good?" she asked.

Adrenaline was already racing through my body from the first part of the run. "Let's do it!"

We entered Juicer and I immediately realized how much bigger the whitewater was than it had looked from the road. I dug my paddle in with every shred of energy I could pull from the muscles in my shoulders and core. I trailed Sage like my life depended on it. The features were so big that I was too terrified to mess up. Boof, charge right, boof, boof, boof. My heart was exiting my body through my throat, but I was still upright at the end.

Just one monster left – Crunch. We hadn't scouted this rapid from the road, but Sage had told me to boof over the holes the entire way down the right side of the river. We entered and I couldn't see an end to the waves and holes. I stayed as closely behind Sage as possible, feeling like my safety was inversely proportional to the distance between us. Right at the beginning I caught the edge of my kayak on a change in the current, turning me the wrong way. I was about to drop sideways over the first of what looked like ten massive holes. Quickly catching a tiny eddy above the drop, I reset. Sage disappeared in the whitewater chaos ahead of me. I would have to do it without her. I took a deep breath and entered the main current again with better angle and speed. At the bottom I let out a manic laugh in semi-shock. I felt like I had blacked out as I fought my way through. I didn't look like a pro in Crunch, but I didn't flip, and Sage cheered for me as we continued downstream.

As the shock faded, I was overwhelmed with a surge of emotions. Pride, fear, stoke, and gratitude swirled through my mind and flowed to every cell in my body, leaving me electrified for days. This, I decided, is how I want to run new rivers.

Into the Flow

The first rays of cold morning light are just starting to peek through the treetops. Icy streams trickle down from the forest above, weaving through the moss-clad rocks of the canyon wall, finding their way always to the waiting river. Jenny and I snap our skirts over our cockpits without speaking, our breath forming miniature clouds in the early morning air. We slide our boats into the water and steer our bows into the current.

We both have work in a few hours. There will be co-workers to chat with, spreadsheets to organize, and emails to send. But the early morning is ours. We carve in and out of eddies, flowing over and around the rocks, using the current to move our boats and to move us.

Sometimes we paddle quickly and efficiently in the early mornings, and other times we savor the quiet moments between

Finding peace on the river. Photo by AJ Frank.

My first time on Canyon Creek of the Lewis River in the Pacific Northwest. Photo by Ben Goulder.

rapids like sipping coffee. Today, we linger and in a calm section we drift gently apart. I lean back, rest my head on the stern of my boat, and close my eyes, letting my mind drift too. My body fills with gratitude for this regular Wednesday morning. But no day is regular if it starts like this, and I know the rest of my Wednesday will carry a little extra magic, captured in the frosty morning. Tasks to be completed at work. Taxes to be filed. Groceries to shop for. The river rinses away the flurry of thoughts and slips each one into the cold water with a *plop*.

More than yoga, I prefer this surrender on the river. I am content as a temporary part of this moving landscape. In moments of fear in big rapids I have to dig deep to find resolve and strength to power through. Sheer stubbornness keeps me trying to roll up when the river is holding me under. I love tapping into that fire, fueling the adrenaline-filled moments of pure focus and commitment. But I also cherish these hushed moments, gently flowing over water-worn rocks.

I sit up, breaking my reverie, and see Jenny paddling ahead of me. She is a bright splash of Gore-Tex against the living backdrop of moss, water, and stone. I dig my paddle into the water to catch up, ready for the next rapid.

CHAPTER 6

Paddling in Paradise: Rafaela Sánchez Castillo's Kayaking Journey in Ecuador's Jungle Rivers

By Denisa Krásná

Rafaela (Rafa) is a spirited 14-year-old kayaker from Ecuador. She was born in Quito but calls Puyo her home. Nestled in the transition from the Andes to the Amazon, Puyo stands as a gateway to the rainforest with its verdant landscapes, cascading waterfalls, and winding rivers. The greater surrounding provinces of Pastaza and Napo serve as a hub for kayakers, both seasoned enthusiasts and novices alike, drawn by the allure of navigating the jungle rivers.

From a young age, Rafa found herself immersed in a vibrant kayaking community surrounded by paddlers from around the world who flocked to Ecuador in pursuit of their kayaking dreams. In this mixture of local and international paddlers, she found inspiration and camaraderie.

Rafa has been kayaking since she was 11 years old, finding her passion for kayaking early in life, inspired by her father's own love for the sport. His personal journey into kayaking was laid out by his parents, who one day made an unexpected investment – they purchased kayaks. Despite living far from the rivers in the bustling capital of Quito, they were determined to learn. Their desire led them to the waters of Baños de Agua Santa, a picturesque city under the shadow of the majestic Tungurahua volcano, where they honed their kayaking skills. Eventually, Rafa's grandfather passed the boats to her father, laying the foundation for her own journey into kayaking.

Rafa's own introduction to kayaking began with trepidation, as she recalls her first experience on the river with Kayak Club Ecuador under the guidance of Gabriel Garbin in the nearby city of Tena. At first she was gripped by fear. Yet, amid the rush of adrenaline and the connection with friends, she found satisfaction and exhilaration, marking the start of a lifelong bond with

Rafa practicing on the river of her home country, Ecuador. Photo by @nickaobenalcazar.

Rafa on the Misahuallí River in Ecuador. Photo by Luigi Castilloni.

the sport. “Despite initial worries, I felt a lot of tranquility and trust in the people around me,” Rafa recalls of her first kayaking memories.

For Rafa, kayaking transcends mere sport and adventure. It serves as a sanctuary for her mind, a place where the stresses of life dissipate and she finds peace in the rhythm of the river. “When I’ve had a bad day, or when I’m going through a bad moment, I go kayaking and it helps me relax. Suddenly, everything is forgotten.” Kayaking, for Rafa, is also a conduit for forming deep connections with her teammates, a chosen family that shares her passion and pushes her to new heights: “It’s a very special bond that I’ve formed during this time with my crew.”

In Ecuador, while whitewater kayaking has gained popularity as a sport and recreational activity, female participation in the sport is noticeably lower compared to their male counterparts. As a consequence, Rafa paddles almost exclusively with men, which leaves her yearning for a different dynamic: “They are very respectful, very cool, but I miss that feminine energy.” Lately, there has been a growing movement to encourage and empower girls and women to participate in kayaking and other outdoor activities, through initiatives such as women-only paddling events. Rafa was part of one such paddling experience exclusively with women, alongside her friend Fátima Naveda, where she was grateful for the power of feminine energy, a welcomed change-up from her usual male-dominated outings.

Through her years of kayaking, Rafa has undergone a transformation, evolving from a girl easily deterred by setbacks to a determined and resilient athlete. Kayaking became her crucible for resilience, instilling in her the invaluable lesson of perseverance: “When I started kayaking, I was frustrated very easily and wanted to give up. But through kayaking, I learned to try, try, try, try, until I get it.” This newfound mindset has transcended the waters, permeating other facets of her life, empowering her to confront challenges with steadfast determination and resilience.

She credits her coach, Billy, for instilling in her the perseverance to overcome obstacles both on and off the river. One defining moment stands out in Rafa’s memory, a testament to the dedicated support of her coach. She recounts a harrowing experience on the Piatua River, marking her first encounter with its challenging rapids. As she was navigating through the smooth boulder gardens, she flipped and had to swim. “I went through a lot of holes and I was already super, super exhausted – I couldn’t take it anymore. Then I got stuck in a really big hole. At that moment, I just wanted to let go.” But Billy came to her rescue and got her out of the hole. “I got out, but he got stuck. He stayed for a long, long, long time to the point where he swam. He was throwing up when he got out on the shore; that hole was super nasty.” Rafa knows Billy risked himself to save her, and it is this memory that reinforces her trust in her crew and their willingness to sacrifice for one another.

The intensity of the ordeal left Rafa shaken and emotionally overwhelmed, prompting her to momentarily contemplate abandoning her passion for kayaking altogether. Yet, amid the turmoil, the sense of camaraderie within her team became unmistakably clear, reaffirming the depth of their bonds and the lengths they would go to support one another. Despite the

Rafa with her coaches and friends from Kayak Club Ecuador. Photo by Gabriel Garbin.

trauma of the experience, Rafa emerged from the river with a newfound appreciation for the unwavering solidarity of her team.

While she returned to the river, fear became a common companion for Rafa, manifesting itself in moments of uncertainty on the river. Admitting fear is a common emotion in kayaking, and she describes instances where she feels paralyzed upon entering certain rivers, overwhelmed by the dangers they present. In her earlier years, Rafa recalls being more susceptible to fear, often finding herself in tears amid moments of uncertainty on the river. However, as she has matured, she has developed coping mechanisms to manage her apprehension: "I was limiting myself in being able to move forward. But I have learned to breathe. I learned to distinguish if it's just fear or it's me protecting myself from danger. And if it's fear, I say, Rafa, breathe."

With the guidance of her coach and the support of her team, she's learned to distinguish between rational caution and irrational fear, empowering her to push her limits and quell her anxieties. Rafa has gained confidence in her abilities and her readiness to tackle varying levels of difficulty on the river. She emphasizes the significance of communication with her team, acknowledging when a situation surpasses her current skill level and asserting her boundaries accordingly. Rafa recalls a pivotal moment on the Jatunyacu River. After flipping in an intimidating rapid and getting stuck in a massive hole, she was engulfed with fear and uncertainty. She recalled Gabriel's persistent advice: "Try another roll, another roll, another roll, one more, give it another roll." Returning to the river after the ordeal, she

Learning to breathe through fears on the river. Photo by Luigi Castilloni.

navigated the same rapid with newfound determination, overcoming her apprehension to paddle a clean line. For Rafa, this moment epitomizes what she considers success in kayaking: "to overcome your fears and move forward little by little."

In navigating the challenges of kayaking, Rafa often grapples with external pressures and internal expectations. Whether facing formidable rapids or daunting obstacles on the river, she finds herself subjected to the well-meaning, but sometimes overwhelming, encouragement of others urging her onward. But Rafa doesn't easily give in to external pressure. Through the support of her team, and her own introspection, she has learned to discern between genuine risk and undue pressure. Recognizing her safety and well-being ultimately lie in her own hands, she has cultivated the strength to assert herself and say no when necessary. "When I really see that it's a danger, that something can happen to me, that I'm not ready for that, I say no. And I say to my coaches, 'I'm sorry, I'm not ready for this.'" In doing so, she has embraced a newfound sense of agency and autonomy, navigating the waters of kayaking – and life itself – with greater confidence and conviction.

In December 2023, Rafa participated in the Cosanga Race, an annual kayaking competition organized on the Cosanga River in the jungle-clad mountains of Napo. Reflecting on her experience at the Cosanga Race, Rafa recounts a mix of emotions. Participating for the first time, she found herself confronted with the reality of inequality within the competition. There were significantly fewer female participants than males. While the expert category had separate divisions for men and women, the intermediate and beginner categories were combined for women. "This seemed too unfair to me. We didn't have the same opportunities to win." Despite the challenging conditions, and the frustration of competing against a division dominated by more experienced participants, Rafa's love for competition remains undiminished. "I like competing! I like the feeling before competition, feeling nervous, but at the same time you know you can do it. It's a beautiful experience." Looking ahead, Rafa expresses a genuine fondness for competing and hints at a desire to continue testing her skills in future races.

As she looks ahead to her future in kayaking, Rafa outlines her current and future goals with a sense of determination. She reveals her immediate focus on preparing for high-performance training with Kayak Club Ecuador, aiming to continue her journey toward more challenging whitewater. Looking further ahead, Rafa sets her sights on a formidable challenge: paddling the Topo River in Río Negro, close to her hometown. Renowned for its difficulty, this river is accessible to only the most skilled paddlers, earning it a legendary status in the kayaking community. Despite the daunting nature of the task, Rafa expresses a deep-seated desire to fulfill this ambition – a goal she has harbored since the outset of her kayaking journey.

Yet her favorite river remains the Jondachi as it joins the Hollín, located in Napo. With an abundance of waterfalls cascading into it from the canyon walls, the river is known among kayakers for its striking features and spectacular rapids. Rafa describes it as a river of unparalleled beauty and energy,

Rafa, finding courage and joy in her passion for kayaking. Photo by Luigi Castilloni.

enchanting her from the moment she set foot on its riverbank. The sheer majesty of the landscape, punctuated by numerous waterfalls, left an indelible impression on her. For Rafa, the Jondachi–Hollín river section embodies a sense of serenity and exhilaration – a place where she feels truly connected to the natural world and invigorated by its power. "I entered the river and felt such a beautiful energy, such a pure energy, which I could enjoy in its entirety."

In her kayaking endeavors, Rafa experiences a profound connection with nature, finding solace and beauty in the environments she encounters. She reminisces about the allure of rivers like Misahuallí and Jatunyacu, where she feels immersed in the tranquility and splendor of the natural world. "When I entered the river, it felt so beautiful, it was like nature was welcoming you, like it was saying, come, come, come, come, come closer." However, her admiration is tinged with sorrow when reflecting on the impact of mining activities, particularly on the Jatunyacu River. Rafa laments the extensive degradation caused by mining, witnessing firsthand the devastation of once-pristine landscapes and natural environments.

Rafa describes the stark transformation that has occurred over time. When she first visited Jatunyacu, the pristine beauty of the wild river captivated her. What was once a serene haven for the Indigenous communities and kayakers alike has now succumbed to the pervasive influence of mining activities. As Rafa reflects on the current state of Jatunyacu, she observes with a heavy heart the encroachment of mining infrastructure along the riverbanks. The once-vibrant greenery and natural rock bed has given way to a landscape dominated by industrial activity, leaving only pockets of untouched riverbank amid a sea of mining operations.

Mining endangers kayakers themselves. On one occasion not so long ago, Rafa and her team were navigating downriver when they encountered a harrowing confrontation. A miner, wielding a gun, was aiming it at them. "I didn't know what to do because nobody is prepared for that situation." Rafa recalls numerous other instances where their kayaking days were disrupted by hostile actions. "There have been many times in a row when they have thrown stones at us when we were only going down the river."

Her experiences with mining-related conflicts underscore the urgent need for environmental protection in Ecuador. Rafa expresses frustration at the government's inaction in addressing these issues, attributing it to corruption and vested interests within the political sphere. She highlights the irony of Ecuador's status as a tourist destination juxtaposed with the environmental degradation wrought by unchecked mining activities. Rafa advocates for swift intervention to curb further environmental degradation and preserve Ecuador's natural beauty for future generations.

In her role as a kayaker, Rafa actively contributes to environmental conservation efforts. She prioritizes spreading awareness about the current state of rivers and their ecosystems, regularly engaging in conversations with friends and fellow enthusiasts to highlight the pressing issues facing these natural resources. Rafa emphasizes the tangible impact of pollution on river health, noting the prevalence of litter during her paddling excursions. Committed to taking practical action, she makes a habit of collecting trash she encounters along riverbanks and in rivers, often stowing discarded bottles and other litter in her kayak for proper disposal. Through her advocacy and hands-on conservation efforts, Rafa strives to instill a greater sense of responsibility and stewardship toward protecting the environment among her peers and within the kayaking community.

Despite the challenges she faces, Rafa remains undeterred in her passion for kayaking and her commitment to preserving the natural environment. Amid the thrill of competition and the beauty of nature, it's the sense of camaraderie and shared passion that Rafa cherishes most. For her, kayaking isn't just a sport. It's a way of life, a journey filled with challenges, triumphs, and the unbreakable friendships forged on the water.

PART II: ROCK

Climbing

It goes, boys!

—Lynn Hill after the first free ascent of the Nose

Climbing is a multifaceted sport that encompasses various disciplines, each with its own challenges, techniques, and rich history. From the vertical walls of indoor climbing gyms to the towering peaks of remote mountains, climbing captivates adventurers and athletes alike, offering a unique blend of physical prowess, mental fortitude, and a profound connection with the natural world.

The history of climbing spans millennia, evolving from a necessity for survival to a popular recreational and competitive sport. Ancient cultures engaged in climbing for various purposes, such as hunting, gathering, and religious rituals. Early evidence of climbing dates back to prehistoric times, depicted in cave paintings and archeological findings.

Anna Šebestíková on Czech sandstone. Photo by Standa Mitáč.

Mountainous regions like the Alps and the Himalayas have long been sites of human exploration and ascent. In the 18th and 19th centuries, climbing began to take on a more recreational form in Europe, with notable ascents of peaks like Mont Blanc and the Matterhorn. The late 19th and early 20th centuries saw the development of mountaineering as a sport, with organized clubs and the establishment of climbing routes and techniques. In the mid-20th century, the focus shifted to rock climbing, with the emergence of new equipment, techniques, and climbing disciplines. Today, climbing encompasses a wide range of styles and disciplines, the three major ones being mountaineering or alpinism; trad, or traditional, climbing; and sport climbing.

Mountaineering, or alpinism, stands as the epitome of climbing exploration, representing a fusion of technical proficiency, mountaineering prowess, and a deep connection to the world's most formidable and remote mountain environments. From the rugged peaks of the Rockies to the soaring summits of the Andes, alpinists embark on audacious expeditions to ascend towering peaks, traverse icy ridges, and navigate treacherous glaciated slopes, confronting a myriad of physical, mental, and logistical challenges along the way. At the heart of alpinism lies a relentless pursuit of adventure and exploration, as climbers venture into some of Earth's most inhospitable and awe-inspiring landscapes.

The demands of alpinism require climbers to possess a diverse skill set honed through years of training and experience. Mastery of technical climbing techniques, including rock, ice, and mixed climbing, is essential for navigating steep and exposed terrain. Alpinists must also possess a keen understanding of mountain weather patterns, avalanche dynamics, and high-altitude physiology, enabling them to make informed decisions and mitigate risks in remote and unforgiving environments. Furthermore, alpinism demands exceptional levels of physical fitness, mental resilience, and teamwork. Climbers must acclimate to extreme altitudes, endure harsh weather conditions, and manage limited resources and equipment while maintaining focus and clarity of thought in high-stakes situations. Success in alpinism often hinges on effective communication, trust, and collaboration among team members, as climbers rely on each other for support and safety throughout the expedition. Alpinists experience beauty and solitude amid the vastness of the mountains, forging a deep and enduring bond with each other and the landscapes they explore.

Trad climbing, or traditional climbing, represents a return to the essence of mountaineering where climbers engage in a deeply immersive and adventurous experience on natural rock formations. Unlike sport climbing, which relies on pre-placed bolts for protection, trad climbing involves placing and removing removable gear as climbers ascend, leaving no permanent traces on the rock. The essence of trad climbing lies in its emphasis on self-sufficiency and problem solving. Trad climbers must possess a comprehensive understanding of various types of protective gear, including nuts, cams, hexes, and slings, and know how to select and place them securely in cracks, fissures, and other natural features of the rock. This intricate process demands meticulous attention to detail, as the effectiveness of the protection directly impacts the safety of the climber.

Moreover, trad climbing requires a keen sense of route finding and navigation. Trad climbing routes follow natural features of the rock, requiring climbers to discern the best line of ascent based on the terrain and available protection opportunities. This aspect of trad climbing adds an element of exploration and discovery. In addition to its inherent physical and technical challenges, trad climbing creates a strong sense of community among climbers. Trad climbers often form close-knit partnerships and share a mutual respect for the traditions and values of the sport. They uphold a code of ethics that prioritizes environmental stewardship, leave-no-trace principles, and responsible climbing practices, ensuring that future generations can continue to enjoy the beauty and majesty of natural rock formations.

Sport climbing, characterized by climbing routes equipped with permanent bolts and anchors for protection, has seen a surge in popularity in recent decades. Originating in Europe in the late 19th century, sport climbing evolved from traditional mountaineering techniques and has since become a distinct discipline in its own right. Climbers ascend routes of varying difficulty, relying on strength, agility, and technique to navigate challenging sequences of holds and movements. Sport climbing routes are equipped with permanent anchors, known as bolts, which are drilled into the rock. These bolts serve as fixed points of protection, allowing climbers to clip their rope to the bolts as they ascend, thus reducing the risk of a potential fall. This setup provides climbers with a safe and controlled environment to push their physical and mental limits without the added complexity of managing their own gear placements.

One of the defining features of sport climbing is its accessibility and inclusivity. With the proliferation of climbing gyms and development of outdoor crags around the world, climbers of all ages and, increasingly, all backgrounds can experience the thrill of sport climbing. Sport climbing routes vary in difficulty, offering a wide range of challenges for climbers of all skill levels. From gentle slab climbs to steep overhangs and intricate technical sequences, each route presents its own set of obstacles that requires strength, agility, and precise technique to overcome. Whether climbing for recreation, fitness, or competition, participants often find connection with fellow climbers, sharing beta, encouragement, and a passion for the vertical world. The sport's emphasis on progression and self-improvement promotes a culture of lifelong learning and exploration, inspiring climbers to pursue new challenges and expand their horizons both on and off the rock.

The gender gap in rock climbing has historically been notable, though it has been gradually narrowing over the years. Traditionally, white men dominated the sport, reflecting broader societal attitudes and perceptions about gender and physical activities. Stereotypes about strength, risk-taking, and athleticism often were barriers to women participating in climbing or pursuing it seriously. Additionally, the lack of female representation in climbing media and the scarcity of female role models further contributed to the gender gap.

At the end of the last century, the American climber Lynn Hill redefined gender norms within the sport. One of her most iconic accomplishments came in 1993 when she became the first person to free climb the Nose route on El Capitan in California's Yosemite National Park, a feat previously considered impossible. Her ascent not only revolutionized the sport but also challenged conventional notions of what women could achieve in climbing. Hill's remarkable abilities and unwavering commitment proved gender was not a limiting factor in climbing, paving the way for greater recognition, respect, and opportunities for female climbers worldwide.

In recent years, there has been a significant shift in the climbing community. More women are participating in climbing than ever before, and there's a growing recognition of their achievements and contributions to the sport. Efforts to promote inclusivity, provide mentorship opportunities, and create supportive climbing environments have helped to encourage greater female participation. Additionally, the rise of female-led climbing events, initiatives, and media representation has played a crucial role in inspiring women and girls to pursue climbing.

Despite these positive developments, the challenges of the gender gap in climbing are amplified for minoritized groups, including women of color, 2SLGBTQIA+ individuals, and those from other marginalized communities. These groups face intersecting barriers related to gender, race, sexuality, socio-economic status, and other factors that impact their experiences in the climbing community. Minoritized groups encounter unique obstacles such as lack of representation, discrimination, and systemic biases within climbing spaces. Issues of access to outdoor climbing areas, cost barriers associated with gear and training, and feelings of isolation due to underrepresentation can further marginalize these individuals. Additionally, concerns about safety and inclusivity may deter minoritized groups from fully engaging in climbing activities.

Historically dominated by white men, the climbing community has made strides in recent years to promote diversity and equality within the sport. Organizations like Brown Girls Climb, Indigenous Womxn Climb, and the Global Climbing Initiative have emerged to support and empower minoritized women and underrepresented groups in climbing, providing a welcoming and inclusive environment for climbers of all backgrounds and identities. Continued advocacy, education, and the fostering of inclusive spaces are essential in further closing the gender gap and ensuring climbing remains accessible and welcoming to all individuals, regardless of their gender, race, sexuality, ethnicity, nationality, age, and socio-cultural background.

In *Flow* we aim to serve as a platform that amplifies the voices of minoritized climbers, contributing to the diversification and representation of underrepresented groups within the climbing community. *Flow* provides a space where these voices are heard, stories are shared, and experiences are celebrated. By highlighting the achievements, challenges, and perspectives of minoritized climbers, we strive to promote greater inclusivity, understanding, and appreciation of difference within the climbing world. We believe in the transformative power of storytelling and in the importance of creating an inclusive and equitable climbing environment for all as depicted within the pages of this book.

CHAPTER 7

Mountains in My Blood: Tracing Ancestral Paths

By Janel Lynn Rieger-Chávez

I remember the moment I knew I belonged in the mountains. I was at Mom's home and, as usual, my Nahua Mamma was feeding me too many tamales, beans, and "pink rice" – that's what I called it as a child, but really it is just rice cooked in tomatoes. We were discussing the hibiscus plant blooming flowers and what kinds of teas we could make when I got the good news. I had been accepted into the Rock Guide Course and received a scholarship. I told Mamma and we both had a moment of dancing and some tears of joy, and then Mamma said the most powerful words to me: "Of course you are to become a mountain guide. Our people were born in the mountains. We lived there, created family, and roots. The mountains are in your blood, *mija*, and our Native ancestors will always guide you."

I am the daughter of a migrant Mexican farm worker, Sara, who blossomed into a loving mother of three and brought us to Minnesota to have a better life in the United States. Growing up, the words "education is your freedom – work hard and you will be okay" were told to me almost everyday when I went to school. To my Mom, having the chance for her daughters and son to have an education meant EVERYTHING. And, well, there isn't a day that goes by that I don't think about this.

But, really, this is something that all children of migrant workers and immigrants, first or second generation, know. It motivates us, it haunts us, it controls us, and, like my Mom's words, it gives us freedom. Freedom from hunger, racism, sexism, work fatigue, abuse, and poverty. Freedom to experience joy, love, identity, humanity, and the wonders of the world. But here's what every one of us also knows – we know the pressure of succeeding, of proving others wrong, and of making sure the house is always clean, like "Mom, why do we need to wipe down the bathrooms every damn day?"

With that comes a sense of constant urgency to achieve whenever possible. I don't think I experienced a true feeling of rest until I reached my 30s. This is why so many of us are

Discovering my love of climbing. Photo by David Elliot.

out here crushing it, making noise, doing it all, and everyone is like, "Wow, you must have so much energy," or "Wow, you must be so smart." This is said in ways that are surprising, as if an Indigenous Mexican woman couldn't make it, couldn't succeed, couldn't do science. This part of my story is essential to the kind of climber I've become. It's the origins of my love for mountains and for mentoring in our community. So here is a small part of that and the love of climbing to follow.

So I went out and decided I wanted to pursue the hardest of degrees: chemistry and engineering. AND LET ME TELL YOU, IT WAS SO FREAKING HARD. Why? Because I grew up in a small town that didn't have the resources to teach me advanced math as a kid, and my mom, despite being a genius out there speaking two languages, just didn't get the opportunity to learn this as a child. Her life was a different one, where school was not a priority or really an option. After sixth grade, she worked to help the family and that's just how it was. So I had to do the most embarrassing thing and start in a class called Math 60. What does that mean? Well, basically I started out with rudimentary math. Yeah, before algebra, before trigonometry, there's Math 60. Guess what's next? Math 70, Math 80, and then, finally, I was at college algebra. TWO years of my life just to get to college algebra, but I knew I wanted this.

After taking my prerequisite classes at a community college, I cried without hesitation for hours when I saw my acceptance letter to the College of Engineering at the University of Minnesota. Uh, what, is this real? Here's my ticket, to FREEDOM, to YOU'RE GOING TO BE OKAY. MOM, I'M GOING TO BE OKAY.

So there I was, often the only BIPOC student in the classes, often ignored when in small groups, often told, "Wow, good for you, must be so challenging." And it was. I was usually the only student in the class working 30 to 40 hours a week and being a full-time engineering student. When I said I could only study after 11 p.m., it was because I was working at a restaurant and then headed to Caffettos coffee shop to study until 1 a.m. Then I would go home, pet my attention-starved cats, review my work for the next day, and get around five hours of sleep most nights if I was lucky. I remember this feeling I would get in my legs and feet where it was painful to walk, like my feet weighed a ton but somehow they were also still numb. I was exhausted from waiting tables for eight to ten hours. I would wake up feeling my body beg for rest, but the urgency to work harder, to get an education, was stronger. So I got up, thinking the pain makes me stronger, thinking I'm so lucky I have heat and water at home. Thinking, *I need to just keep moving*. Now, looking back, I'm not really proud of that time. I don't wish that upon anyone. But it was ingrained in me that if I wasn't exhausted, was I even thankful for the sacrifices my ancestors made? It's a heavy thought that never really left me.

When I graduated, the first thing I did was sleep for ten hours. I did this for almost three to four months straight. Sleep to me was the grandest of all gifts of graduating. And then there was climbing. Upon graduating, things like time and money began to be a thing. I could do things besides study and work. I could have fun and experience joy, and maybe even hobbies. Okay great, so here I was trying this new sport I'd never heard of called climbing.

My climbing origin story is like many. I tried it out because some friends were doing it in college. Then, after I graduated, I started climbing three to four times a week in the gym and wanted to make the transition to outdoor climbing. Well, there I was stuck. I would ask my friends to go, but often they would just have me belay them on their projects or ignore me like I was invisible. They would take me to crags that were not beginner-friendly and be like, "Oh yeah, sorry, you probably can't climb that."

At the time, it made me feel so small, like this wasn't possible and I should move on. I also noticed no one at the time really looked like me in the climbing scene. The gym and crags were filled with white men and some white women, including my friends. Ask and check in with anyone from the BIPOC community that climbs with you. I guarantee they have felt out of place, small, unwelcomed, and that they needed to code switch. I remember heading home one of the nights and was told, "You just need to climb harder and then people will want to climb with you." I wanted to cry on the car ride home, I wanted to scream at them, and I wanted to prove them all wrong. And so that's what I did.

I had to get outside. I wanted to climb some big mountains, so I had to make some room for myself in this white, male-dominated space. So I put in the work. I found the only BIPOC climbers in the gym and we began our outdoor journey. We learned traditional climbing and focused our energy on crack techniques. I would spend hours climbing on the crack wall memorizing "finger stack equals 0.4 to 0.5 cam, knee lock equals #5 cam, and so on." To me it was art, it was science, a puzzle, and I wanted to have all the pieces to make it work. Finally, it was time for my hard work to shine. I was headed on my first climbing trip where I would be leading everything. I was so psyched, though my cams were just a little too shiny. It was time to scratch them up.

I arrived at Red Rock Canyon, in Nevada, in the spring. It was warm and the desert had its own vibe. You look out and see cactus, bushes, birds, and sand. Then in the distance you could see mountains striated with sunset reds as if the sky painted it and never left. I hiked out on the approach with my good friend Joey. He was an ex-marine turned math professor and overall just a joy to be around, unless you were rude or crass. Then he would hold nothing back, and I loved that about him. As we reached our first climb, I racked up probably too many cams, but hey, it was my first multipitch climb. As I tied into the rope and did our safety checks, my heart was beating so fast that the sounds moved slower and the sun felt hotter. I was ready. Pitch 1, cruised up it, pitch 2, no problem, pitch 3, what fun, pitch 4, little spicy run out, and the final pitch, hey, I'm on top of this thing. What I didn't say to Joey until a few years later is what the middle-aged white men said to me at the belays as I came up to build an anchor. First anchor, "Well look at you," second anchor, "I didn't expect it to be you again leading," third anchor, "You should build your anchor here and you'll need so and so cam. Here I can show you," fourth anchor, "Wow, isn't that cute. You led the whole climb. You want a photo to show your future kids?" For the rest of the trip, I pretended as if that never happened. You have to or you'll be swarmed dizzy with micro-aggressions. You

Climbing in Devil's Lake, Wisconsin. Photo by Akira Maples.

just have to move on, or that's what I've always thought I needed to do. Now life is a little different in my community. But that's later in this story. Just wait, it's worth the wait.

After five years of climbing, I began my journey as a mountain guide. My guide course was in a place called Eldorado Canyon in Colorado. This place was legendary. Known to be one of the most "sandbagged" climbing destinations.

I definitely felt a lot of things – scared, motivated, and ready to prove them all wrong. I could do this. So I trained. I mean, I trained *a lot*. I went climbing outside as much as I could. I went to the Midwest's most legendary sandbagged destination, Devil's Lake. This was home to some of the scariest 5.6 traditional climbs you'll ever find. Add in wasps' nests in the only hold on the blank wall with little to no friction and small gear placements to make it quite the experience. All good, 'cause I was out there cruising on the 5.10s and 5.11s and some of the scariest 5.6s I've led, *ever*. And then off I went to Colorado.

I arrived in Boulder about a week before my course started. I wanted to get used to the terrain, to feel the mountains, connect, and breathe. And to get used to the altitude so I wasn't gasping for air during my course. I was so lucky to climb with my friend Sergio. He was learning the ropes of trad climbing but was already a strong climber. One thing I loved about him was his ability to be humble and gracious.

Story time. Often, when I've mentored men there has always been this weird energy. At first everything seems good, but later the lack of humility shines. This would lead to them telling me, "I know what to do. I'm a strong climber." This happened to me in El Potrero Chico in México. I was mentoring a man who was mostly a boulderer and had never climbed multipitch routes. I kept asking him questions to make him feel comfortable and confident on the climb. This was also to review that he understood what he had learned and how to problem solve when necessary. His response was filled with *I know more than you now* vibes, and this should have been the first red flag for me. I was still new to mentoring, so I didn't realize this at the time. Later, we were climbing a longer route called Time Wave Zero. I asked him if he knew where the pitch goes and if he wanted to look at the topo map and number of bolts to help guide him. He was already upset because he was unable to lead one of the 5.11 routes lower down, while I was able to lead it with no takes or falls. He grudgingly said, "I got it okay," and then about 15 minutes later a refrigerator-sized rock came flying at me.

What happened was he went off route on a sport climb. Rather than down climb when he didn't see a bolt, or check the topo, he chose to continue to climb up over 20 feet (6 m). He grabbed a loose rock off route, fell over 30 feet (9 m) with rope drag, and sent the rock flying down at me. The falling rock missed me because I was able to just barely move out of its way. If I hadn't had the room or reflex to move the right way, I would have been dead. After I rescued him off the route, he proceeded to have no humility. It's as if he was disconnected from the fact he almost killed both of us and could have killed other people climbing below us.

I was in shock but found my peace with the experience. Because, for me, this was also a moment to have humility. Really, this could happen to anyone, whether beginner or experienced.

We've all sent a rock or a carabiner down accidentally. I think where I felt it was remembering how fragile we all really are. This was the first big climbing accident to happen to me and the result could have been different. They say when you start climbing you have this huge bag of luck since you are climbing easy terrain and low-risk, high-reward climbs. However, when you become more experienced, your bag becomes smaller and smaller. This is because often as experienced climbers we forget how fragile we really are. We forget our humility. We forget that, yes, even we need to do safety checks, check the topo, pause when it doesn't seem right, and check our mood. This sometimes means turning around when the climbing chemistry is off.

Happily, I got a second chance at this climb when I went back in 2023 with Ya, one of my favorite climbing partners. We cruised it and had so much fun. It felt right this time and it will be a day I remember forever. So thanks, Ya, in case I haven't told you that. You made that day really special, and I'm thankful to have other BIPOC women to climb with on hard routes.

Okay, back to Eldorado Canyon. After spending a week climbing with my friend Sergio, I was incredibly privileged to connect with a local climber and mountain guide named Meg. She is a force of nature. She is the kind of climber that instills confidence in you, makes you want to try hard, and supports you. This was something I'd never experienced with other climbers. Up to this point, the majority of my climbing partners were men. I was mentoring other women but had no women/nonbinary climbing partners that were at my level of climbing or stronger. The day I met Meg, it was a hot day in October. We got straight to business, racked up and made our way to the first route. That day we climbed three or four routes in a row and ended the day with practicing short roping down the mountain. This experience was one of the most beautiful moments of mentorship and friendship in climbing for me. Because of Meg I felt like I belonged in Eldorado; that this was my space too. Afterwards, I reflected a lot on this experience. I knew I wanted to make this more of a regular thing. Climbing with strong women was night and day compared to my experiences climbing with men. Not saying I didn't love my male climbing partners, but this was next-level feelings and I couldn't wait to make this the reality of my life.

The guide course was ten days of climbing, learning, and being tested. There were six students and I was the only woman in the course with five white men. I was a little intimidated, and I wasn't sure how much I should code switch. I decided I would be 100 percent me. That is, coming from a Latin and Indigenous culture. Meaning loud, matter-of-fact, encouraging, and showing up with joy. If I'm trying to hide who I am, then how am I supposed to focus on climbing, safety, and showing my knowledge? This is just a reality for a lot of the BIPOC community. Code switching in white spaces means we are not fully showing up as who we are with our ancestors' blood.

We spent three to four days in Eldorado Canyon, climbing some hard technical climbs. We learned to short rope on third and fourth class descents, lowering techniques, rescue, and client care. During this course we were divided up into two groups. This allowed for a three-to-one student to teacher ratio when on terrain. For me, the course went great. I was crushing all the climbing, content, and client care. It felt like I was supposed to be in this space. In our group, I was paired with two unique climbers that have very different styles and risk tolerance. One of the climbers was a very strong climber but lacked the mountain sense of safety and risk management. His systems were not dialed in for anchors, gear placement, and transitions between pitches of climbing. This resulted in being put in some unsafe situations while hanging off a mountain, sometimes hundreds of meters off the ground. Because of this, I let the person and the instructor know about my discomfort with his risk assessment. The other person in my group felt the same and did not hold back at all. As the course went on, the person was given less autonomy to belay without an instructor. We all continued with the course.

At the end of the course we had a meeting with the instructors to get feedback and find out if we passed. I was overjoyed to find out I had, in fact, passed! They then shared feedback and advice for my future in mountain guiding. This is where the joy diminishes. You see, while trying to be constructive, they told me I might need to tone down my personality, as in not be so loud when climbing. This included my encounter with calling out the person in our group for their risk assessment while climbing and giving me advice on how to be more cordial. While their intent was good, they were missing something very big. First, the other white male in our group had yelled at this person, while I chose to have a conversation with them. However, this was not mentioned at all in their exit meeting. Of course, the double standard was there, but that didn't bother me as much as the second thing, which was that being loud, having big energy, and expressing my joy are integral parts of my culture and what makes me who I am.

You see, they missed the reality that the majority of mountain guides are white males. There are a small number of female-identifying guides and even smaller numbers are Latina or Indigenous. Therefore, their data is biased since they lack diverse data collection, even though it wasn't necessarily their intent. However, not having a larger data set of what a guide looks like or acts like means my being loud, energetic, and joyful was seen as a weakness. It did not fit into the norm that is centered in patriarchy and European whiteness. After this encounter, I felt confused and a little sad. Talking to other people in my community and other BIPOC female guides helped me understand why the instructors were biased. The reality is being my full self is what makes me a good, smart, and risk-aware mountain guide. Without this, I lose so much of who I am, my instincts and knowledge that were passed down from my ancestors. So I moved on and rejected this part of the assessment. I am a loud, energetic, and joyful mountain guide, and this is one of the most beautiful gifts I've received from my ancestors.

After this course, I wanted to continue the work I did in the community but think bigger. As I started to look at our community, I noticed a gap in alpinism. You see, I had the privilege to be taught ice climbing and alpinist techniques by someone in our own community.

When I first sought out ice climbing, I wasn't really sure how I would respond to it. I mean, I've always loved the heat, sun,

Learning to ice climb at Sandstone Ice Park in Sandstone, Minnesota.

and warmth of summer. Winter to me meant seasonal depression and dreading the thought of going outside. Well, who knew I could love something more than rock climbing! Here it was climbing frozen water and I was enthralled. I bought boots and found myself excited to ice climb even in below-zero temps. I remember that holiday week, it was still COVID times so I didn't go home to see my family. To make the most of it, I met up with my friend Dave. He's an ice farmer and actuarial scientist. Both things may be subjects many of us have never come across, but it simply means he helped create our ice climbing park and is really good at math. I remember we climbed to the point of me getting the screaming barfies, which is essentially when your hands are so cold that when the blood rushes back to them you get this feeling like you want to throw up but also laugh and make loud noises. Ice climbing – such an elegant sport.

After that day, Dave forwarded me a post made by local climber and alpinist Scott Backes. In it he wrote that he was giving away ice tools and to write him a reason why you think you should get them. At the time, I didn't really know much about the history of ice climbing or alpinism, so I didn't fully understand who I was writing to. I began with a picture of my first time ice climbing. In it I'm wearing jeans that are soaked and a puffy, with the biggest smile on my face. I followed it up with my story of rock climbing, my work within the community, and my love of crack climbing. I wrote, "I want to take my climbing to the next level. I want to climb some really big mountains. And I want to take the community of underrepresented climbers with me on these adventures." This must have spoken to him, because the next thing

I saw was a message letting me know he would be giving me the ice tools and an offer to ice climb together to help me take my climbing to the next level. I was psyched, but it wasn't until all my ice climbing friends were freaking out with excitement and jealousy that I finally googled him and found out he was one of the pioneers in alpinism and had some pretty big accomplishments to show for it. As I read in awe of his story, I also began to feel nervous. I mean, was I going to make a fool of myself in front of this legend?

The day came and I met Scott at Sandstone Ice Park. At the time there wasn't a lot of ice, so we were going to be dry tooling and mixed climbing. This meant we would climb the rock and thin ice with our ice tools. The day went by and I was putting my everything into getting up these difficult routes. By the end of the day, he invited me to continue climbing with him. Thus began a mentorship and friendship I will always hold close to my soul. Because of his guidance and general psych of climbing, I was motivated to begin my journey in mountaineering and alpinism. I trained like it was my purpose, ice climbing three to four times a week and endurance training, which was new to me. During my first season of ice climbing, I led a WI4, climbing Mount Baker/Koma Kulshan and Mount Rainier/Tacoma, and climbed some classic alpine routes in Washington Pass. That small kindness of Scott's to mentor me in climbing began a chain of events I couldn't have even imagined in my wildest dreams.

As my journey continued, I learned to ski, took an avalanche course, trained, and read every book I could on alpinism and endurance training. My dreams were coming true. I had climbed

Ice climbing Night Fall in Grand Marais, Minnesota. Photo by Taylor Krosbakken.

really big mountains and I was glowing. During this time, I was also mentoring others in ice climbing within the BIPOC community. I started to form a wonderful group of BIPOC climbers that wanted to learn how to ice climb. Then the next big idea came to me. The Midwest is very flat, therefore training for big mountains is difficult to do. When I asked the members of the BIPOC community I was climbing with if they had ever thought about mountaineering or alpinism, there was a big resounding "yes, but." Yes, but is it safe for people of color? Yes, but how do we even train on flat land? Yes, but am I strong enough? I realized there was a deep disconnect with the idea of even training for a big mountain in the Midwest BIPOC community. There were those who were interested, and those that dreamed but never really saw this as a reality. So it was time for me to put the work in for my community in a way I had never imagined. And this was the formation of the Flatlanders Ascent. An all-BIPOC group of climbers training to climb a really big mountain.

Training began immediately and it included crevasse rescue skills, terrain study, rope management, and a lot of endurance training. One of my favorite moments from these training sessions was when we went to a park in South Minneapolis. We were going to practice self-arresting in case of a fall into a crevasse or on steeper terrain. This meant falling and sliding backwards down a sledding hill and then somehow turning your body around to plunge your ice axe and crampons into the snow to stop the fall. One by one, everyone practiced, learned, and laughed a lot. We then proceeded to learn about snow anchors and we found a larger pile of snow on a corner of a residential neighborhood. Here we were, with ice axes and our crampons on a Monday, just digging in the snow and testing the strength of our picket anchors. It was pure joy. We were just a group of BIPOC climbers learning skills to be independent and dedicated to learning, training, and creating space for ourselves and our community.

The day of the Flatlanders Ascent rolled closer and we were making some waves. Before we took off for Washington to climb a really big mountain, Koma Kulshan, also known as Mount Baker, we were asked to be on the news. It was beautiful to see the group speaking about the joy of the mountains and this incredible journey we'd been on. When we arrived in Washington, I realized we only had one day for our weather window and it was of course the first day. Our original plan had been to hike up to base camp, spend the following day practicing our skills, and then make the ascent that night. Instead, it turned into hiking to base camp, taking a nap in our puffy jackets, and then waking up at 12:30 a.m. to begin our way up the snowy glacier. And let me tell you, this group – despite being sleep-deprived – was stoked. We ate some food, melted snow for water, and roped up. We had two teams with five people on each rope. I would be leading and the second group would follow our path. As we looked up the mountain, we could see faint signs of climbers' headlamps. They looked like dancing stars as they moved slowly to the top of the mountain.

It was finally happening: ten BIPOC climbers were climbing a really big mountain. During training, I taught them to listen to their bodies and continue to always eat when they could and hydrate. As we made it to the crater, we stopped to take the temperature of the group. I could see some of us were feeling the mountains and needed to rest. So, as half the group made food and melted snow for water, the rest of us headed up the last part of the climb. As we climbed, we saw a lot of guided groups and smaller groups of friends. None had all BIPOC climbers. This was apparent as the people asked me, “Oh, are you a guided group?” or “Are you all from so and so city? There’s a lot of your kind of ethnicities there.” And “Wow, good for you guys.” This really didn’t seem to dampen the mood at all, though. We were doing the thing and didn’t really care what others thought. There was one moment when I realized how incredibly well this group had trained. As we headed up the Roman Wall, which is notoriously the steepest part of the climb, we noticed guides and their clients struggling. At one point, a client was feeling very uncertain and needed to climb through to get to flatter terrain. I told the group to self-arrest on the side so they could pass. And just like that the group knew exactly what to do, and as the person passed I couldn’t help but feel so proud of them and their accomplishment. We proceeded up the steep terrain and there they were, front-pointing, sidestepping, and crushing their first mountaineering climb.

As the sun was fully peaking in the sky at about six in the morning, we took the last steps around to see the summit of the climb. The wind severely picked up at this point. The kind of wind that reaches out to take your breath. It left a sting of cold on my skin and I looked to see how they were doing. “Hey Flatlanders, we good?” I looked out at them and they were all smiling so big, or at least that’s what I thought since we were covered up to protect ourselves from the wind. I forgot who said it, but someone pointed out, “Hey, is that the summit or a false summit?” There it was, the summit. With the dry snow and wind, it looked like a flurry of sparkling dust. At this point we were able to de-rope and make our final 10–15 steps. And one by one we reached the top and stood together at the summit of Koma Kulshan. As we stood there, five BIPOC climbers from the flattest of lands, I couldn’t help but feel our ancestors celebrating with us.

For this next part I need you to do two things. One, you will need to cue a song to play, “Ella Baila Sola,” by Eslabón Armado and Peso Pluma. Have it ready for the moment, so you feel it too. Now, it’s important you take yourself into this moment. Leave your surroundings and immerse yourself in this moment with me. Here, I’ll take you there. The summit of Koma Kulshan – it’s silent, you think, but then you truly feel it. The wind whips so strong it burns your cheeks and takes your voice. Your body is screaming at you, as you haven’t really stopped moving since dusk. Finding your balance on glacier ice that has existed longer than anyone on the mountain. The snow is so dry it is easily carried into the heavy air. You try to squint your eyes as you catch the shimmers from the snow glowing and reflecting from the sun. And, as you look out, beneath you see the clouds below you. Yes, that’s right, you’ve made it to the clouds. There are no more trees where you stand, only ice and snow. Below you can see a faint path of where you were and what you will still need to follow to make it back home. You’re cold, tired, and your stomach

Feeling the joy of climbing. Photo by David Elliot.

feels as if there are butterflies moving in it like subatomic particles in an excited state.

I brought you here so you could feel with me what I was so privileged to feel. Here I stood doing something my ancestors never even dreamed possible. And then my soul began to swell as my eyes grew heavy and I felt it. (Cue the song above.) As we stood there, I felt our ancestors among us. I felt their stories of struggle, hope, and love. I felt my *abuelita* looking out at her daughters in México in the warm desert sun. I felt my mother and her weight of purpose to our family. I felt my great *tia*, her empathy as she tamed snakes and brought them to safety, despite people's fear. I felt my Tia Guadalupe, as her kindness toward all living beings made me who I am. I felt my ancestors' choices to be strong when everyone saw them as weak. From the time of the Aztecs, as my Mom would tell me, "They would just eat beans and tortillas and run across the desert. As they're warriors, and we are from them." My ancestors surrounded me, and I thought, *Now they can rest for me. Their mija is living their wildest dreams*. Living but, most important of all, filled with joy.

GARMIN

CHAPTER 8

From Bustling Delhi to Himalayan Peaks: Finding My Inner Child

By Kavitha Mohan

I have always envied people who knew since childhood what they wanted to do with their lives. When I used to meet individuals so driven and passionate, I often wondered why I hadn't found my passion yet. When I interacted with such motivated people, my insecurity would creep in and tell me I was probably just meant to do a nine-to-five job, as I didn't have the courage to live a life full of uncertainties. After all, a known devil is better than an unknown angel. Some people find their passion so early in their lives and continue to excel in the "prime" of their lives. In my "prime" I was lost, confused, and filled with anxiety and numerous insecurities. I was uncertain about the person I was and what I wanted to do with my life. Now I realize that not knowing was the best thing that happened to me. It pushed me out of my comfort zone, and made me explore and understand myself better and eventually find my true passion for climbing and connecting with my most authentic and joyful self.

I come from a very humble background in South India, from a state known as Kerala, also known as "God's Own Country." Unlike with most families in India, I was blessed to be born to educated and progressive parents. My mother was a French professor and my father was a forest officer. Thanks to my father, I was lucky enough to be exposed to the wild beauty of nature as a child. My childhood was filled with long hikes through sun-kissed golden meadows. I would wake up to the chirping birds, early visitors from the jungle to our hut, then take an afternoon dip in the river and enjoy the beauty and sound of the nearby waterfalls. It felt more natural to me to lie in the lap of nature than live in a concrete building. However, life took a different turn and I grew up to become a chemical engineer working in one of the busiest cities in India – New Delhi.

After graduating with an engineering degree in 2012, I soon found myself working with a reputable multinational company in the oil and gas sector in New Delhi. In the initial days, I was keen on adapting to the new job and excelling at work. The job was taxing and demanded long working hours and sometimes entailed extra work hours on weekends. I slowly started to give

Climbing in my home country, India. Photo by Rahul Yelange.

up the hobbies I enjoyed as the job started to eat away at my personal time. The toxic work culture made me miserable and I slowly ended up losing my identity. My life revolved around work and sometimes partying with my friends. I felt myself struggling to put up with the toxic lifestyle and it took me some time to understand I was falling into depression.

During my time in New Delhi I made a good friend, Prasanna, who was madly in love with the mountains. As our friendship grew stronger, I would join him on his mini escapades to the Indian Himalayas. The Himalayas were mighty and breathtaking. I had never seen anything like them in my life before. In the mountains, I could feel an instant energy shift. I felt my anxieties slowly drift away and I started to feel like a child again. With a few nudges, I soon started to travel solo to the Himalayas. As COVID-19 hit, and remote working became an option, I started to backpack through the Himalayas, especially in the Indian state of Uttarakhand. I felt so tiny in front of the mighty Himalayas, but I knew I belonged there. This is a place where I could be completely still as I gazed at their beauty and magnificence. I knew from within this was the place where I wanted to live.

As I traveled and met more people, I heard about a few mountaineering courses that one can complete to learn the ways of the mountains and eventually go on some exciting expeditions. I found that to be encouraging, but I felt I wasn't ready for that yet. I was physically unfit and undisciplined. I decided to pause that idea and see what other options I had. As COVID-19 subsided, I had to go back to the office. However, my perspectives on life had changed and I wasn't ready to go back to that monotonous, stressful lifestyle. I contemplated leaving my job, but I was unsure if I could live with the precariousness and lack of security. I kept recalling memories of those happy childhood days, when you are your truest self. My happiest memories were holding my father's hand and enjoying our walks through the lush tropical forests in Kerala, savoring a chocolate ice cream and truly enjoying every lick, and, amusingly, getting excited about balancing on the wall between my house and my neighbor's. I remembered enjoying every bit of adventure I could have, but more so I also adored the simple things in life back then. I knew by now that people clung to their unhappy lives because they feared uncertainty and lack of security. I didn't want to be that person anymore. There was no lingering doubt in my head. I knew I had to take a leap of faith in myself and quit my mundane job.

Nevertheless, it wasn't an easy decision to leave my job and all the luxuries that came with it. In order to find my passion, I had to be fearless. Quitting my unhappy job was just the first step. I had just turned 30. I wasn't looking forward to questions from society. It is unusual for an Indian woman to remain unmarried in her 30s and follow an unpredictable path with uncertain outcomes. I have seen a lot of talented women giving up their dreams to fulfill their partner's happiness. I have already seen my gifted sister juggle her life with her job and kids, stressed out and not able to find much time for herself. I didn't want such a life and realized I wanted to live for myself.

After leaving my job in 2022, I was uncertain and clueless about what to do next. The happiest memory I had was in the mountains, so I decided to start my journey in the Himalayas. I searched for some volunteering options in the foothills and soon received an offer to work with an NGO named Avani, located in the Kumaon region of Uttarakhand. This NGO had come up with an interesting technology to generate electricity out of pine needles. In the early days, the forests of Kumaon region of the Indian Himalayas were covered with oak trees, which provided valuable resources such as firewood and fodder for the local communities. Over time, pine trees replaced these forests. The pine needles that cover the forest floors are highly flammable and are one of the leading causes of forest fires in Kumaon. I found electricity generation from pine needles a viable solution to reduce forest fires. However, after a few weeks I had a lingering feeling in my heart this wasn't my passion and I wasn't truly excited about it. This was merely a curiosity to learn, and I felt that something else was waiting for me. I was slightly disheartened, since I was back to where I had started. However, the only way to find my passion was to remain true to myself, and so I decided to leave.

I explored more places in the coming months and met a few impressive women who had started some brilliant ventures to help the locals in the mountains. All these ventures seemed unique and inspiring, but none of them resonated with my heart and with who I am as a person. I wasn't ready to lose hope yet. A few months later, I got a call from one of the places I used to stay and work remotely from the foothills during COVID. I had become close friends with the guys there, and they knew I was traveling nearby. They needed immediate help to run their resort-style homestay, and I really wanted to save some money until I figured out what I wanted to do next. The homestay, situated on the banks of the sacred Alakananda – a tributary of the holy river Ganges – was magical. A renowned whitewater kayaker ran it and many whitewater kayakers trained there. I slowly learned how to manage the guests and helped the chef to prepare his dishes.

One day we took some of the guests to the river for a swim in the shallow area. I wasn't really a good swimmer. In fact, I was extremely scared of water. Nonetheless, I wanted to push my boundaries and foolishly dove in. I couldn't handle the currents and needed help from one of the kayakers to pull me out of the water and swim back to shore. Later that day, he teased me for my swimming skills and for nearly drowning. It felt horrible to be teased in front of everyone. I felt the episode to be demeaning, but it motivated me to learn how to swim. I asked him if he would teach me to swim because he was an excellent swimmer, and he slowly agreed. I took my time to get comfortable with water first and practiced regularly in the pool after finishing my work. I watched YouTube videos for some tips and continued to experiment with my style. I gradually started to get better at swimming.

After seeing my hard work, the owner of the homestay decided to teach me some stunts in whitewater kayaking. However, I wasn't really physically strong then, and the moves did not come effortlessly to me. A few boys would tease me about my lean body and taunt me to try yoga and easier sports. Sometimes they would jump in to show how easy it was for them. I would smile back, hoping for the day when I would become better and stronger. The fellow kayaker who taught me how to swim shared some captivating stories about climbing in India and about some of his female friends who climb. I had never heard about climbing until then and I didn't know what the pursuit entailed. Climbing isn't a popular sport where I come from and I had no access to it. Yet I felt very curious to explore.

I decided to research more about climbing in India. I would spend my time after work watching videos of other female climbers and understanding the sport. I read about different types of climbing – top rope, lead, bouldering – and also about accessible climbing destinations in India. My initial days at the homestay were great, as I was growing and learning more about the outdoors and about running a lodge. However, as months went by, my stay started to become more daunting. After a long day, the boys would resort to late-night revels. I slowly started to receive uninvited attention and this made me feel very uneasy. I decided to leave and returned home to my parents in Kerala. My supportive mother welcomed me with open arms and good food. She believed in me blindly and this restored my faith in myself. After a few weeks, my sister invited me to Bangalore to babysit my nephews. Hampi, a popular climbing destination in Karnataka, India, is just an overnight train journey from Bangalore. After lending a hand to my sister for a few weeks, I decided to venture out to Hampi. I was clueless about what to do and where to start when I got there.

After an overnight train journey and a one-hour bus ride, I reached Hampi, the old capital of the Vijayanagara Empire and a UNESCO World Heritage Site. I traveled to the small settlement of Hanumanahalli in Hampi, after crossing the Tungabhadra River by boat and then sharing a tuk-tuk with the local kids. I discovered a small local climbing rental shop, Golden Boulders, run by an experienced local climber in Hanumanahalli and decided to drop by in the evening as a start. I moved on to a popular stay in Hampi for climbers so I could meet and interact with other fellow climbers. While getting a late morning coffee in the dining shack, I quietly noticed a group of Western climbers chitchatting and having their brunch after an early morning climbing session. I initially felt too overwhelmed to speak to them but later mustered enough courage to go over and ask if I could join them. They welcomed me with ease into their small group and we soon started talking about our travel adventures. I effortlessly became friends with Ayce, the only woman climber in the group. She had been exploring Hampi for a few weeks and knew most of the boulder areas around the place. We planned to meet up and go climbing in the evening. Luckily, two more young girls from Austria joined our group later in the afternoon.

We excitedly planned an all-girls climbing session and this made me feel instantly comfortable. The two Austrian girls, Anna and Patricia, were school friends and had been traveling through Asian countries for a few months. The four of us hiked toward the bouldering area in the evening, getting acquainted with each other along the way. Despite our age differences, we instantly connected with each other. Our conversations were smooth and effortless. I recall being both nervous and excited to try my first boulder. The girls were very kind to find an easy balancing route

On my first boulder project in Hampi, Karnataka. Photo by Ayce Cersa.

for me. They climbed first so I could review their beta and understand the movements in climbing. The moment I touched the rock, I knew I belonged there. Even though I watched the girls, I still struggled to recognize the handholds and footholds. They looked so tiny and my fingers barely had any strength. The girls called out the holds for me while I climbed, and my adrenaline helped me reach the top.

When I climbed, I felt completely mindful and thought of nothing else but the boulder itself. My overthinking self surprised me by being quiet while climbing. Later on, I watched the girls maneuver through some crazy routes, and I would gaze in awe, thinking that someday I would be able to climb like them. We had only known each other for a few days, but we grew close to each other very quickly and soon became like sisters. Anna and Patricia were strong technical climbers, and they pushed me to become better each day. I am so grateful to have met them in Hampi. I owe my perfect start to climbing to these girls. They made me believe in myself again, connecting me to the adventurous girl I was as a child. I slowly started to believe I might have found what I was searching for. Every morning we would have a quick breakfast at 6:30 a.m. at a small outlet run by the locals and then hike toward the numerous bouldering sites around the area. I would practice on some easy routes and later just watch others climb, learning from their moves and techniques.

A few weeks later, the local climbers announced an international climbing competition in the restricted climbing area near the Virupaksa temple in Hampi. I wasn't really good at climbing, but I was eager to see the routes in the restricted area and interact with more women climbers. The Austrian girls and I decided to go to the competition together. The girls wanted to have some fun and try driving a two-wheeler with the three of us on it. We had a few falls and laughs before reaching the site of the competition. The first boulder of the competition was a highball. The boulder had very good holds and I flashed it with the help of the girls. Climbing down from the highball was scarier and it made my legs tremble. Even though it was a competition, the participants were supportive and friendly.

Everyone was helping each other with the routes and techniques. As the routes got harder, I realized I needed to work on my finger strength. I used my natural flexibility and height to my advantage. The climbing competition helped me to assess what I needed to work on and how to use my strengths to my advantage. I had started to fall in love with climbing, not just the sport but also the community. I met some Indian climbers from Bangalore and Delhi, and they advised me to start climbing at indoor gyms in the cities to build strength and technique.

One evening the girls invited me to swim in Sanapur Lake. Little did I know that by "swimming" the girls meant cliff jumping into the lake. I had only recently learned how to swim and I had never swum in open water before. I was terrified, but I still wanted to jump in. The memory of nearly drowning in the river at the homestay took over. The girls took turns jumping in and hiking back up to the cliff multiple times. They could see the fear in my eyes but also sensed I wanted to jump. Patricia, an exceptional swimmer, jumped into the water right away to give me some confidence. She waited for some time in the lake to assure my safety in case I decided to jump. Anna realized I was still scared. She took my hand and we jumped off the cliff together. This was the day when I truly admired the power of female friendships. They sensed my emotions and protected me. They never belittled my fear of water but merely stood close and supported me.

A few days later, the girls decided to continue their travel adventure to the Philippines. I contemplated staying in Hampi a bit longer, but it didn't feel the same without the girls. I tried to see if I could find some local jobs in Hampi to continue climbing. However, the season was nearly ending and most climbers were leaving. A local climber advised me to try some indoor gyms in Bangalore to work on my climbing techniques. So I returned home and started searching for jobs there. Soon after, I managed to get a chemical engineering job as a scientist at a Saudi-based research organization. The universe indeed helps you to achieve your dreams if you have the will to pursue them. I was leaning toward some popular gyms in Bangalore initially, but they were very far from my office and it was not practical to commute in the traffic. I searched for gyms closer to my work and eventually managed to find a small climbing gym for beginners called Urban Climbers approximately seven miles (12 km) from my office. I decided to rent an apartment close to the gym so I could stay late on weekdays and spend a good amount of time there on the weekends. I was very lucky to have found this gym, because the owner, Mr. Rahul Yelange, was not only an excellent climber but also an avid mountaineer. He has summited close to 30 Himalayan peaks, including Mount Everest. His experience guides him to motivate individuals in the right direction and provides him with a keen eye to see a climber's weaknesses to be worked on.

The first month of climbing was exhausting and sometimes a bit overwhelming. I was not very good at it and I felt physically weak. My body was not balanced and I was mostly scared of falling on the mat from a height. I could barely hold on to sloppers or climb on the sloped walls. I had to work hard to ascend even the easy routes. However, I started to improve in a month's time. Unfortunately, I broke my ankle in a foolish slacklining incident. I felt devastated because I had just started to improve and the thought of not climbing for months saddened me. I wasn't ready to let go. I continued to go to the gym with my walker to work on my upper body strength. I was determined to build my strength and trained my fingers during these months. Once my cast was removed, I worked on improving my ankle strength and started to climb again within three months of my fracture. Magically, my climbing improved because of the strength training I did during the break.

As months went by, my strength and technique continued to improve. My body felt more balanced and the strength in my fingers gave me more confidence. I started doing dynamic moves with more grace. I realized that climbing is more of a mental game than about strength. Some days, when my mind is not in the game, I fail to grasp the holds. Only when I truly commit and really want the hold does it come naturally to me. I realized that to become better I had to be more disciplined in my habits. I changed my lifestyle completely, from eating to

Bouldering in Ramanagara, Karnataka. Photo by Rahul Yelange.

Ice climbing in Leh, in northern India. Photo by Atul Suresh.

sleeping. I believed only consistency and discipline would give me the results I was aiming for. I could slowly see myself becoming a different person – someone I never imagined I could be a year previously. Even my vacations slowly evolved from relaxed sightseeing to climbing adventures. One day, when we were climbing outdoors in Ramanagara, a small settlement near Bangalore, I met a teenage girl who had just started to climb. She was struggling to climb an easy route. By then my fingers were strong and I could easily ascend such routes. She was impressed with my strength and how quickly I reached the top. She came to me and mentioned she wanted to train to become a better climber. That day I realized I could mentor and motivate another woman.

We started going on mini outdoor climbing adventures. The regulars in our gym had become a close-knit community and we planned our first climbing adventure in Tail Baila in Maharashtra in December 2023. Climbing in the Sahayadri range is not an easy feat. The big holds on the basalt rock in the Sahayadri hills may look inviting, but the tighter you grip, the more likely you are to fall off. The rocks are loose and one must rely on their instincts while climbing. We were a group of nine people (three women including me) and we attempted our first multipitch climb in Tail Baila. We pitched our tents at the base of the hill and hiked up to a temple, which is the base of the multipitch climb. The first pitch was relatively easy, with just one technical move. However, the height and the fall into the valley below made our legs tremble. After climbing the first pitch, we anchored ourselves and rested in a cave nearby, sharing stories and jokes. The start of the second pitch was hard, with inaccessible, crimpy handholds. I slowly started to lose hope after a few tries. My lean body swung against the rock as I took multiple falls while trying the challenging move. However, we kept going and managed to ascend and reach the top of the rock tower. We were blessed with stunning views of the valley below. We rappelled down at sunset and went back to our campsite. We distributed our chores equally, from setting up tents to picking up firewood for cooking. We cooked a tasty Indian meal, shared some silly ghost stories, and slept peacefully that night. We tried a few more climbs for the next couple of days and then returned to Bangalore with good memories and lessons learned.

Our next escapade was even more exciting. We decided to go to Leh, in the north of India, for ice climbing. Leh is a city in the Indian union territory of Ladakh. It is a cold desert and has dry mountainous terrain with beautiful landscapes. After an overnight flight from Bangalore, our team reached Leh. Coincidentally, there was an ice-climbing festival going on in Leh and a number of people from all over the country were visiting there. We were lucky to have good access to the walls and snacks to re-energize our spirits. The winter had arrived late in Leh and the temperatures dipped to as low as -4°F (-20°C). Nonetheless, the snow-capped mountains were breathtaking and we were teleported from a busy city to Narnia.

The ice-climbing group was a small group of six and I was the only woman in the group. We acclimatized ourselves to the chilly winds and to the new elevation of 11,562 feet (3524 m)

for the first couple of days. This was my first experience ice climbing and facing extreme winters. Sadly, I ended up getting my period with heavy cramps on the day we decided to ice climb. I didn't want to miss the day, so I quickly took some painkillers and headed out. We practiced a few basic techniques on how to walk with crampons and wield the ice axe. The boys began to experiment and climb an easy route. The chilly weather made my cramps worse. I quietly decided to take an easy day and not strain my body further. I wished for a woman companion that day and sincerely hoped I could avoid explaining my inability to climb.

However, the next day I was determined to climb the ice wall. The winter had become fiercer the next morning. We woke up to a mild snowfall and barren lands carpeted with snow. The snowfall increased as the day progressed, but we cautiously drove to our climbing destination. After a small hike to the ice wall, my turn had come to try the wall. I felt a gush of anxiety as I started to climb an unknown terrain. The snow continued to fall as I climbed and covered my goggles. My hands went numb after some time and I couldn't go all the way up. I tried a few more times in vain. I decided to call it a day and went back exhausted, ready for bed. The next day, I was committed to trying again. The snowfall had reduced, but the sun mocked us, playing hide and seek. As I climbed, I felt more comfortable that day and managed to ascend the wall with the cheerful support of the boys below. My hands were numb and tired because of inefficient stroke technique. I took the remaining day to work on my technique and hang out and joke with the boys. By the end of this mad adventure, we transformed into a small family, witnessing one of the most savage winters and still emerging victorious.

Even though my climbing adventures have just started, I am hopeful for more challenging ones in the future. Climbing has changed my life and has brought a sense of purpose back to me. I have become a more disciplined and mindful person. Once I started training for climbing, I realized that excelling at a mountaineering course is within reach. I have now applied for my basic mountaineering course in the upcoming year, and I continue to train hard after work hours. I cannot wait to go on expeditions in the Himalayas and see what surprises life has planned for me. I had to take a long journey to discover my passion for climbing, mostly because I never had any exposure to it. But, as I eagerly look forward to the mountains that beckon, I am reminded that the journey to this point has been as rewarding as the peaks that await. With every step, I embrace the unknown, understanding that through adversity we truly find ourselves. And so, with each sunrise, I greet the horizon with anticipation, ready to write the next chapter of my adventure, one climb at a time.

In Hampi, India. Photo by Denisa Krásná.

CHAPTER 9

Cordada Libertad: Climbing for Freedom and Self-Discovery

By Marianna Tarczyńska

Some people are made out of fire and water and have to learn how to deal with those contradictions. Accepting who we are is a crucial step in self-development. In my case it was done through extreme sports such as climbing and mountaineering.

Climbing helped me to explore the potential of my mind. Being several times so close to death made me feel more alive and deeply connected to my true self.

The journey still continues.

I will share with you some parts of it.

From Corporate Confines to Andean Peaks

My professional background is in software engineering. After several years of working in IT in various corporations in Poland and Great Britain, I decided to make a radical change and found myself drawn to Ecuador. I was growing weary of Europe and its consumerism, and the stifling corporate environment. I yearned for a different world. The allure of Ecuador's natural beauty, glaciers, and absence of harsh winters was compelling. I bought a one-way ticket. Soon, I made Ecuadorian friends who introduced me to rock climbing, and I began training.

Within half a year, I managed to complete the challenging Sphinx multipitch route with a difficulty rating of 6c. This climb wasn't a no-fall zone, but climbing its 18 pitches with just six months of climbing experience was a significant accomplishment for me. After another year, I completed my first 7a route, and within two years I had progressed to climbing 7b. After three and a half years, I tackled my first 8a route. Climbing at a difficulty of 7b, which many believed would take ten years of training, was something I accomplished after only two years, and in my 30s.

Being a woman in this male-dominated sport wasn't always easy. I often felt underestimated, and many told me that certain achievements were not within my reach. However, I was determined to prove them wrong. I would climb as hard as the men, gender notwithstanding. Training was demanding, and it came

At the summit of the Sphinx in Ecuador. Photo by Elisa Toledo.

with a fair share of challenges, including full-body pain, two sprained knees, wrist tendinitis, and a back contracture. Rock climbing is a high-risk sport, and falls often result in a surge of adrenaline. Injuries are also a frequent outcome of overexertion. I had to learn to listen to my body, rest when necessary, and cope with the humility of experiencing injuries even when I was in top form. Climbing, at its core, is about making split-second decisions under pressure and stress, and it helped shape my character.

Over time, I found myself excelling in leadership roles rather than being a follower. I made friends in my new South American life and began organizing trips on my own. I didn't need to be guided by more experienced mountaineers to learn from them. I learned to trust my intuition while pushing my boundaries.

This transformation also impacted my professional career. Just four years after taking up climbing, I secured sponsors from Petzl Ecuador, La Sportiva Polska, Deuter Polska, and GoPro Ecuador. I also completed an instructor course and began sharing my knowledge with others. My lifestyle became centered on climbing, and I started seeking work that allowed for a flexible schedule, whether as a tour leader or engaging in web design, logo creation, or photography. What mattered most was not just what I did but also how I did it. I preferred direct contact with clients without intermediaries, which allowed me to have more control and clarity, ultimately enabling me to concentrate on training and climbing.

Another challenge was navigating the male-dominated environment of climbing. I tolerated friendly teasing, but I detested discrimination. Over time, my climbing friends recognized me not solely for my gender but for my courage and determination as I climbed progressively more advanced routes. Engaging in high-risk sports improved my memory and provided me with a sense of belonging. In this community, we shared a common passion, enthusiasm, and goals. The male-dominated environment I found myself in gradually evolved into a respectful community where tolerance and mutual support proved invaluable during difficult times. When you're on the rock face, you are detached from reality, focusing solely on the next move you must make. Each climb is a vertical puzzle. You're perched on a tiny foothold, secured only by a rope. Three meters below is your last quickdraw, and you're thinking about your next move. You might fall, but that's also where the fun and growth comes from. You have to fall many times before you can succeed, in climbing and in life.

What follows are accounts of expeditions that illustrate the transformative journey mountaineering and rock climbing have sculpted within me. Through recounting these expeditions, I hope to convey the profound impact mountaineering has had on my journey of self-discovery, from the corporate confines of Great Britain to the rugged peaks of Ecuador.

Liberation

Since I was 16 years old, men have been paying attention to me, making me feel self-conscious. Over time I got used to it and connected with my feminine side. I used to wear high heels, dresses, skirts, and light makeup. Then I discovered another world – the mountains and their winter summits. I questioned again what is feminine. Here, clothing must be warm and waterproof. You experience exhaustion and bone-chilling cold, but true joy lies in finding your path and seeking the summit. In the mountains we are all equals; a storm doesn't care if you are a man or woman.

In 2014 I relocated to Ecuador. Naturally, I felt compelled to ascend the highest peaks in this country. I didn't know anyone in the mountain climbing community here, so I began acclimatizing on my own, starting with the volcanoes Rucu Pichincha, Rumiñahui, and El Corazón. I relished the challenge of finding my way and the adrenaline rush, especially in more exposed sections. As a photographer, I shared my journey through pictures. Before long, I received an invitation to join an expedition to the Cayambe volcano.

Cayambe is not a technical climb, but it soars at an altitude of 18,996 feet (5790 m) above sea level. To put this into perspective, the highest peak in Europe, Mont Blanc, stands at just 15,771 feet (4807 m) above sea level. Cayambe is a thousand meters higher, which means lower oxygen levels.

The invitation came from my friend Santiago, and even though I didn't know anyone else on the team, I decided to join the expedition. We consisted of three women and three men. However, when we reached the base camp, Santiago told us we would regroup. I was initially puzzled but accepted the group's decision. It turned out we would split into two separate teams – one with the three women and the other with the three men. I found this arrangement appealing.

On the night of our summit attempt, we woke up around 11 p.m., sipped some hot tea, and donned our mountain layers. We tied into the rope and proceeded slowly, avoiding extended stops. In contrast, the men pushed on as swiftly as they could.

After an hour, we reached the glacier, where we strapped on our crampons. While we sat and rested, we noticed a group descending – it was Santiago's team. He informed us that one of the other men, John, had reacted poorly to the altitude, forcing them to descend. Despite our slower but measured pace, our women's team reached the summit. It was then that I conceived the idea of climbing mountains exclusively with women. This gave rise to the Cordada Libertad project. I firmly believe women can be just as strong as men, and that, with proper training, nothing can hold us back. There is no greater form of empowerment than supporting one another in the freedom of the mountains.

Cordada Libertad became a beacon of empowerment, a testament to the strength we find in supporting one another amid the freedom of the mountains. In breaking free from conventional norms, I discovered a sense of liberation and a community of women united by the shared passion for reaching new heights and defying limits.

Empowerment

A colleague reached out to me. "Marianna, I want to climb Cotopaxi, but I have arrhythmia."

I replied, "Okay, we'll acclimatize and take it easy. We'll assess how you feel."

Our journey began with hikes up Rucu Pichincha and Iliniza

Norte, where Magda had no trouble with acclimatization. So I decided she was ready for Cotopaxi.

We set out early, proceeding cautiously. When we reached an altitude of approximately 18,373 feet (5600 m) above sea level, Magda mentioned she felt cold. I offered her some warm tea from a thermos, but it didn't seem to help. After she ate some energy bars, I asked how she was feeling. She admitted to feeling dizzy, and I decided we should start descending. Anxiously, she inquired, "Am I okay?" I reassured her that she looked fine, but that it would be best to descend because she seemed fatigued. She relaxed and we slowly began our descent, taking pictures and conversing along the way. Magda left some rocks behind on the mountain as a marker of her achievement, symbolizing the burdens she carried in her abnormally beating heart.

We reached the safety of the shelter around nine in the morning, where we sat down and enjoyed hot chocolate. It was then I told her honestly, "Magda, when we were up there, your lips had turned blue and you were extremely cold. Going down was the right decision." With a frightened look on her face, Magda began to tremble with the onset of a panic attack.

I monitored her condition. Magda gradually calmed down and apologized for her episode. I was filled with relief as we continued our descent, sharing jokes on our way to our car at the trailhead.

That evening, while at home, I sat and reflected on the experience, pondering my ability to manage her arrhythmia in the mountains but not the panic attacks. What if the panic attack had occurred at a higher altitude? Had we narrowly escaped a dangerous situation?

The phone rang. It was Magda. She thanked me, saying, "Marianna, this experience has changed my perspective on the world." Relief washed over me. I realized that empowerment goes beyond the summit. It's not just about conquering mountains or reaching heights. It's about understanding our limitations, facing our fears, and making choices that prioritize our well-being. Magda's journey showed her inner strength and resilience. In that moment of vulnerability, she discovered a newfound courage within herself, acknowledging that true empowerment comes from embracing our vulnerabilities and learning from our experiences. As I listened to Magda's gratitude over the phone, I understood that our shared adventure had not only changed her perspective on the world but had also deepened my appreciation for the transformative power of empowerment, rooted in both physical and emotional strength.

That night I slept peacefully.

Stubbornness

Cotacachi is a unique mountain. At an altitude of only 16,220 feet (4944 m) above sea level, it is unglaciated. Despite lacking a glacier, the peak is notably "crumbly" with loose rocks. My first attempt to summit it was with my friend Michal, who was visiting Ecuador to see his family. We both agreed on Cotacachi as our challenge. After researching online, we found two routes: one on the eastern wall and one on the western wall.

At a junction marked by a *Y*, we chose the path along the eastern wall. This variant was said to be more difficult, but we had confidence in ourselves. Navigating through rocky terrain, Michal followed me closely. Eventually, we reached a channel that led to the summit. Roping up, we started to climb into the chimney. Rain suddenly began to fall, signaling an approaching storm. "Let's turn back," urged Michal. Although we were just 230 feet (70 m) from the summit, I agreed with him and we decided to descend.

A month later I returned to Cotacachi, and this time my team was composed of my friends Pepeins and Ivan. The entire mountain was covered in snow. Staying on route was a challenge, but we persisted against the strong winds. Once again, at the *Y* junction we chose the eastern wall. We reached the chimney leading to the summit ridge, but as chunks of ice and rock started to cascade down in the strong winds we decided to turn back once more.

Undeterred, I returned to Cotacachi with just Ivan, determined to reach the summit. This time we came prepared for any eventuality of snow or ice with cams, crampons, and ice axes. It was foggy, but the winds were manageable. We reached the junction and, again, chose the right path. We reached the chimney, but again rocks started to plummet from the summit. We quickly retreated to a wall that offered protection from the barrage and traversed to another chimney. We couldn't see where it led as it spiraled upward. Roping up, I climbed with a passion fueled by the challenge of this summit.

A serac above me was melting, dripping ice-cold water. Ice falling from a serac is like getting hit by a boulder and can have dire consequences. I ascended as quickly as possible to get out of the danger zone, placing protection along the route as the terrain crumbled around me. Climbing higher and traversing, I reached a stable boulder and set up an anchor, realizing then that my clothes were soaked through from the melting ice. Ignoring the cold, I shed my wet sweatshirt to put on a jacket to belay Ivan up to my anchor. It was foggy, but it appeared we were on the right ridge. To confirm, we checked our GPS, which read 16,220 feet (4944 m) – we had reached the summit!

We snapped a few photos before beginning our descent. We carefully descended through the chimney and further down through crumbled rock. We broke apart the serac from above to prevent it from falling on us. Upon reaching stable ground, we untied from the rope and I started leading the way down.

Without warning, a rock came flying down from above and struck me in the head. I felt it hit my temple, the spot on my head least protected by my helmet. Instinctively, I clung to the nearest rock to avoid rolling down the slope in case I passed out. I waited for the pain to pass, thankful to remain conscious.

We continued our descent with extreme caution, carefully following each other until we finally reached the car. Our ascent had been risky, but reaching the summit was immensely rewarding. We were proud that we had successfully navigated an unknown route to avoid the falling rocks and found our way through the fog to the summit. We shared our GPS route with friends who were eager to repeat it. A month later, I received a call: "Marianna, you are incredible! How did you manage that route?"

The crux of our stubbornness lay not in defying nature but

Leading ascents with Cordada Libertad. Photo by Elisa Toledo.

in learning to adapt to it. Each setback became a lesson, each challenge an opportunity for growth. As I reflected on our triumphant ascent of Cotacachi, I realized stubbornness, when channeled wisely, can be a powerful force. While our journey up the crumbly slopes was marked by setbacks, challenges, and moments of doubt, in the end, our stubbornness transformed into a narrative of resilience and tenacity. It was not just about reaching the summit but about embracing the challenges while acknowledging the risks. As I hung up the phone, I couldn't help but smile, knowing that our story had become an inspiration for others to face their own mountains, whatever they may be, with unwavering determination.

Risk

In the Peruvian Andes, we reached Chopicalqui High Camp, situated at an altitude of 17,388 feet (5300 m) above sea level. My climbing team included my friends Kevin and Edwin, and John, whom I had just met. Once on the glacier, I regretted that all I had was just a three-season tent. I came up with the idea of using our ice axes, trekking poles, and snow stakes to reinforce the tent. It worked, and we hoped it would survive the night. Now all that remained was to prepare a meal and rest briefly before our summit attempt.

As we settled in for sleep, one of the men began to make advances toward me. We were just friends, but he seemed unable to understand that. So often women are expected to return or tolerate these advances and aren't appreciated solely for their skills and accomplishments. I don't accept this attitude. Just as in the city, in the mountains we are equals, and we deserve respect.

At 11 p.m. we woke up to begin our summit attempt. A discussion ensued. I pointed out to Kevin that he lacked respect for women. Part of the group suggested we discuss it later. I disagreed, emphasizing the problem existed at that moment, therefore it was necessary to stand up for myself right then. I tied into the rope, but due to stress, I forgot to tie the clove hitch knot that closes the loop.

We started the ascent. I was leading the route. After two hours, we reached a wall with two options for continuing. I opted for the right, which was less steep. I realized I needed a second ice axe, so I took off my backpack. Edwin, who was tied to us on the rope, insisted I should take in the slack of the rope, even though he should have waited at this point. To prevent further complaints, I took in the slack. At that moment, a small rock broke loose from above, and I lost my balance. I managed to stop my fall with a small hold a meter down. It was at that moment I realized I hadn't secured a clove hitch on the rope. At this point, I had a loop of rope around my neck, passed over my head from taking off my backpack. If not for my grabbing the hold to stop myself from falling farther, the rope could have strangled me. Calmly, I tied the clove hitch, but I dared not mention to the rest of the group just how close I had come to a tragic accident. We continued our ascent.

In that precarious moment, I found myself contemplating the significance of life. Perhaps some higher power wanted me to remain in this world. As though I have something important to convey or achieve. I asked myself, *Who am I? What is my purpose?* These existential inquiries echoed through the frozen air, emphasizing the fragility of life and the importance of living authentically, despite the risks. As we continued our ascent, I carried with me a newfound appreciation for the significance of every step, every breath, and every question that propels us forward on our journey.

Vulnerability

I have always been drawn to the idea of exploring new routes in the mountains. There is still so much to discover here in Ecuador and, for any mountaineer, climbing a new route is a prestigious achievement. The opportunity finally came. Alongside my friend Maciej, we decided to climb Iliniza Norte from the east wall.

Iliniza Norte is a rocky formation with an elevation of 16,818 feet (5126 m). It's a bit less crumbly than Cotacachi. Our plan was to establish a new route from the east wall, where there are only a few recorded ascents. We reached the east ridge. With our ropes, cams, and stoppers, we planned to first traverse then locate the exit of the chimney leading to the summit.

I took the lead for the first two pitches of the traverse. The first 197 feet (60 m) didn't require placing runners, as the terrain was relatively straightforward. However, I reached a large boulder that needed to be climbed around. I contemplated whether I should set up an anchor here, but it didn't seem too complicated. I decided to just place the rope behind the boulder for a belay and continue simul-climbing.

Carefully, I repositioned the rope and hugged the boulder, attempting to step onto its other side. In that precarious moment, the boulder unexpectedly dislodged and I fell. Time seemed to slow down. Instinctively, I turned my back to it to protect my face. The massive rock passed over me, and I found myself hanging on the rope. The air was filled with the smell of crushed rock. Maciej asked if I was okay. I cautiously responded that I believed I was, but I needed some time for the adrenaline to subside. After a moment, I assessed the situation objectively and determined that the only casualty was my backpack, which had been slightly damaged. We decided to continue the climb.

We eventually reached a vertical section where I set up an anchor to belay. Maciej took the lead for the first pitch in this section, and then it was my turn to lead the next one. Maciej led the last pitch to the plateau. At this point, it would have been possible to turn back since our route converged with the normal one. However, what is establishing a new route on a mountain without actually reaching the summit? We pressed on to the summit and then descended using the normal route. We agreed not to mention the incident with the dislodged boulder to avoid diminishing the significance of the first ascent of the new route.

In the pursuit of new heights and uncharted routes, vulnerability becomes an inevitable companion. The climb up Iliniza Norte's east wall epitomized this truth. Confronted with the challenge of forging a new path, I encountered a moment of intense vulnerability. As I was hanging on the rope, the scent of crushed rock lingered, a reminder of the fine line between conquest and humility in the face of nature's raw power. Yet, as the adrenaline subsided, a determination emerged unscathed. The decision to continue, to press forward and reach the summit, epitomized the spirit of exploration – one that acknowledges vulnerability but embraces it as an integral part of the mountain's unpredictable dance.

Taking the Lead

Chimborazo stands as the highest peak in Ecuador, towering at 20,547 feet (6263 m) above sea level. It is the second most popular ascent in the country after Cotopaxi. My friend Lidia had made multiple attempts on Chimborazo in the past, but had yet to reach the summit. At this point, we had already completed numerous successful expeditions together, including technically challenging climbs like Iliniza Sur, Cayambe, and Cotopaxi. I hoped this Chimborazo attempt would be the time she reached the top.

Although it was my first attempt on Chimborazo, I was determined to make this ascent. We established our base behind the second shelter, and due to strong winds, we set off late, around noon. It was bitterly cold, but the conditions were relatively stable. We roped up, and I started leading the route.

As we made our way to a rock formation known as the Castillo, someone shouted, "Mariannaaaaaaa!" I couldn't identify the person beneath the helmets and warm face coverings, but if he knew my name, he must know me. It was only after a while that I recognized Santiago. He explained that his partner couldn't continue, and they were going to descend with one of the guides. Santiago, however, felt capable and asked to join our team. After

Leading an ascent with Lidia on Iliniza Sur. Photo by Jaris Aizprua.

some consideration, I agreed, but with one condition: we would reach the summit. "Are you sure you are up for it?" I asked. "Yes, yes, I am feeling strong."

We accepted Santiago to the team, and our journey continued. We eventually reached the ridge, where the strong winds sent shivers down my spine. Ignoring the initial signs of hypothermia, we encountered another group that had decided to turn back. They greeted us, and I was so cold that when I responded I sounded like Donald Duck. They suggested we should also descend, but I decided our team would carry on. Thankfully, Lidia had chemical hand warmers, so we stopped briefly. I stamped my feet, donned an extra pair of pants, and removed my shoes. Santiago warmed my feet in his hands, and we placed the warmers in our boots. Feeling somewhat rejuvenated, we continued our ascent.

By around 8:00 p.m., we stood at the summit, our lips having turned blue, but we were filled with satisfaction. Now we faced the descent. Descending from Chimborazo is notoriously dangerous, as rocks tend to fall. It was late for us to begin our descent, but the cold worked in our favor, stabilizing the snow. We made our way down without any complications.

Our ascent had been a success, and it reaffirmed my belief that women can lead, with teams of both women and men. Following this ascent, Lidia found motivation to lead other mountains, and I felt genuinely happy for her. After years in mountaineering, she had finally taken on a leading role. It was then that I began to see the broader idea behind the Cordada Libertad project. Climbing mountains among women is just the first step. We, as women, possess the same leading abilities and must strive for independence and inspire more women to believe in themselves and take the lead in every aspect of their lives.

Mentorship

When I met Elisa, she had no previous mountaineering experience, but she exuded both contagious kindness and incredible strength. Naturally, I believed she had to become a part of Cordada Libertad. I started teaching her from the beginning – belaying, basic climbing skills, and how to use crampons and ice axes. However, what set her apart as an excellent student was her voracious appetite for learning.

Our first climb together was Cotopaxi, standing at 19,347 feet (5897 m) above sea level. Elisa displayed unwavering determination. We started as the last team to leave base camp that day and reached the summit first. Subsequently, we embarked on Cayambe. But I didn't want this to be just about reaching the summit. I aimed for Elisa to become independent in her climbing pursuits.

On the first day, we practiced glacier skills and ice climbing. Elisa had no prior experience in this area, so we began with some low-to-the-ground traverses without ropes on safe terrain. Then I spotted an inclined ice wall for practicing ice climbing techniques. I climbed it first to set up an anchor to belay Elisa. She performed surprisingly well for her first time.

We returned to our tent to rest and plan the summit attempt for the next day. This time I intended to let her lead. We set off around 1:00 in the morning, first tackling some rock climbing. Upon entering the glacier, I allowed Elisa to lead when the terrain was more straightforward, but I led in more complicated sections. We continued without issues.

At Cayambe, there were two options for reaching the summit in the final part of the route. One involved heading straight up through the crevasses, while the other required traversing the lower summit known as Santa Barbara, which was technically easier but longer. As we reached the plateau, the fog started to thicken, severely limiting visibility. We were very close to the summit and I made the decision to continue, despite the poor visibility, before descending.

We couldn't see much, but we opted for the traverse option, as it was a more straightforward route. However, this led us to a massive crevasse that proved impassable. I decided to climb straight up from there, using my intuition as my guide. We reached a ledge next to a steep inclined snow wall. I traversed before climbing straight up again. The fog was so thick that I couldn't see anything except the inclined wall. In a brief moment of visibility in the swirling fog the summit was revealed. We were so close. We followed the snow ridge to the left and climbed the final incline. In no more than 20 minutes, we reached the summit. Even though we had no views, we were satisfied with our ability to push onward and find our way through the challenging conditions.

After taking a few pictures, we began our descent. It started snowing as we were retracing our steps, covering up the holes our crampons and ice axes had made in the ice. The guiding holes became completely covered and we were surrounded by a vast whiteness. I began searching for more footprints, but there were none in sight, and I couldn't find any other markers.

We continued down cautiously until I finally found a footprint – eureka! After following it for about two minutes, Elisa pointed out, "Marianna, it's our footprint from the last 15 minutes." I felt a sharp stab of disappointment, but there was a silver lining: at least we weren't lost yet. We waited, hoping the fog would temporarily clear.

In these conditions, all we saw was white – not even shades of gray or black. To determine I wasn't snow-blind, I asked Elisa if she could see anything and she confirmed she couldn't see anything either – everything was white. The only logical decision was to wait. We didn't move and hoped the fog would dissipate, even for a brief moment. After about an hour of staring into whiteness, we had a fortunate break of about ten seconds. I immediately spotted the way, and we continued the descent confidently.

We finished the long descent with windburned faces but feeling very positive. We had managed to navigate our way out of the situation without requiring help or rescue effort.

In the aftermath of our challenging descent from Cayambe, I couldn't help but marvel at Elisa's growth throughout our journey. From a novice in mountaineering, she had transformed into a resilient and independent climber. Our mentorship, focused on fostering not just summit achievements but self-sufficiency, had borne fruit on the icy slopes. In the face of thick fog and challenging conditions, Elisa's determination and adaptability shone through. As we successfully navigated the treacherous descent, our shared satisfaction was not just in conquering a summit but also in empowering Elisa to confidently find her way through adversity. Our journey exemplified the essence of mentorship – a collaborative ascent that goes beyond peaks, creating resilient climbers capable of navigating life's complexities with newfound strength and independence.

Growth

Reaching the summit of Cayambe led to another project with Elisa, the ascent of Iliniza Sur, which stands at 17,267 feet (5263 m). Iliniza is a technical mountain, its difficulty contingent on the conditions. Elisa was more than prepared for such a climb. She exhibited determination and decisiveness, and was physically strong. Climbing with her was not only rewarding but also enjoyable. We shared many laughs and discussions about life along the way.

Our first task was to reach the shelter, a 2–3-hour hike. We rested there, planning to depart around five in the morning. The weather conditions were perfect – no wind, rain, or snow. We easily made it to the next part, the chimney, and tied into the rope. I took the lead in this exposed section, involving about a 60-degree slope. Since there was no snow, we decided to climb it simultaneously. Elisa demonstrated remarkable strength and focus. We then traversed an exposed plateau, and I was confident enough in Elisa to have her lead this section. She excelled once again, and we reached the summit at around 8 a.m. We took photographs and savored the view. The descent took about two hours, and when we reached the base, I asked Elisa, "Was it harder than Cayambe?" She replied, "No, Cayambe was more challenging." I couldn't help but admire her attitude. She was undeniably strong.

Once we entered the shelter for some tea and energy replenishment, Gato, who was the head of the shelter, remarked, "Girls, you don't look tired at all. Wasn't it too easy for you?" I responded, "Oh, yeah, it was a piece of cake." Elisa laughed, and Gato suggested, "Maybe you should go for Iliniza Norte." I replied, "Why not?" and, turning to Elisa, asked her, "How are you feeling? Are you up for it?" She replied enthusiastically, "Yeah, let's do it!"

Iliniza Norte is the twin peak to Iliniza Sur. It lacks a glacier,

Elisa leading on Iliniza Sur. Photo by Marianna Tarczyńska.

but on that day it was covered with snow, increasing the difficulty of its rocky ridge. We traveled light, without crampons or a rope, only carrying waterproof clothes, helmets, and gloves. We had to be cautious, given our fatigue from the climb that morning, and navigated carefully through the exposed rocky terrain. Despite our tiredness, we maintained an efficient pace, reaching the summit around noon. We took some pictures before descending back to the shelter in stable conditions. By around 2 p.m. we were packing our bags in the shelter and descended to the car, arriving at about 4 p.m.

We were proud of our climbs, and I was genuinely happy for Elisa. This endeavor had its challenges, particularly on Iliniza Sur on the incline, where a fall could lead to serious injury. Iliniza Norte presented its own risks due to exposed rocks covered in snow. Fortunately, we had a favorable weather window that allowed us to make both summits in a single 12-hour push. Elisa continued to excel in strength and skill, and I was excited for future climbs with her. What challenge was next for us?

Solitude

Celso Zuquillo is a significant rite of passage for climbers in the Ecuadorian Andes, known for its challenging ridge. The route is characterized by crumbly rock, ice, and snow in a volcano-alpine style, along with intimidating exposure. Elisa and I had already climbed Cotopaxi and Cayambe together and she'd proven herself ready for something more difficult, so I proposed the technical Celso Zuquillo route.

Our ascent began with a climb to the shelter at an altitude of 15,748 feet (4800 m) above sea level. We rested and planned our 4 a.m. morning start. When we woke up, there was no wind, indicating a potential weather window. However, conditions changed, and it began to drizzle. The combination of fog and darkness made it challenging to identify the route elements. We decided to bivouac until the first light to rest and reassess our south-facing route.

We found a small rock pit that was quite snug. I lay down on the ground, while Elisa sat beside me, and we exchanged jokes to pass the time. As daylight broke, I quickly spotted our route. We reached the mountain ridge at around 7 a.m., where I set up an anchor using slings and led the first pitch – a traverse between rocks, snow, and ice. I placed two runners along the way in case Elisa fell as she followed. I climbed to the top of the ridge but struggled to find a stable rock for an anchor. I moved higher and found a solid boulder to build a secure anchor and belay Elisa. Elisa climbed confidently and steadily behind me.

It took us three hours to cross the ridge, mostly simultaneously climbing. I belayed Elisa on the more exposed sections until the summit. We took pictures at the summit before embarking on the descent, but it was already 11 a.m. and fog began to envelop the mountain. Heavy snowfall in the preceding days had created potentially unstable conditions. We decided to take a cautious approach, which meant waiting. We found a small hole cave in the rocks and sat on our backpacks, drinking tea. We put on all our clothes to keep warm in the freezing temperature as we listened to the ice and snow slipping and moving outside. I thought about retracing our path down the mountain ridge, but Elisa told me she didn't think she'd be able to manage the descent that way.

During this time, a rescue team was organizing to help us, but I was wary of descending in the fog with poor visibility and unstable snow. Even with the pressure to start descending, I opted to wait for more favorable conditions.

Around six in the evening, as the last rays of sunlight finally broke through the fog, we began to see more clearly. I quickly identified the descent path. The traverse was quite exposed, with seracs above us and a crevasse below. I took a meticulous and calculated approach, making sure not to get too close to any potential hazards. I had Elisa belay me to the other side, moving carefully and delicately like a ballerina across the accumulated snow. I belayed her to me and we continued climbing down simultaneously. When Elisa suggested using the radio to inform the team of our progress, I agreed. They promptly informed us we had taken the wrong path and advised us to stay where we were.

It was not an ideal spot to wait, with seracs above us. The way we started descending looked right to me, but if it was the wrong way, as the rescue team had informed us, it would be better to go back to the rock cave, where we had been waiting before, to protect us from falling rocks. Trusting the team, we headed back, repeating the exposed traverse. Shortly after, they radioed us again, saying they saw us and that we were on the right descent route after all.

Feeling somewhat demoralized, we restarted the descent, following the route we had already climbed down before climbing back up again. The rescue team reached us and we were grateful because we were exhausted.

I felt disappointed because we climbed so well for the technical ridge climb to the top, only to struggle on the descent. The challenging descent led me to contemplate my decisions and the need for a GPS device. We should have had one, and wouldn't have had to second-guess if we were on the right path down. I wanted to come back and climb the mountain properly.

The following March I had the opportunity to return to this route with my friend Camila. Our plan was to ascend and descend the same way. After I arranged the permits for our climb, she cancelled at the last moment due to work commitments. In the end, I decided to proceed alone. I already had the necessary permits, and my plan was to deceive the authorities into believing it was an acclimatization trip, not a technical ascent.

Upon arriving at the hostel in the evening, I greeted Gato. After I reheated some soup and prepared for a nap, he discreetly inquired about my plans, whether I intended to take the normal route or Celso. I responded, "Celso," and we agreed on a radio check at 5 a.m.

I set out at 4 a.m., with no one heading to Iliniza Sur that day. Instead, most climbers headed to the twin peak, Iliniza Norte. I appreciated the solitude of the climb. Around 6 a.m., I reached the entrance to the ridge, which was now covered in more snow than before. My thin, softshell gloves that allow me to use my ice axe were not warm enough to keep my fingers from starting to freeze. In the middle of the traverse, I had to stop and scream in pain, rubbing my fingers to warm them up. Ten minutes later,

I switched to another pair of waterproof gloves, and the pain subsided.

The most exposed part lay ahead, but I climbed confidently with my warmed hands. Next, there was a crack in the rock to climb and I placed some cams for protection. I noticed a large rock to the right was unstable and I avoided touching it to keep it from coming loose. To progress upward, I stood on one cramponed foot in the crack, the other on the rock, with both hands gripping small edges while wedging my knee into the crack. I stood up on my foot to reach my hands a little higher, readjusted my knee, and repeated little by little to continue up.

As I approached the last off-width section, I went to take out my phone from my pocket and it slipped out from its protective cloth, dropping onto the snow below. I couldn't waste time retrieving it, so I continued and used my backup phone to capture photos of the summit. On my descent, I decided to retrace my steps to search for the dropped phone. I could see where it hit the ground but no other evidence of where it fell after. It was just a material thing; I let go of trying to find it.

While I could have chosen to descend the normal, easier route from this point, I followed my original plan to descend down the ridge I climbed up. I reached the crack I had climbed up and started to descend. I jammed my hands in the crack, then my knee, and then I moved my hands down and stood on my crampons in the crack. I repeated these steps until I reached the base of the crack.

Around 10 a.m. I was back at the traverse, and the improved conditions made the journey easier than during the early hours. I proceeded cautiously, avoiding the loose boulders, and climbed down without placing protection. After navigating the last exposed sections, I reached the base. The fog had rolled in, obscuring the passage to the north face of the mountain. Relying on my GPS, I determined the right path, and an hour later I was back at the shelter.

I realized I had forgotten my radio check-in with Gato, but he was calm and said that bad news usually traveled fast. As I retraced my steps, both physically and metaphorically, I found myself contemplating the essence of solitary climbs – moments of resilience, self-discovery, and the unwavering pursuit of summit aspirations. The solitude of the mountains became a reflection of inner strength and the indomitable spirit that continues to propel me toward new challenges. This solitary ascent would be etched in my memory for years to come, a blend of challenge, perseverance, and introspection in the high mountains.

Freedom

Solo climbing has always held a special fascination for me, and the next natural step was to try free solo climbing. Free soloing means climbing without a rope, where a fall could result in severe injury or fatality. There's a route on Rucu Pichincha called Prudencia Z, rated at 7a, and I felt confident on it. After analyzing the movements and sequences, I believed I could climb it without the safety of a rope. This route involved tricky moves, friction steps, small crimps, and long reaches, with precision being essential. It was a style that suited me.

I kept my intention to free solo to myself. I decided that, the next time I climbed the route, I would imagine not having a rope as a mental exercise. While practicing with this mental image, the pressure got to me and I fell.

I realized I needed to change my strategy. On my next attempt, I brought fewer pieces for protection, using only three for the entire climb. I didn't fall this time. I then progressed to climbing the route with only a single piece of protection (just before the crux). And on the third attempt, I used a rope, but without clipping it into any protection. The only thing missing was attempting the climb without a rope.

On the following day I returned to the route. I started by climbing it with a rope, then with fewer pieces. Then I left behind my harness and rappelling rope. Without the harness, I felt free. I was solely focused on the movements and sequences, just as I had planned. The climb went smoothly, and I reached the anchor. I put my harness back on for the rappel down. I felt a profound sense of fulfillment. I had successfully climbed a route graded 7a without any gear.

Free soloing Prudencia Z, where precision and mental fortitude were paramount, was a defining moment in my journey. The melding of movement and sequences, unburdened by the safety net of ropes, encapsulated the essence of true liberation. The anchor reached, and with the harness back on for the descent, I carried with me a newfound understanding of freedom in its purest form.

Connection

The natural progression was to climb a multipitch route without a rope. In Cojitambo, we have the country's longest multipitch route called Langarota, rated at 6b+ and soaring over 984 feet (300 m). The grade might not be extremely high in terms of difficulty, but it's a slab route, which means the holds and footholds can be very small. I had climbed this route twice in the last month while giving climbing lessons to clients. When guiding, you don't want to fall, so I felt well prepared.

The day was sunny and no rain was forecast. I packed a small backpack with my phone, harness, chalk, slings, a 23-foot (7-m) cord, a descender device, and two pieces of protection. I had thought through various scenarios and prepared accordingly. I decided to climb with a harness on, and if it started raining, or if I felt uncertain at any point, I would clip into the nearest bolt and look for a solution. I also had the cord for self-rescue if needed.

I started at the base of the rock, put on my headphones, and played some music. I slipped on my harness and climbing shoes and felt my adrenaline rise. *How would I feel on the rock?* I had never attempted such a long free solo before. I started climbing and passed the first few bolts, my movements and thoughts flowing smoothly. All I could focus on was the next move. I couldn't remember every specific move on the route, but many of them came naturally, almost intuitively. I had control.

As I progressed to the fourth pitch, I entered the slabby section with small holds and tiny footholds. I had used plants to hold on to last time. I decided not to invent new moves and stick

Rock climbing the Estivo route in Cuyuja, Ecuador. Photo by David Diaz.

to what I knew. I stood on the edge, used the overgrown grasses on the rock to find balance, and carefully moved on to the right footholds and crimps. Eventually, I reached the bigger holds and made my way to the ledge before the fifth pitch.

Pitch five involved overhangs, large rock blocks, and friction steps. Some blocks were loose, so I had to be cautious, continuously checking them. Next was the sixth pitch, which had great holds and made me feel confident. The last pitch required weaving between rock and grass to reach the summit of Cojitambo. I checked the time and found I'd completed the entire climb in just one hour.

I felt a sense of accomplishment climbing it alone. No one had seen me, which made the experience even more gratifying. No one knew where I was or what I was doing. Climbing without a rope was a release, freeing me from my thought patterns and letting me connect with my true self.

Who Am I?

> *I believe that – if we are honest with ourselves – the most fascinating problem in the world is: who am I? What do you mean, what do you feel when you say the word "I"? "I, myself." I don't think there can be any more fascinating preoccupation than that, because it's so mysterious; it's so elusive.*
>
> —Alan Watts

For a long time, I struggled to answer the question of why I engage in mountaineering. I view it as a form of liberation and a means of self-exploration. It has played a significant role in shaping my personality. While some expeditions have been mentally more challenging than others, especially with adverse weather conditions, a positive mental attitude goes a long way in pushing forward.

I relish the independence I experience in the mountains, whether I'm part of an all-women team or venturing out on my own. In these environments, I feel closely connected to nature, and when facing life-threatening situations, I become acutely aware of the present moment and a heightened sense of being.

In dangerous situations, I rarely dwell on thoughts of death. Instead, I am focused on taking swift and effective action. There is no time for lengthy analysis. My primary fear is injury, as not everything is within my control, and I acknowledge that one's fate is uncertain.

Tragically, I witnessed the aftermath of accidents involving friends during a descent from the nearby Mount Carihuairazo. A group above them lost control and slid into other climbing parties, resulting in three fatalities and four injuries. In a separate incident, a boulder spontaneously dislodged and fell onto climbing routes in Rodadero, resulting in an immediate fatality. The longer one is involved in the sport of mountaineering, the more frequently you hear of such accidents and the loss of fellow climbers. These sobering events serve as a reminder of the inherent risks and uncertainties in the pursuit of mountaineering, and they reinforce the importance of preparedness, safety, and awareness in this challenging and rewarding endeavor.

Why do we climb and risk our lives? Near-death experiences and the instinct for survival can help us understand the fundamental meaning of existence. They teach us to accept the world as it is and enable us to forgive past wrongs done to us. Is it an addiction? In a way, yes, but what are we not addicted to in our lives? We need morning tea or coffee. We love apples or bananas. Our clothes must be the right colour. We become addicted to things, places, flavours, and people. It's all part of human nature.

Extreme sports provide an avenue for breaking away from our regular reality to reflect on our values. They help us appreciate the transient nature of existence and what we have in the present moment. This raises questions about our shared humanity, our consciousness, and the awareness that the past shapes the present and the future. Breaking free from the constraints of the past and maintaining an open mind toward what's to come is true freedom. It's about recognizing the past's influence while remaining open to new possibilities.

Extreme sports, like climbing, also provide a unique opportunity for women to find a balance between feminine and masculine elements. They challenge and break stereotypes about how a woman should look and behave. Women can embrace their beauty while also being strong, determined, and capable. This ability to shatter traditional gender norms empowers women to redefine their identities on their own terms.

It's essential to understand that our perception of the world is a subjective reflection of our thoughts. We are the creators of our own reality. If we see negativity or judgment around us, it often mirrors the feelings and qualities within us. By recognizing this, we can choose to focus on positivity, beauty, and strength in both ourselves and others. To find happiness, we must see the world as it is and continue to believe in ourselves and others, without passing harsh judgments.

Climbing has taught me humility and self-discovery. It's a journey into one's own psyche, a process of confronting and overcoming fear, and a means of forging one's character. It brings you in contact with people who accept you for who you are, with each person offering their unique perspective on the world. There isn't a single "right" way of seeing things; our diverse viewpoints are all valid. Our brains are incredibly powerful and can shape our reality. We are both the actors and creators of our experiences.

In the mountains, we learn the beauty of life lies not in its predictability but in the courage to confront the unknown. As we navigate the precipices and peaks of our existence, we are not merely spectators but active participants, shaping our reality with resilience, determination, and an unwavering belief in the limitless possibilities that lie ahead. In embracing the enriching lessons of climbing, we discover the true summit is not a destination but a continuous journey of self-discovery and transformation.

CHAPTER 10

Vertical Reflections: Navigating Life, Identity, and Risk in Alpine Climbing

By Sydney Pham

I think about death a lot more than the average person. Don't get the wrong impression – I am not apathetic toward life, it's the exact opposite. I am an alpine rock climber and mountaineer. I push the boundaries of gravity for no reason other than pure desire, motivation, and dedication. Death is a risk of climbing, a component that must be heavily considered and mitigated at all costs. Most people do not risk their lives to do their hobby, so I have to ask myself, *Why do I do this? Why do I put myself through experiences that are undeniably just plain hard, for fun?* I have found the answer is very simple. It is one of the only times I feel completely myself.

I am a queer Vietnamese American woman born and raised in Washington state. I grew up very curious about the world around me and was lucky to have grown up surrounded by such beautiful, lush, mountainous scenery. I connected with the outdoors from a young age with the influence of my Vietnam War refugee parents through family road trips, picking fruit from fruit trees, and fishing and harvesting on Puget Sound. As I grew up, the way I connected with the outdoors changed, but I stayed constant in my youthful curiosity about the outside world. I faced many challenges as a second-generation Vietnamese American woman and share many of the same struggles bicultural people face as they find a place for themselves in the world. My journey to self-discovery is intimately intertwined with my outdoor pursuits and how I came to call myself a rock climber.

I struggled a lot as a child with the pressure to excel and carried with me many values that had been instilled by my immigrant parents such as shame, duty, and excellence. In my elementary years, I wanted to be the perfect Asian girl for my parents. Obedient, poised, excellent. I loved doing the things I was good at, such as soccer and math, and detested anything that made me feel inadequate, like playing the piano. I craved praise and affirmation from my parents but rarely got it. It was a cycle of desire and disappointment that ultimately led to very low self-esteem and self-doubt. Heading into my high-school years, I was a shy and quiet girl. Someone who didn't take up much space. I did what I was told.

On Mount Stuart in Washington state. Photo by Lauren Bolin.

I had spent my entire life up until that point trying to make my parents proud of me. I picked up tennis, found I had a natural gift for it, and pursued it at a high level. I spent hours before and after school attending lessons and hitting practices with my father. I was obsessed with tennis, but, in all honesty, I'm not sure I really enjoyed it. Part of me believes it was a way to get my father's attention and hold it. He would show up to all my matches and silently watch from the sideline. Occasional claps after a good shot, and the more common silent disappointed head shake after an unforced error, were all I ever got from him, but he showed up and, deep down, I craved that. I was good, but I wasn't great. I competed in the highest division state tournaments playing singles, which is a fair accomplishment in itself, but in the end, I choked. I wanted so badly to be great, but I wanted it for approval and not for myself. I felt like I let my father down and felt intense shame because of that. I quit tennis completely after that last state match. I have struggled with this theme my entire life.

Aside from my athletic pursuits, I was an above-average student. I graduated high school with a high, but not perfect, GPA, to the disappointment of my parents. Throughout my life I've had ideas of what I wanted to do as a career but was never sure. These ideas ranged from a baker when I was young to more realistic ideas, like a sports medicine doctor and a computer scientist, as I grew up. I would proudly present these ideas to my parents and anxiously await their reaction. *Will they approve? Will they "let" me be these things?* That was all I was considering when looking for a career. I never put any real thought into what I liked or wanted to do with my life; it was mostly a journey for affirmations. I ended up going to school to become a nurse after a lot of pressure from my parents. They felt it was a stable and respectable job with multiple career directions after graduating.

Up until college, I'm not sure I made a real decision for myself in my entire life. I had no sense of autonomy. I felt I had a duty to my family to make them proud. After all, they had fled a war-torn country to provide me with all the opportunities I had. Who was I to let them down? Unsurprisingly, this mentality, combined with moving hundreds of miles from home for college, guided me into a deep depression. I had no idea what to do with myself, so I hid in my single-bed dorm room day in and day out, only going out to go to class and get groceries. The wondrous feelings of freedom and exploration that many college freshmen experience were lost on me. I kept my head down, got good grades, and largely didn't push myself to make new friends or try new things. I had zero self-confidence, no passions of my own accord, and no sense of self. For once in my life, no one was watching over my every move and telling me what to do, and so I was lost.

I faced many struggles on my journey of self-discovery and, as I have struggled with anxiety and depression my entire life, I wanted to be happy more than anything else. I slowly started to push myself out of my comfort zone and started to break out of my shell. I joined clubs and made some acquaintances, but it wasn't until I joined the Spokane Mountaineers in Spokane, Washington, that a leaf turned over in my life. I had started backpacking in high school with friends and stopped throughout college, but I still had my longtime love and interest for being in the outdoors. The backpacking in Washington is stunning, as the terrain is filled with steep granite peaks and snow-capped volcanoes. My heart was captivated by these spectacular landscapes, so when the opportunity presented itself to learn how to climb these mountains, I found the courage to jump into a passion that was all mine.

I attended a three-month-long Mountain School put on by the Spokane Mountaineers in 2018 where we participated in classroom sessions, as well as weekend trips outside. I showed up, eager to learn, but once again largely kept to myself. I chatted with classmates who sat next to me during class, but I was shy and would flee after class ended, weaving between the other students who often stayed to chat. We would go on the occasional overnight weekend trip to practice our newfound skills, such as self-arrest and glacier travel. Instructors would encourage us to pair up and find a tent partner, but I opted out because I was too shy to ask anyone to camp with me. Instead, I carried a small one-person bivy sack and shivered by myself all night. I did want to make friends and feel like I had a place to be myself, but I lacked the social skills and confidence to express myself freely. Things changed for me, however, when I met a man in my class named Charlie LaBrie.

When I met Charlie, he was 58 years old. He had lived many lives by that point in his life. He grew up in Minnesota but moved to Spokane three years prior and attended Mountain School with his wife. He had been a rock climber for over 20 years by this point, but glaciers were new and interesting to him. My immediate impression of him was that he had a youthful energy. I could tell he liked to talk, and he liked to laugh. He made friends easily, and by the second week of Mountain School he knew everyone in class by name. I liked saying hi to Charlie when I walked into class because he always made me feel seen. At the end of our three-month course, we were set to do a graduation climb up in the Canadian Rockies on a peak called Athabasca. It was a ten-hour drive and we were encouraged to carpool. Charlie and I had talked only a few times at this point, but I was thrilled when he offered up a spot in his van to drive up to our climb. I happily accepted. In the smaller setting of the van, I felt like I had the opportunity to take up more space. And, by the end of the graduation climb weekend, I felt lucky to have made some friends – it only took me until the last weekend of Mountain School!

In addition to alpine skills, we also covered rock climbing in Mountain School. I had previously rock climbed in a bouldering gym but never outside, until one outdoor weekend session where we went to a local crag to practice different skills. I loved it! I thought it was very thought-provoking and engaging. So, when Charlie began inviting me out to some local rock climbing after Mountain School had ended, I was eager. As I began learning more about rock climbing, I started to realize how niche and challenging it was. One mistake or lapse in judgment could be devastating.

I learned about the difference between sport and trad climbing. Although I was interested in sport climbing, which is generally considered safer, I was more eager to learn how to trad climb.

With my mentor, Charlie LaBrie, in Squamish, British Columbia. Photo by Sydney Pham.

Mastering this style of climbing takes many hours of practice placing gear that won't fail in the event of a fall. It also requires a headspace of climbing above a piece you've placed yourself, where trust is paramount or else fear and self-doubt will creep in. Most people (me included) start with sport climbing, as it is safer, easier to learn, cheaper, and there is often more of it around. Even if you are interested in traditional climbing, there are so many barriers to becoming competent at it. In particular, because of the danger aspect of the sport, mentorship, classes, and guidance are crucial to avoid injury or death. Luckily for me, I found myself a brilliant trad climber who was eager to take me under his wing: Charlie.

I'm not sure exactly how I became interested in traditional climbing, but I do remember the excitement and obsession I felt when I did. We started off on the ground at a local crag, plugging gear into cracks while Charlie explained the physics of a fall and how to judge whether a placement is good or bad. There was a lot to consider, such as the angles of a fall, the quality and texture of the rock, and the shape and depth of the crack. Charlie was adamant that I be as safe as possible while learning these new skills, which consequently required me to be very patient. Being on "lead" is when you are the person climbing and placing protection as you go. One person leads a route and the other follows, cleaning the route of the gear the leader had placed. This is by far the much safer role, as a fall is not nearly as consequential. After leading a route, Charlie would have me follow, asking me if I noticed anything about his gear placements, taking all opportunities to offer a window into his mind. We often grabbed beers after our climbing sessions and chatted about climbing. Me, the apprentice with a mind full of wonder, and Charlie, the mentor, eager to teach. Despite my impatient requests, Charlie didn't want me to lead any trad climbs until I had followed many routes and mastered the basics. This was frustrating to me, but I appreciated his care and attention.

There is something to be said for spending time with older and wiser people, not just in rock climbing. Charlie had been trad climbing for as long as I had been alive, and in that time had learned many lessons. An experienced mentor in climbing could be the difference between life and death. While Charlie was a good trad climber, he was an excellent alpine trad climber. Alpine climbing adds many more complex layers to trad climbing. This climbing style often involves long approaches carrying overnight gear, as well as all your climbing gear, just to get to the base of the climb. These climbs are often very remote and wild, meaning you must often use your instincts to find the correct way to navigate your way up the peak. Alpine climbs are also often very long. Using a multitude of skills, you navigate your way from the bottom to the top of peaks, sometimes thousands of feet high. It is common for these climbing days to be 16-plus hours long, all while maintaining the focus necessary to avoid any lapse in judgment that could result in a catastrophic mistake.

My first alpine climb was the West Ridge of Mount Stuart, a 9,415-foot (2870-m) prominent mountain in the Cascade Range in Washington state. I had backpacked near this mountain before and had noticed and admired its grandiosity. I was thrilled to try to climb it. We set out from the parking lot midday and

Enjoying alpine trad climbing in Grand Teton National Park in Wyoming. Photo by Tyler Cebulla.

made camp by 5 p.m. A short first day to make for a shorter approach the next morning. The Cascade Range is a place full of awe and natural beauty, so just being out there was wonderful. We passed many parties on our approach, as it was a popular day hiking and backpacking area. I remember running into a middle-aged woman with her children that day, and she asked if we were climbing Mount Stuart. We proudly said, yes, we would try tomorrow. She commented that she didn't understand how people could have the desire to do something like that, but that she admired our drive. We set up camp in the shadow of Mount Stuart. The mountain was commanding. Huge, pointy, and daunting. That night, I couldn't control my excitement. I had never felt that kind of enthusiasm for life before. I was so happy to be alive and found this colorful vibrancy was hard to contain inside of me. At that moment, I felt like I could fill up rooms with my energy. I was bursting.

We were up before sunrise the next morning and quickly packed up our camp. We had a long day ahead and started our hike to the base of the granite rock wall with vigor. After a couple hours, we found ourselves in a gully surrounded by granite. The rock formed these amazing ledges that led the way up. We looked at our guidebook and decided we had found the right gully to ascend and continued upwards. After not too long, Charlie suggested we stop and put our helmets on. While we were not yet doing technical rock climbing, the gully was prone to rockfall. Charlie cautioned me to stay close to him and avoid kicking any rocks down the gully. A falling rock will cause more damage if it has the opportunity to gather speed, so it was best if we stayed close together. This environment was completely foreign to me. I had never been in a place where natural danger existed all around and a slipped foot could mean death. We ventured upward in the gully for hours. It was steep and strenuous, but it was beautiful and rewarding. I remember stopping to catch my breath and looking around, the sunrise hitting the granite and making it shine with an orange hue. The only sound was our breathing in the cold morning. My legs and lungs hurt, but I was happy.

As we reached the top of the gully, Charlie and I got turned around. We weren't sure which direction to go. I was eager to keep moving and felt frustrated to be waiting around as we looked at the guidebook, so I told Charlie I would look around the corner for a path. At this point, the gully had turned into a ridge. I followed the ridge to the left and found myself on a pile of large boulders. They rested on each other and I climbed up and over them. I continued in this direction, peering my head around corners, looking for any sign that people had come this way before. After a few minutes, I heard Charlie shouting that he had found the way. I turned around and began to climb the rocks back to Charlie. I had both my hands and feet on some boulders and, as I began to step upward, one of the microwave-sized blocks my foot was standing on gave way. It tumbled downward and off the cliff below me. For thousands of feet it fell as I listened to it bang and bounce off the granite, until it finally found a resting place at the bottom of the mountain. Luckily, the blocks my hands were on held in place. I climbed out of the predicament I had gotten myself into and joined Charlie. He asked what the noise was, and I explained I kicked a rock down. It wasn't until after I had gotten off the mountain and put some separation between this experience and me that I realized the gravity of what had just occurred.

Thankfully, the rest of our ascent was less eventful. We found our route and continued upward, utilizing our skills to mitigate risk and navigate the alpine environment. At one point near the summit, I was belaying Charlie from a ridge. The wind was howling, I was as cold as I had ever been, and I was exhausted from the last 12 hours of effort we had put in. We were in the clouds, but occasionally they would break and I would get a view of Stuart Lake far below me and I could truly see the grandeur of the place where I stood. Little did I know that the perplexity of alpine rock climbing in that moment would be the catalyst for the lifestyle I would come to pursue and thrive in. The summit was an alluring accomplishment, but the journey was the gift.

After this trip I was consumed by alpine trad climbing. I planned all my time off from work around taking trips to climb mountains. At that point in my life, I had graduated from nursing school and was working night shifts as an intensive care unit (ICU) nurse. I worked six nights in a row from 7 p.m. to 7 a.m., sleeping during the days, completely flipped from the rest of the world. I was then granted eight days off where I could run off to the mountains and completely remove myself from society in a different way. Work drained my soul, and the mountains filled me up. It was an unsustainable lifestyle.

As I entered the ICU, the COVID pandemic hit the world, and suddenly my work environment was filled with so much death and fear. At 22 years old, I was jaded, lonely, and burnt out. The only reason I stuck with this job was because of my goal to become a certified registered nurse anesthetist (CRNA), which required ICU experience. While I had made great strides in my personal life to make decisions for myself and do the things that made me happy, my career path was much more complicated.

Throughout college, my relationship with my parents had become very tenuous. I was tired of doing everything they asked of me without question. I began to push back and confront these feelings and the vicious cycle of expectation and disappointment. As I started to come into my own person, my parents felt I demonstrated a lack of respect and duty to family. We became estranged. I began going to therapy, where my therapist encouraged me to set boundaries with my parents and told me that I couldn't control them, only my side of the relationship. But I knew how much I was hurting my parents in the process of self-discovery. I didn't mean to. I was just trying to be myself. I felt shame and guilt for not being what they wanted, but I fought these feelings and held steadfast on certain aspects of my life. It was easier to do with personal things like my body and my hobbies, but my career felt different.

Growing up poor after fleeing their home country, my parents had a work ethic that is still unmatched by anyone else I have ever met. They valued success, and to them that meant status, money, and reputation. And, despite my reluctance, I realized later in life the power of these things. At a certain point in my life I had to analyze my career goals and the direction I was headed. I didn't want to live my life for my parents, but I couldn't deny they had influenced me so much that I wasn't clear on the differences between what I wanted versus what they wanted. But one thing was for sure: I still wanted to make my parents proud, and it hurt me deeply to be seen as a disappointment. Becoming a CRNA meant I would be completing a respected doctorate program to take up a profession that was high in demand, with a salary as generous as a nurse could make. Ultimately, I decided that compromise was one of the best things I could do for my family. I would continue to wholeheartedly pursue my passions in rock climbing and decided this passion was enough to balance out the lack of passion I felt for my career. Undoubtedly, this career would provide me with the stability and freedom to do anything I wanted with my life, which I have come to learn is all my parents ever wanted for me anyways.

I believe my experiences with alpine rock climbing changed the trajectory of my life. As I grew as a rock climber, I found courage and determination inside of me I didn't know existed. It wasn't a process that was as simple as climbing immediately resulting in confidence. No, it was riddled with challenges and barriers I would come to be very familiar with. I came to see that I fell in love with a sexist, gate-kept, male, white-dominated sport. Most of the people I have climbed with outside have been straight white men. I have been talked over, discredited, and not seen. Despite my experience and skill, I am often overlooked as a person of value in the outdoors. I have been on alpine rock climbs and run into other parties who ask for information about the route, except they only talk to my male partner, even though I am the more experienced climber. As a queer woman of color, I rarely run into people like me in alpine rock climbing. There are many things I attribute this to, including a lack of mentorship, cost, and general inaccessibility.

Charlie was a gift to me. He was so eager to take on a shy, queer woman of color as his mentee. He saw something in me and he believed in me. The amount of time and effort he put into me and our relationship was priceless. Without him, I would have had to take many classes (largely led and attended by white men) at very high costs, only to gain the skills but with no guarantee of a climbing partnership. Women who are just beginning in this sport are often seen as weaker, burdensome, or only as a potential romantic partner. It takes countless trips to become

Teaching with Climbers of Color. Photo by Peter Lin.

a competent alpine rock climber, which is not possible for lots of people due to financial constraints. And the gear required for alpine rock climbing can easily exceed thousands. I recognize all these barriers to entry and am so thankful for all the opportunities I have had to get to where I am. I would love nothing more than to facilitate change.

Before I went back to graduate school, and inevitably had to shift my priorities toward my schooling instead of my outdoor adventures, I had the opportunity to work with a few organizations that aligned with my values regarding accessibility. I applied to become an ambassador for the Cairn Project, a nonprofit whose mission is to nurture the next generation of empowered and self-confident girls through outdoor adventure by providing small grants. I helped to raise money for this cause by launching a campaign with the goal to climb 25 pitches of alpine rock during the climbing season of 2022. I had never had much of an online presence and initially felt uncomfortable in this role as a fundraiser, feeling awkward as I announced my upcoming climbs and adventures to potential donors. But as the donations came in, I felt very affirmed in my role as an outdoor woman supporting other women.

I was invited to speak for the Sierra Club's Asian Diaspora in Solidarity group, where for the first time in my life I began to really think about how my childhood and upbringing impacted my journey in the outdoors. I gave an hour-long presentation about how I became a woman in alpine rock climbing to other Asian people and felt an instant connection and validation of my struggles. I realized that my experiences as a queer Vietnamese

American woman trying to find her place in society were not unique to myself. At one point during my presentation I was reflecting on how the shy girl I used to be would never have given this presentation but that telling my story was more important than my feelings of being uncomfortable. Despite the inherent aversion I felt toward taking up space, I learned I needed to if I wanted to break down barriers for others like me. For one of the first times in my life I showed up as my true self to strangers, and their reception was nothing but positivity and even gratitude for my vulnerability. I then accepted a position to be an instructor for Climbers of Color, a nonprofit organization based out of Seattle, Washington. Its aim is to promote diversity, equity, and inclusion in the climbing and mountaineering communities by providing mentorship, technical training, and access to key resources like scholarships and gear. My experience teaching crack climbing technique and trad climbing with Climbers of Color was nothing but positive.

I took on the role as an instructor with eagerness and was thrilled to be talking to people about my favorite thing in the whole world. I had thought about teaching climbing before this opportunity presented itself but talked myself out of it because I felt too intimidated by the idea of instructing a group of white men. I feared putting myself out there only to have my experience discredited or invalidated like it had been in the past. But I have found that most people of color are a safe place for me. Our shared experience of being members of marginalized minority groups means we know what it feels like to be excluded, and Climbers of Color is built to do the exact opposite. It provides a place for students to learn, ask questions, and have access to resources, but it also provided me with a place to shine, speak freely about rock climbing, and feel seen and heard. When I finish graduate school, I plan to continue instructing with groups like these, volunteering my time and expertise in the hope of sparking change.

Far from the shy, quiet girl I once was, I now describe myself as confident, bold, and competent. I have developed from a girl who didn't take up much space to a woman who demands space. Early in my climbing career, especially on mountaineering teams, decisions would be made on my behalf that I didn't necessarily agree with, but I didn't feel like I had a place to disagree or share my thoughts. I would let myself get steamrolled until I found the confidence to believe what I had to say was worth something. I came to believe I deserved to be in these spaces. I am a very strong alpine rock climber with valuable experiences and have a lot to offer to the climbing world. So I do what I can to share my experiences, skills, and wisdom with folks who want to learn, especially those from marginalized communities like mine.

So, back to death. That day on Mount Stuart with Charlie was one of many close calls I have had in the mountains. After I walked away from that, I realized just how close I was to falling thousands of feet to a terrible death. The only reason why I didn't was sheer luck. So I vowed to learn what I could to become competent, to practice and read up on skills to be a better alpine climber, and to never let my or anyone else's ego get in the way of safety in the mountains. I choose to venture out into the alpine world with just what I can carry with my own two feet,

Demonstrating crack climbing technique with Climbers of Color. Photo by Peter Lin.

to ascend and descend large, remote, wild peaks, only to return to where I started. There is an insightful quote I enjoy by the French writer, René Daumal:

> *You cannot stay on the summit forever; you have to come down again. So why bother in the first place? Just this: What is above knows what is below, but what is below does not know what is above. One climbs, one sees. One descends, one sees no longer, but one has seen. There is an art of conducting oneself in the lower regions by the memory of what one saw higher up. When one can no longer see, one can at least still know.*[3]

The mountains have shaped me in so many ways I can't keep track of them all. From growing out of my shell and discovering my own voice to finding courage and grit inside myself and finding community among like-minded people. I choose this life because I couldn't imagine it any other way.

CHAPTER 11

From Czech Sandstone to Mountain Cracks: Learning through Ascents and Falls

By Anna Šebestíková

TRANSLATED FROM THE CZECH BY DENISA KRÁSNÁ

Climbing serendipitously stumbled into my life. Since childhood, I've spent ample time in nature, particularly exploring forests and rivers with my outdoor club. At 13, my mother enrolled me in a climbing club, setting everything in motion. Back then I never imagined it would become such a passion. As the years pass, my dedication to climbing deepens as I am driven by exploration across various disciplines. Despite the shifting focus, certain aspects continue to captivate me: the boundless variety of movements and the camaraderie inherent in the climbing community.

Climbing has become an integral part of my life. It serves as relaxation, one of the few activities where I can truly unwind. When I climb, everything else fades away. My mind must be focused, leaving no room for distractions. I must concentrate on the present moment, assessing my surroundings. *What are the next steps? Where should I place my hands and feet? How far am I from the safety of the next spot where I can place protection? Where can I place additional gear? What happens if my planned sequence fails?*

Everything flows naturally. My body responds to the commands of my mind without hesitation. There's no space for intrusive thoughts to disrupt my flow. I'm intimately acquainted with my body, able to assess what I can safely attempt at any given moment. Crack climbing is my preference. I fully embrace the idea that a crack essentially serves as one long hold, alleviating additional concerns. I don't need to scour my surroundings for holds like in face climbing, which minimizes variables. When I climb cracks, fear seldom enters the equation. I have confidence in myself. I understand that success relies solely on my abilities. The deeper I wedge my body into the crack, the less fear I experience. Hence, I'm unfazed by longer distances between gear placements.

Face climbing presents a different challenge. Variables multiply,

Face climbing in Wadi Rum in southern Jordan. Photo by Šimon Janošec.

Climbing at Adršpach in the Czech Republic. Photo by Jakub Friewald.

and I usually need to have more protection. *What if my foot slips? What if a hold breaks off with me?* I strive to maintain control over every aspect of the climb. However, there are instances where my influence over the outcome is limited. I prefer to climb with certainty. I only allow myself to fall when I'm confident nothing untoward will happen to me. Only when my mind deems the situation safe. In such cases, I'm untroubled by the prospect of a substantial fall. I enjoy the mindset. I like to have perspective and to climb to heights where I have a view. It imbues me with a distinct sense of liberation and, often, relaxation. While my body engages in the physical demands of clinging to the rock face, my mind finds solace, fully immersed in the act of climbing.

Mountains offer me the greatest sense of peace. Whether I'm scaling a towering wall or traversing along the peaks, I find peace in their presence. Combining the beauty of climbing with the grandeur of mountains creates an experience that is truly exceptional. The most cherished moments occur when my partner and I embark on a journey on our own. I frequently opt for less popular routes to avoid running into other climbers. Then I can savor the tranquility and the majestic scenery of the mountains in a unique manner. In the mountains, I rest and perform at the same time, and that's what I find so profoundly fulfilling.

Crazy

I perceive success in climbing as something truly extraordinary. It's something I plan meticulously in advance and must work hard for, giving my maximum effort. However, most of the time, I don't set specific goals, and even if I do, the satisfaction from achieving them quickly fades away. For me, success isn't solely about long-term accomplishments. What are more important are freedom, independence, and the opportunity to spend time outdoors. Climbing is an ideal companion in this pursuit. I dislike being confined indoors in the city for extended periods; I need to escape outdoors. I prefer to get away. I'm not saying I dislike the hustle and bustle of the city. Occasionally, I appreciate things like culture or romantic dinners. Yet excess of anything isn't good. Frankly, I'd rather enjoy a pint at the local pub after a day of climbing in Adršpach. Although I'm not from there, nor have I ever lived there or spent all my free time there, this place has grown close to my heart. I fell in love with it from the first encounter. I've never been in such a beautiful place. I love the rocks and the climbers who frequent it. Adršpach has become a second home to me.

Adršpach, situated in the northeastern part of the Czech Republic, boasts a mesmerizing landscape characterized by towering sandstone formations, some of which reach heights of up to 460 feet (140 m). These unique geological features have been sculpted over millennia by natural forces, resulting in a breathtaking array of cliffs, pillars, and intricate rock formations. Tourists can explore the area's labyrinthine pathways, discovering hidden gorges, caves, and tranquil ponds along the way on a circular hiking trail. But, for climbers, Adršpach is often paradise and hell at the same time. I first visited there in 2016, when my friend and I were simply passing through during a long-distance hike. We came from the city of Teplice nad Metují, and it was already pitch dark when we arrived. Somewhere in the middle of the tourist hiking trail, we dropped our backpacks and decided to camp overnight. We had no idea where we were at that moment. The next morning, I couldn't believe my eyes. I was astonished by the breathtaking scenery around me. We completed the entire circuit, including various detours. The endless labyrinth of sandstone towers interspersed with cracks fascinated me. Until then, I had only climbed on sandstone once, at Prachov in Bohemian Paradise, where my friends and I nearly killed ourselves while trying to climb some of the routes. Bohemian Paradise, located about an hour and a half's drive northeast of Prague, also features high sandstone towers that form several sandstone towns, creating a fairy-tale-like landscape. But climbing there is challenging and often dangerous due to the fragile rock and lack of protection. And so, when I looked at the monumental towers of Adršpach, I couldn't fathom how I could ever possibly climb there. Nonetheless, I felt a strong pull to return and try it at least once.

It didn't take long for an opportunity to arise. In 2017 I was deeply focused on climbing competitions and even maintained a somewhat systematic training regimen. On the way back from one of the qualifying competitions, I met Zbyšek, who spoke about Adršpach. Assuming he was familiar with the area, I promptly agreed to visit there together.

Shortly after, we finally were able to make the trip happen. Dolní Adršpach Station: the train halted at the platform. However, Zbyšek led us away from the towers to a nearby climbing area. The following day, he took the lead most of the time. I wondered why we weren't climbing in Adršpach, just across from us, in the rock town. Zbyšek replied that we could try a known route there, but I would need to lead the entire climb because he was scared to climb in Adršpach. "Sure, what's the problem?" I replied. "Let's do it. I enjoy taking the lead on climbs."

We packed our gear and headed across the road. After a while, we found the start of the route, Přes Fichtli na Milence (Over Fichtli on Lover's Tower). Until I looked up and saw the initial chimney, I had no idea what to expect. Unfortunately, I was only wearing a tank top and shorts on that sunny afternoon, leaving little protection between my body and the rock. Moreover, I had forgotten my climbing shoes. "If you manage to lead the whole thing, I'll lend you mine, and I'll climb barefoot behind you," Zbyšek offered. So we agreed not to go back for them. I still had no clue what lay ahead. Nevertheless, I managed to make my way up through the narrow chimney and all the others that followed it. I reached the top, scraped and bleeding. Signing the logbook and looking out from the highest point onto the surrounding towers was an unforgettable experience.

A few weekends later, I tackled my first crack climb at Prachov in Bohemian Paradise. Just one crack move that couldn't be avoided – a mandatory jam. I had no clue how to handle it. I took a break for a while, and when I reached the top I declared that cracks were nonsense, that I never wanted to climb them again. If only I had known at the time...

In the summer, I returned to Adršpach and climbed several easy classics, mostly routes with face climbing and chimneys. However, it became evident to me that if I aimed to climb here, mastering crack climbing was essential. The towers in Adršpach are predominantly smooth, with few handholds on the rock. This means that, apart from the classic crack climbs, most routes here tend to be quite difficult. I realized I had two options: tackling modern, technically demanding routes with widely spaced protection, or opting for cracks, which, despite having fewer bolts, present a less daunting challenge compared to bare walls. Despite my initial reluctance, I decided to pursue this path.

I started with my plan toward the end of summer in 2017, during the annual International Mountaineering Film Festival held here. My more experienced friend offered to lead a route in Adršpach and I could follow. I wanted to tackle a crack climb and was determined to do it. The crack was damp and covered in greenery, and it progressively widened. I began the climb in shorts, a T-shirt, snug competition climbing shoes, and without crack gloves to protect my hands as I shoved them in the cracks for grip. The first challenging section came after roughly six feet (two meters). Moreover, my buddy's advice was not particularly helpful.

"What should I do here?" I shouted at him. "Just jam your hand in there," he said. "Nothing special." Although I had done it before, it really hurt without crack gloves. I managed to make my way up through the initial green, slimy corner, only to realize it was just the beginning. What followed were a few moves in a fantastic hand jam in the now dry rock toward the bolt. And then it was time to take a break again. "And what do I do here?" I asked my friend. "It's too wide." He replied from above, "Put two hand jams side by side." *What?* I had no idea what that meant, but I managed to figure out how to stay in the crack. However, I mostly used the rope to assist me up. It definitely didn't look like continuous climbing. In the end, though, I managed to scramble to the top. It was an extremely difficult and painful experience as I jammed any body part I could into the rock crack, but instead of being deterred, I wanted more.

Courageous

Because I survived my early struggles with sandstone climbing, I figured there was a good chance I could survive anything. Sandstone climbing in the Czech Republic is unique and holds a somewhat notorious reputation among climbers worldwide. What sets Czech sandstone climbing apart are the rock's fragility and the need for climbers to exercise extreme caution. The sandstone is notoriously brittle and prone to erosion, making it exceptionally delicate. Climbers must navigate routes carefully to avoid damaging the rock and endangering themselves and others. Moreover, traditional protection methods like cams and nuts could easily harm the soft sandstone and are therefore strictly forbidden. Fixed protection is very scarce, with the first piece often up to 50 feet (15 m) above the ground. Otherwise, climbers either rely on slings and monkey fists made of ropes that can be wedged in the crack. Many climbers thus view Czech sandstone climbing as daring and even reckless due to the inherent risks involved. The combination of technical difficulty, unpredictable rock quality, and the need for delicate movement makes climbing in the Czech Republic a test of both skill and courage. It requires climbers to possess not only physical prowess but also a deep respect for the rock and a willingness to accept the challenges it presents. For many, however, the rewards of stunning beauty and exhilarating climbing are worth the risks.

Undoubtedly, luck accompanied me during many climbs. The following summer, I returned to Adršpach with a clear goal: mastering crack climbing. My friends gave me some great advice: “Every time you’re coming back from the rocks, stop by the route Tréninkovka (Training Route). The lower part of the route is a perfect hand crack. Climb it up and down, depending on how you feel.” It didn’t take long before I felt comfortable hand jamming. Well, when the jams held, that is. During my second visit to Teplice, I went to a route called Prásknutí bičem (Whip Crack) with a friend. It’s a beautiful, quite well protected crack, with a corner hand crack that smoothly transitions into a roof. However, in the roof, the crack widened a bit, and my small hands didn’t feel secure there at the time. Fear of falling headfirst led me to withdraw my legs from the crack twice in a row, jumping down onto the slab below. At that moment, it didn’t seem strange to me at all; I felt fine. But my friends found my move exceptionally crazy. This climb, among others, earned me a humorous nickname that reminded me for a long time of what a daring, or reckless, move it had been.

In spring 2018, I dedicated time to exploring other sandstone climbing areas. I didn’t have a specific plan. I climbed either based on recommendations or simply chose routes that caught my eye. Once at Skalák (Hrubá Skála, Bohemian Paradise), I relied on a borrowed guidebook to select my climb. However, the assigned difficulty often doesn’t align with reality. This wasn’t something I initially anticipated. Despite the challenges, I persevered through the route and returned safely to the climbing pub in the evening, where I was told it was one of the seldom climbed and relatively serious routes in the area.

Different

“You ride well, Anna!” says a friend on a cycling trip. “Come on, man, I feel like a snail compared to you,” I reply. “Well, yeah, but sometimes you forget you’re a girl.” Yes, that sometimes happens to me. I’ve always compared my performance to those of guys. I grew up in a group of boys and quickly became one of them. I did water sports with them, ran up hills, and increasingly forgot I’m actually a girl. I became immune to stupid remarks aimed at me. It took some time, but, eventually, I accepted my body as it is. I got used to my wide shoulders after a few years. I knew that, if I wanted to climb, I wouldn’t be able to change my body.

But men often underestimate women. There are plenty of girls around me who can outperform guys in endurance sports. Not me, because I don’t put in as much time running or cycling, simply not as much training overall. I just try to work hard enough so as not to be a burden to my partners. But in climbing, this is different. The thought, *If some blonde girl can climb it, then I have to manage too, right?* frequently occurs to guys. Naturally, they seem to have more confidence. I’ve never heard anything like this from girls. During my initial years on the sandstone, there

Climbing Czech sandstone at Adršpach. Photo by Standa Mitáč.

were several instances when guys underestimated me. In some rare cases, they were correct to doubt me. However, with time, things settled down. I learned to assess what I could do and what I couldn't. I grew more confident with each passing year.

I began my climbing journey with a girlfriend, but over time most of my climbing partners turned out to be guys. While I don't often climb with girls, I thoroughly enjoy it when I do. I would like to climb more with girls, but it's quite difficult to find a climbing partner around here that shares similar goals to me. Not that many girls are drawn to climbing cracks in the mountains or in Adršpach. Especially since suffering in wide cracks doesn't appeal to many people, regardless of gender. Also I tend to be rather impatient and often prefer climbing with a partner who can smoothly ascend routes with me.

In June 2019, my friend and I climbed a stunning route, Slunovrat na Starostu (Solstice on the Mayor), in Adršpach, and our friend documented our ascent in a video for an online climbing magazine. I was thrilled that we formed an all-female team, despite some uncertainty until the last moment. I believe our climb demonstrated to the Czech sandstone climbing community, as well as to other girls, that "it goes, boys." This fills me with immense joy. Traditionally, there have been very few female climbers in Adršpach, with most climbers not even considering the possibility of women climbing there. I hope to see such biases vanish. I believe it's slowly happening, with more girls venturing into climbing there. While many start following the lead climber on these routes, some are now taking the extra risk to lead as well.

Stubborn

Transitioning my climbing to the mountains presented quite a challenge. While I'd spent my childhood skiing in the mountains, climbing posed a different set of obstacles. I used to marvel at photos of endless peaks bathed in the setting sun. I longed to be part of that beauty, to see it all in person. However, I didn't know anyone who climbed in the mountains, and the thought of embarking on such journeys alone left me feeling somewhat apprehensive.

At the beginning of 2018, I learned about a project called Sokolíci, a team of young alpinists within the Czech Mountaineering Association. Its website mentioned an upcoming team change, with each cycle lasting three years. Without hesitation, I applied, just having turned 18 and thus fitting within the age limit. I hoped my lack of experience in climbing mountains wouldn't be a significant obstacle. After all, I had climbed several challenging routes on sandstone, hadn't I? I was also motivated, but by what exactly? I couldn't even remember. It didn't take long for me to find out I didn't make the team. I interpreted it in my own way: *They say I'm not good enough?*

I had a strong desire to start climbing in the mountains. During the summer, I primarily climbed in Adršpach and tackled multi-pitches in the Italian Arco. In the winter, my friend and I decided to venture into the High Tatras alpine mountains in Slovakia. It was our first time climbing in winter, but we were undeterred. I rented all the necessary gear, from boots to ice axes. Who needs instructors and advice? We believed we could handle it ourselves.

Climbing in the High Tatras in Slovakia. Photo by Standa Mitáč.

While our ascents weren't particularly noteworthy, we managed to navigate dry tooling and ice climbing successfully. Our summer mountain experiences followed a similar pattern. We were proficient in belaying, and I could place cams, so what could be the problem? Climbing a few mountains in the nearby limestone Austrian Alps taught us a lesson in underestimating the mountains. Reflecting on those experiences, I'm grateful for the journey I underwent independently. However, I wouldn't recommend it to others.

When I reapplied to Sokolíci after three years and was accepted, I felt like I had truly earned that spot. It wasn't until 2021 that I began immersing myself in the real mountains, the ones I had previously only dreamed of. I spent over a month climbing in the vicinity of Chamonix, in France, and it was nothing short of paradise. Adršpach proved to be an invaluable training ground, shaping my skills in ways I couldn't have imagined. With each experience, my abilities steadily improved. We concluded the three-year cycle with Sokolíci with a successful expedition to Pakistan, where I relished a month in the almost untouched valley of Nangmah. Looking ahead, I eagerly anticipate future expeditions and the challenge of scaling more walls in the heart of pristine nature.

Free

Climbing has been instrumental in helping me recognize the significance of freedom in my life. It stands as one of my most cherished assets. I'm thankful for the ability to pursue all that I do. Above all, the freedom to travel without anyone dictating where I can or cannot go is invaluable. However, I do find myself grappling with decision making at times, especially when faced with numerous enticing opportunities from various directions.

During the first wave of the COVID pandemic, I began traveling more frequently. My friend and I borrowed a car from my parents and we spent nearly three months in Spain during the winter. We primarily camped outdoors, either in a tent or under the open sky. We rarely encountered other people and we took all necessary precautions to prevent the spread of the disease. While I climbed daily and attended online classes in the mornings and evenings, my friends in the Czech Republic were restricted to their homes. This situation struck me as truly unfortunate. It was then I realized the profound value I place on freedom and the opportunity to be outdoors.

Since then, my wanderlust hasn't waned. Whenever I embark on a journey, I aim to prolong my stay as much as possible. Being a student with sporadic work as a climbing instructor, my budget is not limitless. Travel itself always constitutes the most significant expense. However, by cutting costs at the destination, the overall trip often turns out to be more economical than regular living expenses. I encounter many people who think this couldn't be true. Over time, I opted to create a sleeping setup in my car. With the help of my dad, I converted my Hyundai Getz into a makeshift camper. Though compact, equipped with a rooftop box, it comfortably accommodates two people. Once it was done, my boyfriend, Ondra, and I set off for Chamonix for a month for the first time. Since then, we've adopted this mode of travel, striving to maximize the number of people we can accommodate.

I was pleasantly surprised by how simple everything became while traveling. Online learning was a perfect fit for me, allowing me to be anywhere and manage my time efficiently. Although I initially studied food analysis, I realized it wasn't the best career choice for me. Instead, I seized the opportunity to pursue a master's degree in data engineering. I'm committed to maximizing my flexibility to work from anywhere in the future. I find great joy in continually learning new and fascinating subjects.

Enthusiastic

From Spain, we seamlessly transitioned to Jordan. I had never visited a Muslim country before, so I had some mild apprehensions. As a precaution, I packed a scarf to avoid offending the local population. However, I quickly discovered that tourists are accepted as they are, and there's no need to overly adapt to the local culture. I was delighted by how friendly and accommodating everyone was. Only in some places did we attract curious stares, especially children. After all, Europeans are still an exotic sight. Most of the time, my male buddies accompanied me. When I went out alone, the only difference was that nobody engaged me in conversation along the way. We went climbing in Wadi Rum, and this time I chose face climbing over cracks.

I decided to climb Rock Empire, a route established by Czech climbers. We climbed several more routes, with the absolute standout multipitch sport route for me being Queen of the Desert. However, we only learned about the main plan of the trip once we arrived. In the village, we met up with two Czech

Climbing in Pakistan. Photo by Standa Mitáč.

friends, who handed us a drill and all the necessary climbing gear for making a first ascent. We had no choice but to get to work. Once we felt sufficiently acclimated to the local rock, we chose a wall that seemed quite solid by local standards. On the first day, we fixed the lower 330 feet (100 m) of the crack, and Ondra began the ascent of the smooth, compact wall looming above us.

After two bolts, I took over the lead. I found myself perched on a wall peppered with only a few small holes. "What if I put another bolt here? After all, we're above that ledge..." I pondered aloud.

"No, keep climbing, it would be embarrassing to have the bolts so close together," came the response from below. Fair enough. However, after a few failed attempts at progressing upward, I concluded it was impossible to continue climbing without risking a fall directly onto the belay ledge.

"I'll place another bolt. What if this turns out to be the crux?" I suggested.

"All right then," the guys relented.

I placed a secure hook and drilled a bolt above my head. This time, I passed the tricky section relatively easily. I managed to place another bolt significantly higher. However, we called it a day after that. We returned a few days later. My friend led this pitch, followed by two more, relying more on trad gear. It turned out the spot where I had slipped was indeed the crux, and the bolt ended up being exactly where it needed to be. I wouldn't say the route was dangerous, but it wasn't overly protected either. It was just right. The crux pitch offers truly beautiful climbing on compact rock. I'm pleased we left our mark in the desert, far from home. I certainly wasn't in Wadi Rum for the last time. I appreciated the laid-back atmosphere where nobody fusses about anything and everything just flows carefree. The only thing I won't miss is the crowing of roosters and the muezzin's call at five in the morning.

Upset

In 2021 I spent a semester abroad in Innsbruck, Austria, one of my favorite cities. After completing my academic obligations, it was time for some fun. However, I didn't get to enjoy it for long. During my first ski touring adventure, I tore the cruciate ligament in my knee. Despite efforts, knee rehabilitation was unsuccessful, and a few months later I faced another setback when I tore my meniscus. This led to two surgeries. Eventually, this injury propelled me forward. During my recovery, I started cycling a lot. Sporadic rides turned into frequent outings several times a week. Post-surgery, in autumn, I acquired an old road bike. Embracing my body's needs, I diligently adhered to exercise routines and climbing sessions. Before I knew it, I was back. Five months after the surgery, I sent an 8a route in Spain, marking a triumphant return a year after my initial injury.

I began writing this story in Sardinia. It's January 2024, and I've finished all my university exams early to extend my time away. The next semester doesn't start until mid-February. After Christmas, bidding farewell to my family, my boyfriend Ondra and I embarked to join friends in a warmer place. Loading our climbing gear and bikes into a rented van, we set out on

At base camp in Chamonix, France. Photo by Ondra Mrklovský.

our adventure. The initial days felt idyllic: spending time with friends, cycling on breathtaking roads, and climbing in Ulassai, Italy. However, things took a turn after a few days. I fell ill, unable to go cycling, and confined myself to bed for most of the following week. Naturally, the experience left me feeling upset; being sick and incapacitated is never enjoyable. Initially, there's a sense of helplessness and asking, *Why me?* If improvement doesn't occur within a few days, mild anxiety creeps in. It comforted me knowing I was still in Europe and only a two-day journey away from home.

To become ill during an expedition would be much more disappointing. For me, illness struck during the summer in Pakistan, fortunately after returning to the valley. I returned home afflicted with encephalitis. Since recovering, even a minor cold feels like a significant ordeal. Fatigue sets in more easily, and headaches make all activities unpleasant. Most concerning is my uncertainty about what my body can tolerate. I've become more sensitive to various stimuli. Wind, cold, heat, noise, and screen time all bother me more than before. While this heightened sensitivity to screen time may seem like a positive side effect, it poses a considerable obstacle for someone who is pursuing studies in data engineering.

This situation has profoundly altered my perspective on everything. It compels me to confront challenges I never anticipated facing. I remain hopeful my body will adapt in due time. While I've encountered health issues before, none have impacted me as deeply as this illness. Its sudden onset caught me off guard. Despite this, I've learned to accept each injury I've faced. In most instances, I've returned with heightened motivation and resilience. Each setback has prompted introspection on the significance of movement in my life, often steering me toward new paths that prove beneficial in the long run. I believe this adaptive process may also apply to the encephalitis I've experienced, although it will undoubtedly require patience and time to fully manifest.

As I finish writing this story, I find myself standing at the crossroads of uncertainty and possibility. The shadow of encephalitis still lingers, casting doubts and fears upon my path. Yet I remain hopeful. Each day brings new opportunities for growth. Though my future will undoubtedly have challenges, I embrace it with a newfound sense of courage and determination. For it is in the face of the unknown that we discover the depths of our resilience and the boundless potential within.

CHAPTER 12

Beyond the Rock Face: Sofia Tapia's Story of Climbing, Healing, and Community Building in Chiapas

By Denisa Krásná

Sofia Tapia is a climber and community leader in San Cristóbal de las Casas. Commonly referred to as San Cris, this picturesque town is situated amid the mountains of the southern Mexican state of Chiapas. San Cris holds significant cultural importance as the ancestral home of the Maya civilization and as the focal point of the Zapatista revolution. Renowned for its vibrant atmosphere, San Cris serves as a cultural hub within Chiapas, drawing in numerous tourists throughout the year.

But, thanks to Sofia, San Cris has also evolved into a gathering place for climbers from around the globe. Many climbers extend their visits beyond their initial plans, enticed by the welcoming climbing community and the array of superb sport climbing routes and sectors that Sofia, along with her husband, Martin, has meticulously developed. Their contributions have transformed San Cris into a sought-after destination for climbers seeking adventure amid its stunning natural landscapes.

Before Sofia's intervention, Chiapas had virtually no climbing scene to speak of. She herself was introduced to climbing approximately a decade ago when she was 20 years old and met the man who would become her husband, Martin Siller. He was an Austrian climber raised in the Tyrolean Alps, which are renowned for rock climbing and mountaineering. It was in this setting that Sofia was first exposed to rock climbing, sparking her passion for the sport. Initially, she only learned how to belay to support Martin's climbs. Together, they ventured into the mountains near his home in Tyrol. However, Sofia's desire for more than just belaying soon grew strong. She yearned to experience climbing firsthand. Her initiation, though, was far from easy. The first time she attached a rope to her harness was on a daunting 500-foot (150-m) wall. It was a challenging introduction, and she also learned how to rappel on that very same day.

Sofia in the Austrian Alps with her husband, Martin. Photo by Martin Siller.

As Sofia delved deeper into climbing, she found herself spending weekends scaling rocks with her two border collies by her side. With each ascent, she honed her skills, gradually mastering the techniques of leading routes. It was during those initial moments of leading that Sofia experienced an awakening – a rush of emotions that ignited her love for climbing. Leading routes made her feel alive: "It woke up a lot of things inside of me that made me feel like a little girl again. Like playing on the rocks."

For the next year, Sofia and Martin embarked on climbing adventures every weekend, immersing themselves in the thrill of sports climbing and multipitch climbing. Unlike many beginners, Sofia's climbing journey unfolded exclusively on natural rock faces; she never set foot in a climbing gym during her early days. Their passion for climbing extended beyond their local crags, leading them on exhilarating climbing trips throughout that transformative first year. Together, they embraced the challenges, the triumphs, and the sheer joy of exploring the vertical world, forging a bond both with each other and the majestic landscapes they traversed.

Soon Sofia and Martin decided to embark on the journey of opening climbing routes together, marking their ascent into the world of route development. Still in Austria, they collaborated to establish two multipitch routes spanning 500 feet (150 m). Their efforts resulted in the creation of Siller Tapia (110m, 8-/8 UIAA) and Cuauhtli (120m, 8 UIAA). Drawing inspiration from the climbing traditions of the Alps, they adopted the custom of naming routes after the climbers who set them. In homage to this

Sofia with one of her border collies. Photo by Tania Sosa Balderas.

tradition, and the significance of their collaboration, the names of both of them adorn their inaugural route. But the choice to name their route Tapia held a significance beyond mere convention; it symbolized Sofia's own identity, as "Tapia" translates to "wall" in Spanish. Thus, their inaugural route not only marked the birth of their route-setting journey but also served as a reflection of Sofia's personal connection to the vertical world she had come to embrace.

But her intense year and a half in Austria was characterized by a whirlwind of events, marked not only by joy but also a profound sorrow. Following her marriage to Martin, Sofia found herself expecting their first child. However, the excitement of impending parenthood was overshadowed by tragedy when she suffered a heartbreaking miscarriage three months into her pregnancy. Sofia was overcome with grief. During this time, the mountains became her sanctuary and offered peace. Through her grieving and introspection, she began to find a new sense of purpose – a resolve to create something meaningful out of the pain and loss she had endured. Sofia found comfort in a different act of creation: "I used it as a motivation to create something. I couldn't create a human life, but I could create a project. I could still give life to something new."

But she also felt the urge to return to her roots in México. Driven by a need for support and a familiar environment, she sought refuge back in San Cristóbal. Returning to México offered Sofia the opportunity to navigate her grief and healing in the warmth of community and the comfort of her home. Recognizing the importance of surrounding herself with understanding and supportive people, she sought out a community that resonated with her values and aspirations. For Sofia, this meant finding a tribe of women who shared her openness and willingness to explore deeper emotional topics, cementing bonds that would sustain her through the challenges that lay ahead.

But climbing was also an important part of her healing process. Just a short distance from San Cris is El Arcotete Parque Ecoturístico, known simply as El Arcotete. Here, visitors can discover caves, traverse hiking trails, and immerse themselves in the embrace of nature's splendor. For Sofia and Martin, El Arcotete held a special allure, not just as a scenic retreat but also as a canvas for their climbing ambitions. After Martin climbed all five existing routes at El Arcotete, Sofia saw an opportunity to expand their climbing horizons. With a bold vision to transform the landscape, they embarked on a mission to breathe new life into El Arcotete's caves. Securing a generous supply of bolts from Martin's mother, who sent them from Austria, they set to work.

Their endeavor was nothing short of audacious – forging more than 40 new routes in the overhung cave. For Sofia, it was a journey of discovery and creation, fueled by a passion for innovation and a deep-seated desire to leave her mark on her beloved hometown of San Cristóbal: "I didn't have the highest level of climbing prowess, but I was fascinated by the creation of new things. Plus, it wasn't the same as doing this abroad. Now I could bring something new to my home." Sofia's dedication to the art of route setting knew no bounds. What drove her most was her commitment to fostering growth and opportunity within her community. Through her efforts, she sought to infuse San Cristóbal with a spirit of adventure, transforming it into a haven for climbers near and far. In the limestone caves of El Arcotete, Sofia found not just a playground for her climbing aspirations, but a canvas for her dreams of empowerment and transformation. With each bolt placed and each route established, she breathed new life into the landscape, leaving an indelible legacy.

As Sofia's passion for climbing blossomed, so too did her desire to share her expertise with others. It wasn't long before Sofia and Martin established Vertigo Rock Climbing, a climbing company that soon became a cornerstone of climbing in San Cris. Vertigo was born from Sofia's vision, and she asked Martin

Sofia teaching others at Vertigo. Photo by Paola Mórelos.

to join her as a business partner. Together, they formed a dynamic team, pooling their skills and resources to bring Sofia's vision to fruition. From the nascent stages of Vertigo, Sofia assumed a central role, taking charge of everything from planning and administration to fostering connections with the Mexican climbing community, collaborating with local brands, and coordinating partnerships that enriched the climbing experience in San Cristóbal. Her days were suddenly filled with a myriad of tasks, from setting new routes alongside Martin to welcoming climbers from near and far with warmth and enthusiasm. Soon Vertigo became a respected business, and each day presented Sofia with new opportunities to impart her knowledge and passion for climbing to eager learners.

Thanks to Vertigo, Sofia built meaningful connections with a diverse array of people. Climbing became not just a passion but a gateway to a vibrant community filled with like-minded adventurers and kindred spirits whose shared love for exploration and connection with nature mirrored Sofia's own. The friendships she has cultivated drive Sofia to continually expand and evolve her projects. Each year has brought new opportunities for growth and innovation, whether through the development of existing climbing areas or the creation of entirely new ones. Today, San Cris boasts nine distinct climbing areas, with approximately 250–300 routes. Sofia's tireless commitment to her craft has played a pivotal role in shaping the climbing landscape of the region. For Sofia, the true essence of climbing lies not just in the ascent of rock faces but also in the connections made along the way.

Through Vertigo, Sofia has also organized many meaningful events and collaborations, extending beyond the realm of climbing. These initiatives encouraged various practices such as yoga, meditation, and healthy nutrition. Sofia strongly believes in the complementary nature of yoga and climbing. Yoga allows Sofia to work with her breathing, balance her body and mind, and achieve a deep sense of inner peace. She perceives a synergistic relationship between yoga and climbing, recognizing the two disciplines complement each other perfectly: "I think that the more I practice yoga, the better I feel climbing." Moreover, by organizing inclusive meetings open to individuals from all walks of life, Sofia seeks to promote holistic well-being and cultivate a deeper appreciation for the natural world, inspiring others to lead balanced and fulfilling lives.

Both yoga and climbing can serve as a means to enter the state of flow. For Sofia, flow entails surrendering to the present moment without attachment to outcomes or preconceptions about life itself: "For me, that means letting go of control and the expectations we have. And learning to trust completely in ourselves, but also in life. To trust in the processes, to trust that everything is perfect as it is happening. To trust in the universe." Central to this state is the connection with the breath, serving as an anchor to the present moment. By connecting the mind, body, and thoughts, one can tap into the essence of flow and experience harmony and alignment. In essence, Sofia views flow as a state of being where the boundaries between self and environment dissolve.

Caring for the natural world is important to Sofia, who views nature as the essence of life itself – a divine, feminine force deserving of reverence and respect. Whether she's climbing in San Cris or exploring new landscapes, Sofia's connection to the environment runs deep. She approaches each new location with a sense of reverence, seeking permission to traverse its terrain and honoring the interconnectedness of all living things: "I like to feel the places, to arrive and ask for permission to climb the rocks. Because, for me, everything has life. Everything around me, including the rock."

For Sofia, environmental stewardship is more than just a personal choice – it's a way of life. She has embraced a vegetarian lifestyle and eschewed processed foods as she is consciously considering the impact of her consumption on the planet and other beings. Her commitment extends beyond dietary choices; she scrutinizes the sources of her purchases, mindful of their environmental footprint and contribution to the well-being of Earth. Living in San Cris, Sofia is acutely aware of the region's ecological challenges, particularly concerning water scarcity and pollution. Recognizing the intrinsic value of clean water, she takes proactive measures to safeguard this precious resource, mindful of the ripple effects her actions may have on the environment.

Sofia also organized regular cleanup efforts in one of the climbing areas she and Martin have developed on Don Lauro mountain, which offers breathtaking views of the town and its surrounding natural beauty. By instilling a sense of environmental consciousness in the community, Sofia inspires others to take an active role in protecting and preserving the natural wonders that surround them. Unfortunately, escalating incidents of violence and insecurity have forced Sofia and others to distance themselves from the area. Sofia recalls the mountain as a place of connection, where climbers gathered to share experiences and create memories. She and Martin put a lot of effort into the development of several climbing sectors on the mountain, so the decision to cease climbing there was not made lightly. However, the safety of climbers and community members became paramount. After one of their close friends was robbed and violently attacked, Sofia and the climbing community took proactive measures, including issuing warnings on climbing platforms. The area was also temporarily closed to public access.

The sense of safety and security, or lack thereof, greatly impacts Sofia's ability to enjoy climbing in places like Don Lauro, especially when considering the added vulnerabilities that women face in such environments. Despite the mountain reopening, Sofia finds herself hesitant to return, particularly when alone or accompanied only by other women. The concerns extend beyond mere access issues; they involve deeper anxieties surrounding personal safety and the potential for violence. The barriers Sofia faces highlight broader societal challenges related to gender and safety in outdoor spaces, especially in countries like México that have high rates of violence. While men may also encounter risks, the repercussions for women can be more severe, intensifying feelings of vulnerability and unease. The inability to enjoy outdoor activities freely and without fear represents a significant loss for Sofia and other women who yearn for the same opportunities as their male counterparts.

Because of the challenges of safety and security, Sofia appreciates the newest climbing area she and Martin developed during the COVID pandemic. Called Peña Maria, it is situated on private property, and as such it offers a sanctuary of natural beauty and tranquility. The requirement of a key for entry ensures a controlled environment, free from the uncertainties of public spaces. Accessible only through Sofia and Martin, who secured a permit from the owners, the area provides a sense of security that resonates deeply with Sofia and her fellow female climbers. It is a refuge where they can fully relax and experience the joys of climbing, revel in the beauty of nature, make meaningful connections, and embark on adventures with a sense of peace and assurance.

But there are also other barriers and challenges Sofia has had to overcome as a woman climber and business owner in the south of México, including the pervasive tendency of most people to dismiss her contributions and accomplishments and attribute them solely to her male partner. Despite her integral role and significant financial and emotional investment in their shared projects, Sofia often finds herself relegated to the sidelines, with credit and recognition directed toward Martin. "In all those years we've been working together, people almost always say, Martin did all that. That's Martin's. Martin's company, Martin's routes, Martin's car, Martin's dogs." The dynamics of being in a relationship with a climber of Martin's caliber further compound Sofia's struggles. Her efforts to support Martin in his climbing aspirations, encouraging him to share his knowledge and engage with the community, often go unnoticed or unappreciated. "I'm Martin's number one fan, but I feel people often act as if they don't realize we are a couple who work together." The cultural fascination with Martin as a foreigner adds another layer of complexity to the situation, perpetuating a dynamic where Sofia feels marginalized and overlooked.

The lack of recognition has taken a toll on Sofia's self-esteem and sense of worth, leaving her feeling undervalued and invisible. But it has also affected her personal relationship with Martin. Two years ago, Sofia reached a breaking point and moved out to a new home in search of clarity: "I was carrying too much responsibility, felt very stressed, and didn't know how to deal with all the problems in our relationship." The process of confronting these deeply ingrained issues was arduous and emotionally draining, but Sofia and Martin ultimately found their way back to each other. Sofia's experience resonates with many women who confront similar barriers and biases in male-dominated spaces. It underscores the urgent need for greater visibility and representation of women, as well as a shift in attitudes and perceptions within the outdoor community to ensure equitable recognition and support for all, regardless of gender, race, or ethnicity.

Sofia finds hope and healing in the company of women, shaping her belief in the transformative power of female camaraderie and support. She has organized several gatherings tailored specifically for women, providing spaces for connection, exploration, and personal growth. These events serve as platforms for women to engage in activities that nurture both the body and the mind, fostering a sense of community and empowerment. Over the years in San Cris, Sofia has met many women climbers from various countries and from other parts of México. Each interaction with these women was significant for Sofia, offering a departure from her usual male climbing companions. They openly discussed topics such as their menstrual cycles and the emotions they experienced while climbing. These conversations highlighted the importance of their shared experiences and the unique bond they formed as women climbers.

Unfortunately, Sofia still hasn't found a stable community of female climbers in San Cris, which is ultimately a tourist town grappling with issues of gentrification and environmental racism. And so Sofia and Martin decided to embark on a new mission: establishing a climbing gym called Skala in the state's capital, Tuxtla Gutiérrez, which boasts a much larger population and potential for growth, as well as lower rental costs. Tuxtla's climbing community is very small, practically nonexistent, providing an opportunity for Sofia and Martin to introduce the sport to a new audience.

Even though their new business requires frequent travel between San Cris and Tuxtla, they believe they are contributing something meaningful: "Our intention of doing this in Tuxtla is to connect with the local people and to connect them with a new sport, with a new lifestyle, to show them that it is possible to do new things, do things where you stay healthy, you stay strong, you stay connected with nature, and that climbing is a very social sport, a sport that everyone can do, no matter their age, their weight, their size. Everyone can climb, it is a sport for

Establishing Skala bouldering gym with Martin. Photo by Sergio Arrehola.

everyone." Including women. Sofia often encounters reactions of surprise from people visiting the gym when they see her with Martin, asking her, "Do you also climb?" For Sofia, these encounters serve as reminders of the ongoing need to challenge stereotypes and promote inclusivity within the climbing community. By sharing her own experiences and breaking barriers, she hopes to inspire more women to embrace climbing and challenge societal norms regarding gender and participation in outdoor pursuits.

Now that the gym has been open for a year, a new world of possibilities opened for Sofia and Martin. Combining both of their businesses, they recently organized the gym's first outdoor climbing excursion, where members ventured into nature to climb on real rocks for the first time. Witnessing these new climbers achieve something they never thought possible was deeply inspiring for Sofia. While her own climbing activities have been limited recently, Sofia finds joy in creating and managing various projects aimed at fostering the climbing community.

Climbing has served as a catalyst in Sofia's life, enabling her to explore her inner self and understand herself more deeply as a person and as a woman. Through climbing, she has gained insight into her emotions, thoughts, and fears, both beautiful and challenging. The sport has become a conduit for tapping into the full spectrum of human experience, from love and connection to insecurity and fear.

Sofia views climbing as a gift that offers her the opportunity to grow and evolve. It allows her to confront her fears, understand the origins of her thoughts, and ultimately work toward alignment and self-improvement. For Sofia, climbing serves as a vehicle for empowerment and self-realization, charting her a path to navigate life's challenges and embrace its possibilities.

PART III: SKY

Highlining

Highlining is a subdiscipline of slacklining practiced at great heights. Slacklining is a dynamic balance sport that has gained significant popularity in recent years, captivating people from all walks of life. At its core, slacklining involves walking, balancing, or performing tricks on a flat, stretchy, dynamic, typically one-inch-wide (2.5-cm) line made of nylon or polyester webbing. The line is anchored between two sturdy points, often trees, poles, or specially designed slackline anchors. Unlike tightropes, which are taut and rigid, slacklines have some give or "slack," hence the name. The tension differs on every line and can significantly influence its difficulty. There are now many different types of webbing of diverse characteristics, each of which requires different tension, otherwise it can get much harder to control while walking. The inherent challenge thus lies not only in maintaining balance and focus while traversing the narrow, often unstable, surface of the slackline but also in the so-called rigging process (i.e., setting up the line).

The history of slacklining traces back to the 1960s in California's Yosemite Valley, where climbers began experimenting with balancing on parking lot chains, climbing ropes, and steel cables. One of these pioneers is Chongo Chuck, whose persona is forever epitomized in the name of one of the three main slackline stands. As a true Yosemite big wall climber, Chongo has lived in the valley for most of his adult life and has witnessed and participated in the evolution of slacklining. However, the true genesis of modern slacklining is mostly credited to Adam Grosowsky, a passionate climber with a keen interest in balance. In the early 1980s, Grosowsky, along with Jeff Ellington, rigged a piece of tubular webbing, marking the official birth of slacklining. Chongo enjoyed the benefits of their creation and became the master of "surfing on the line." He still continues to play on the slackline in the valley yard to this day.

The efforts of the first slackers sparked a wave of enthusiasm among climbers such as Scott Balcom and Chris Carpenter, who took slacklines to the heights and successfully rigged what are considered the first highlines on nylon webbing. While the very first midline was rigged at the Arches in Pasadena, California, the one that made history was a 17-meter-long,[4] 2,887-foot-high (56-foot, 880-m) highline at the Lost Arrow Spire in

Yosemite. It was here where Scott Balcom became the first person to ever send a highline, on July 13, 1985. Even today, Lost Arrow Spire poses a continual physical and psychological challenge for even the most skilled highliners due to its exposed and windy nature. The rigging process is highly technical, encompassing climbing, rappelling, and the creation of anchors in precarious vertical positions, all situated high above the valley floor. Additionally, the lengthy and steep approach to Lost Arrow Spire adds to the overall difficulty of the endeavor.

Throughout the 1990s and into the early 2000s, slacklining gained traction worldwide, spreading across Europe, the United States, and beyond. The accessibility and affordability of slackline kits, pioneered by companies like Gibbon, YogaSlackers, Slackline Industries, and Equilibrium Slacklines between 2007 and 2015, further fueled the sport's popularity. Since then, the slacklining community has continued to grow, with new companies emerging and spreading the stoke of slacklining to enthusiasts globally.

There are now several subdisciplines of slacklining, each with its own unique challenges and techniques. Most practitioners all over the world slackline in city parks, usually in the company of other enthusiasts. They often organize regular weekly meetings where newcomers are welcomed and quickly embraced by the slack community that teaches them the basics of slacklining on what is considered a "baby line," typically up to 20 meters (66 feet) in length. As slackliners progress, they switch from baby lines to longlines. Longlining refers to slacklining over longer distances, often spanning tens or even hundreds of meters, but most commonly seen are lines from around 30 to 100 meters (100–330 feet). Longlining tests endurance, concentration, and the ability to manage the dynamics of a longer line that is more challenging than lines up to 20 meters (65 feet) in length. Finally, rodeolines are also often seen in parks. The rodeoline, suspended higher and sagging close to the ground, is traversed differently, with users often staying in the middle for activities like swinging, surfing, and acrobatics, resembling circus slackropes.

In the heat of the summer, waterlining is also very popular. Slacklines are set over bodies of water, such as rivers, lakes, or even pools. Falling from a waterline results in a refreshing splash rather than a hard landing. Moving water makes waterlining challenging as it confuses the eye and can even lead to motion sickness similar to what is experienced on a rough sea. Another slackline subdiscipline is tricklining, which involves performing acrobatic maneuvers, jumps, spins, and flips on a short, very taut, trampoline-like slackline. Tricklining has become a competitive sport and is understandably very popular among spectators. Trickliners often form separate communities and practice in different settings. It is important to use bouldering crash pads or similar protective equipment, as injuries are quite common.

Highlining is the queen subdiscipline of slacklining. It takes the sport to new heights, quite literally. Highliners rig slacklines at dizzying heights, crossing valleys, canyons, gorges, or urban landscapes hundreds or thousands of feet above the ground. Highlining requires not only physical skill but also mental fortitude and a deep trust in one's abilities and gear, as well as one's teammates. But, compared to activities like BASE jumping or mountaineering, highlining is relatively safe, with most risks occurring during the rigging process rather than while walking the line.

Highlining is practiced with a safety leash and a climbing harness, so the falls are not fatal unless one chooses to free solo and walk without any safety equipment (which is not a common practice but a very personal, often disguised and not talked about, deed). Long highlines are often rigged using a drone and a fishing line. Once the line is stretched across the gap, a paracord can be pulled, followed by two slackline webbings attached to each other using electrical tape. The main line is intended for walking and is slightly tensioned. The backup line hangs below the main line in big irregular loops. Its primary purpose is to serve as a backup and to catch the highliner in case there's a highly improbable main line failure. Its second purpose is to stabilize the main line and make it slightly easier to walk.

Highlining demands extensive time for planning, gear preparation, team organization, location scouting, and rigging, often surpassing the time spent actually walking the line. Hence, it requires extreme dedication and effort from its practitioners. Rigging and establishing new highline projects foster community bonding and create unique connections among rigging crew members who may not share much in common otherwise. The time invested in planning, preparation, and rigging emphasizes an activity that prioritizes the slackline community over individual pursuits, making highlining a lifestyle sport aligned with the values of the so-called slacklife. Slacklife embodies both a lifestyle and philosophical approach centered on slacklining and the attitudes it fosters. The term "slacklife" perfectly encapsulates the essence of the activity and has gained worldwide usage within the slackline community.

Slacklife is fully lived at highline festivals, mostly over the summer. Highline festivals are vibrant gatherings where highliners from around the world come together to celebrate their passion for the sport. These festivals typically take place in scenic outdoor locations known for their highlining opportunities, such as mountain ranges, canyons, or coastal cliffs. Nevertheless, there are now also several urban highline festivals in beautiful medieval locations like Český Krumlov in the Czech Republic where highliners have the chance to walk above old red-bricked houses between castles and churches.

In addition to highlining, these festivals often feature a variety of other activities and events, including slackline workshops, yoga sessions, aerial silking, BASE jumping, outdoor concerts, juggling, and communal meals. Participants have the opportunity to learn from experienced highliners, share tips and techniques, and strike up new friendships within the tight-knit highlining community. The festivals foster a spirit of camaraderie and mutual support among highliners of all skill levels, creating a welcoming and inclusive atmosphere for enthusiasts to connect, learn, and grow together.

In addition to festivals, highlining has evolved into competitive events worldwide. Speedlining has emerged as a popular discipline where highliners compete to cross the line as quickly as possible. However, the most prominent discipline in recent years is highline freestyle, which combines athleticism and artistry in breathtaking displays. It involves performing various tricks, flips, and maneuvers in the middle of the highline, in the so-called trickzone. Participants push the boundaries of what's possible and are constantly coming up with new tricks and combos. Freestylers incorporate elements from gymnastics, acrobatics, and even dance, adding a dynamic and visually stunning dimension to highlining. The growing popularity of highline freestyle reflects the evolving nature of the sport, attracting athletes and spectators alike with its exhilarating displays of skill and daring.

Slacklining, in all its forms, has spread so quickly that the International Slackline Association (ISA) was created. This association aims to support and develop the slackline community, improve communication and informational resources, and enhance the safety of all forms of slacklining worldwide. A voluntary demographic survey conducted by the ISA in 2013 showed that, at that time, 89 percent of the sport's practitioners were men, and only 11 percent were women. By 2016 the percentage of men was approximately 82 percent and that of women was 18 percent. The latest survey of this kind, conducted in 2018, showed that the percentage of men was around 78 percent and that of women was 22 percent.[5] While the gender gap in slacklining is still notable, the surveys show that, in recent years, there has been a growing effort to encourage more women to participate, including in highlining. Female highliners have been actively promoting inclusivity and diversity within the community, challenging traditional gender roles and inspiring other women to take up the sport.

Efforts to address the gender gap in highlining include creating supportive and inclusive environments, providing mentorship and resources specifically for female participants, and challenging stereotypes through representation and visibility of women in the sport. By promoting inclusivity and breaking down barriers, the highlining community can continue to evolve and thrive with greater gender diversity and representation. *Flow* aims to contribute to the growing effort of female representation by sharing stories of inspiring women highliners who dance upon the line, illuminating the path toward gender equality in the realm of adventure sports.

CHAPTER 13

Sky Sisters: Change Is a Thin Line

By Faith Dickey

My life slammed me into highlining much the way a boat runs aground on a hidden reef. I was barreling forward aimlessly at the time, riding the tides of life, when a few chance choices thrust me into the path of outdoor recreation, in the form of an obscure balance sport that hooked me like nothing ever had before.

There were a lot of things to run from in my life, and I was sprinting. Growing up poor in Texas, raised by a single mom with mental illness, bestowed on me a charming post-traumatic sense of humor and an uncanny ability to adapt to chaos. The only thing I knew about moderation was that it had something to do with dieting, so when my hopes and dreams of prestigious university attendance were dashed by financial realities, I took my hard-earned 6,000 bucks and bought a one-way ticket to London, but not before falling asleep driving home from an 80-hour work week and flipping my car. If I needed a wake-up call, that was definitely it. I'd never left the country before, and the unknown abroad was beckoning me.

Highlining in my new home, Moab, Utah. Photo by Max Haimowitz.

By the time I left the United States, I'd recently found slacklining: a silly, uncommon balance activity that involved stretching a flat rope between two trees and walking on it, using your arms to balance. And, despite the obvious uselessness of such a skill, it captivated me. When I stood on that line, even just for a moment, nothing mattered except concentrating and finding equilibrium – the woes and worries of life just faded into the background. It was a welcome escape, but just a hobby, a park activity to do with an attractive tattooed guy with a myriad of easily ignored red flags. I became a slackliner. I vaguely knew that highlining existed, but it was the pre-social media era and I owned a brick phone. Growing up in Texas gave me no exposure to climbing or heights, so as far as I was concerned, my foray into slacklining started and ended a few feet above the ground. Nonetheless, it quickly filled my free time, and when I finally left for Europe, I took a slackline along.

London proved to be a four-month experiment in chaos, as I dated a slew of strange fellows, managed to go through five different cell phones, worked illegally in a few restaurants, and

The first professional woman highliner. Photo by Max Haimowitz.

drank enough beer to expand physically but not spiritually. Luckily, after a few months the tide was going out and change was afoot. I went to Germany and chanced upon a guy who was going to a slackline festival. It was news to me that such a thing existed, let alone enough people to make a whole festival out of it. I had been by my lonesome setting up slacklines in London parks, disappointed that my friends only brought beer and got drunk. I never met any other slackliners, and I was ready to call it FaithLining and monopolize the market. But this guy, who I met on the Couchsurfing website, informed me that, in fact, there was a great festival full of slackliners and you could walk lines over water and even a highline. I had to check it out. I had no idea my life path was about to do a 180.

I took my chonky, beer-drinking body down to the southernmost part of Germany and found myself in a sea of young slacklining men. If there were women other than me there, they were few and far between. I guess London pub culture doesn't boast too many svelte bodies, because I was astounded at the amount of six packs everywhere, yet was unsure if I wanted to touch them or just wanted to have one of my own. I recall feeling doubtful if I belonged in such a fit group of people. I had ridden a lot of bikes in London, but I'd never considered myself an outdoorsy person, let alone athletic. Yet there I was, with my clunky, hardware store ratchet that I used to tension my slackline, a system so cumbersome and memorable that some of the guys I met at the festival only remembered me as "ratchet girl."

Despite my lack of preparation, I hucked myself at the slacklines like I was drinking water in the desert. My lack of aim in

London was entertaining, but finding this whole community of people who slacklined all the time was like a door opening, and I didn't just step through – I leapt. When I got on my first highline, a paltry little urban line between a climbing gym and a water tower, my performance was not an indicator of what was to come. It still surprises me that I kept going after that thrashing.

I had made some friends at the festival, and as climbers they had basic knowledge of tying knots and being safe on highlines, so they accompanied me up the water tower. I borrowed a harness and climbed out the small window, carefully tying on the highline tether to my harness like they instructed me. I was definitely terrified and had never been that scared in my entire life, but I was also stubborn and had survived all sorts of traumatic childhood shit so I wasn't about to look weak. I was a pretty decent slackliner close to the ground, and in theory the highline should have been no different. It was a slackline, just up high. Yet my body was frozen, unable to respond to my mental commands. I sat on the line, tense and full of adrenaline, wondering how the hell I was ever going to overcome the intense aversion to standing up. But I did, and I fell. I swung in my harness, dangling beneath the highline, over and over and over. I managed to climb the leash and get back up a few times, but I was so exhausted that at some point I was stranded, dangling like a beached whale, disappointed in myself and frustrated at my own weakness. The very tall German guy who organized the festival came out and pulled me back up to the highline. *What a relief I wasn't going to dangle forever!* But I knew if I was going to keep doing this incredible sport called highlining, I sure as hell couldn't be the weakest link, and I absolutely needed to be able to get my own ass back up after I fell.

I globbed on to one of my new hot dude friends from the festival and followed him to Chamonix, France, where I bled my way up my first rock climbs in a vintage leather jacket and a dorky helmet I'd bought just for the occasion. I didn't see other women on the rocks, nor did I even realize I was missing them, for a whole world had just been introduced to me and I couldn't believe I hadn't known about it before. Highlining and climbing were the perfect combination of masochism, self-reflection, and intensity, and when I was doing them nothing else mattered. I didn't know how good it could feel to forget everything else in life and become utterly lost in the incredible focus and determination required to do these sports, all while experiencing some of the most breathtaking views nature could offer. Within a few months, my life revolved around highlining, and though I was sure I wasn't any good and my unfit body would hold me back, I progressed surprisingly fast. Who knew that becoming obsessed with a thing would lead to mastery? But every time I went to a festival or a highline gathering, I noticed something: Where were the other women?

I wasn't focused on feminism or women's plight at the time. They were in my consciousness, somewhere filed under "Well, yeah, that's life." I'd been raised exclusively by women, and so I'd never thought or believed women were capable of anything less than men, because I had no reason to. Despite my mother's psychological shortcomings, she was strong and worked extremely hard, and without a father figure I hardly had any examples of

Free solo highlining in Ostrov, in the Czech Republic. Photo by Jan Šimánek.

gender roles to influence me. My mother did it all. My closest friends growing up were also raised by single mothers, so I was literally surrounded by women who had to fill the space that two parents usually shared. When I began highlining, I was sensitive to being the weakest one, because I was usually the only woman in the group, and somehow I felt I needed to prove myself worthy. How did I keep up? I carried heavy – as in 88-pound (40-kg) – backpacks. I went hard on the highline. I swore, and made dirty jokes, and out-vulgured the guys. I was "one of the boys," which at the time I thought was a compliment, because it was always meant as one. I was told I had "big balls" and that I "wasn't like other girls," as if this, too, was the highest of praise. We called each other "bitches," and I heard countless male highliners tell each other not to be "pussies." I often grappled with the concept that I was "different" from other women, because it seemed to me there are a lot of different types of women out there, and why would I be like a guy and not just a different type of woman? I could tell it was meant as a compliment, and I definitely didn't want to be like the other women my male friends were referring to – whatever that meant.

Despite my bumpy beginning, the result of aggressively highlining and beating the shit out of my body led to something. Besides overuse injuries that haunt me to this day, I became one of the best highliners in the world. I set world records that were level with men's. I was the women's world champion of all slackline and highline records for six years straight, some records for even longer. I broke barriers, becoming the first woman to ever free solo highlines. I established countless highlines around the world. Still, for most of my career, I thought my accomplishments were a fluke, some accidental alignment in the cosmos that led to me being good at something. Sometimes I thought about how much work I had put into getting to a high level and a twinge of pride would bubble up, but I quickly silenced it, for to be confident would be egotistical, and I was terrified of looking like an arrogant woman. I had already been called bossy, too feminist, abrasive, bitter, and difficult. I didn't want to add haughty to the list.

In the beginning, I asserted myself into the rigging processes, frustrated by the common occurrence of the men in the group automatically rigging without including me. It took me a year to learn, as I had to repeatedly ask to be taught and incorporated.

If I wasn't fast enough, one of my guy friends would often take the gear out of my hands and do it themselves, something that slowed my learning and frustrated me immensely. I was never a passive type, so I demanded that I participate. I can only imagine how hard it would have been to learn had I not asserted myself. Later, when I was an experienced rigger, men would sometimes just take gear out of my hands, even if I was doing everything correctly. It felt like subconscious entitlement – the world belonged to them in such a deep way they would never think of their behavior as an overstep. Numerous times I was spoken over, my ideas ignored until a man suggested the same thing. I loved my friends, and I loved highlining, but somehow it always felt like I was fighting for an equal space at the table.

Being the best woman highliner in the world was novel, but the true result of that position was learning just how unequal the realms of outdoor sports are. I wanted to be excellent, not *because* I had a vagina but because I was highly skilled. Initially, it seemed I would be praised for anything I did on a highline because I was a woman, yet when I was actually one of the best highliners in the world, there was little to no recognition given. My accomplishments were regularly dismissed, despite being the same or more advanced than my male counterparts. Wikipedia held information about what men in the sport had done but said nothing about women's accomplishments. When a large book about slacklining was published by a renowned Austrian photographer, he included a four-page spread of two American women highlining, but the small corner that held a photo of me had the caption "Faith is a very good highliner," even though I held every possible record at the time. The author made sure to include plenty of pages devoted to the then male world-record holder. I noticed the women with the multi-page spread were pretty and highlined in cute sports bras. Perhaps I was too modest to be photographable?

I devoted my life to highlining and traveled almost nonstop to pursue the best weather, highline projects, and highline communities. I was one of the first professional highliners, along with my teammates, as we convinced several brands that this niche sport was marketable and combined elements of so many outdoor sports and lifestyles. In the first few years, high-level highliners were scarce and spread across the world, and we would often travel to meet them and collaborate on projects. I spent almost a decade enduring sexual harassment annually from arguably the most famous highliner ever, because I thought it was necessary in order to do the big projects he had access to. My male teammates stayed silent, despite the constant gross and vulgar commentary this man subjected me to. My defense was talking back with insults, but it took years before I finally realized that no amount of highlining was worth being around such a person, and that even verbal harassment can be abusive. I told myself I was strong and resilient, and that his words were just words, but the truth was I felt degraded, and even worse, I was mad at myself for tolerating it. This man's highline talents seemed to be a protective armor, and despite a laundry list of predatory behavior, harassment, and criminal actions, he continues to have sponsors, commercial work, and community praise. If you are a famous male highliner, you have immunity. The community will

Poking fun at gender norms in Moab, Utah. Photo by Max Haimowitz.

look the other way when you behave badly, and will even treat you like an icon.

I eventually experienced some professional success, and a few of the jobs I acquired were pivotal to my career. Some, however, were harsh reminders of the inequality women face. One particular job was a highline commercial in the French Alps, but after seeing my picture the production company asked to see "other options." It hired a novice highliner who was unable to successfully walk any of the lines during the shoot, whereas I rigged the lines for her, easily sending them and even doing tricks, before the cameras came out and filmed her struggling and falling. The storyline in the commercial depicted a strong male highliner who rigged the lines and walked and did tricks on them, then supported his weaker female companion, wrapping a blanket around her when she was cold, after she struggled on the highline. They opted to use computer graphics since the talent was unable to actually walk the highline under pressure. It was infuriating. They hired the best woman highliner in the world to set up lines in the background while they perpetuated the trope of a weak woman and a strong man. It was unbelievable even while I was living it. I concluded that, in order to be successful, I needed to be prettier. Being the best wasn't enough, because women's true value lay in their appearance. I used to joke that my quickest route to success would be to get breast implants and teeth whitening, because who cares about world records if you aren't marketable?

When I walked highlines in high heels, it was to poke fun at the stereotypes of what it means to be a woman and the ridiculous beauty standards we are held to. What better metaphor for navigating the world as a woman than teetering on a wobbly tightrope in painful shoes designed by men that literally require balance just to walk in. To this day, all my first ascents of highlines, world records, and creating the first all-women's highline festival pale in public praise compared to my high heel walks. The stunts I did to prove a point literally proved a point. Several commercial job opportunities showed up, asking for someone to highline or slackline in high heels for various media productions. I was excited about the recognition – I was the only person on the planet at the time who had done it. They all asked for my measurements and a picture of my legs, so I sent them over, then I never heard back. Most of these commercials opted to fake the images or use computer graphics. Again, my skills were not enough. My legs needed to look different, my height taller, my waist narrower. Being built like a fire hydrant, my tough, muscular physique, scars, and thick calves were not what the general media was looking for. As if women aren't already bombarded with images that tell us we aren't good enough. Being rejected for jobs calling for my exact expertise reinforced the small part of me that felt ugly and unworthy.

Some of the most breathtaking places to highline are in national parks, popular destinations for all sorts of people, and some of our preferred locations were near trails where tourists stopped to take in the view. I was used to them taking photos of us highlining, pausing on their hikes to watch the spectacular activity of people suspended between cliffs, balancing on an almost invisible rope. Usually they would start by scanning the mostly male group, then, settling on me, would ask incredulously, "You do this too?!" It is likely that if I quizzed them on why it was surprising to them that a woman highlines, they would deny it had anything to do with gender. Yet I was the only one in the group who was asked that question. Clearly, it was surprising for most people to see a woman doing an outdoor adventure sport. It became a dream of mine that, one day, no one would bat an eye seeing only women walking highlines.

From the beginning of my highline career, I knew the ratio in the sport was very far from equal, but I didn't understand why there weren't more women. It was a balance sport, wasn't it? Balance has nothing to do with gender, and in my experience, women were often quicker learners on slacklines. Our lower center of gravity and body awareness seemed to lend itself to the sport. I was certain that other women would excel if they just tried, but how could I get more women involved?

In that first pivotal year, I had a conversation with some Polish women who were beginners, and I discovered that, for them, it felt intimidating and uninviting to be just a few women in the group. They felt pressured to behave like their male highline acquaintances, in those cases by being aggressive about their time on the lines, an approach that didn't feel natural for them. They wanted a quiet, low-pressure space where they could push themselves at their own pace. I suggested we create a women's highline meeting, in other words a festival specifically for women so we could experience being a majority, meet one another, and highline in a supportive, welcoming space. Perhaps by showing the world that women highlined too, more women would get

Women's Highline Meeting in Ostrov, in the Czech Republic.

into the sport. That conversation birthed the Women's Highline Meeting, which I have organized annually for 13 years. It started small in 2009 – I had to have my then-boyfriend help me install the highlines because at that time I was the only woman who knew how to rig in Europe. Six women attended, but even in that small group I could tell there was something special about the atmosphere. It was amazing being a majority, looking around at everyone and feeling allied, knowing we had shared experiences that connected us beyond simply wanting to balance on a rope suspended in the air. It was a type of ease and freedom even I hadn't experienced before.

From there the festival grew, the numbers doubling year after year. Every summer, when the dates for the event would loom and I would start to advertise, I had to face the barrage of men who called me sexist for creating a women's event, or the commentators who claimed highlining had no sexism and therefore didn't need women's events, or even women who stated they would not want to be around only women! At first I was angry, and eventually I simply felt resigned, prepared for the critics. Anytime a woman spoke negatively about the event, I challenged her to attend before making an opinion. In every case where these women accepted the challenge, they left the festival telling me they now understood why I created it, why women's spaces are important. Some even said they couldn't believe it would be fun to hang out with only women until they actually tried it. It was through the lens of this festival that I realized women are not innately competitive with each other, or catty or mean. It's that we are told we're that way, and we are taught there is only one seat at the table for us, so we have to be better than the other women in order to sit there. The self-consciousness that many of us feel is only present when we are a minority. Yet, when you experience a week of highlining, cooking, partying, living, hiking, sharing workshops, and hanging out with just women, there is such a beautiful, supportive atmosphere, noncompetitive, genuine, and motivational. In a group of only women, you get to be whoever you are, and your acceptance is automatic. Your unique journey on the highline is celebrated, no matter where in that journey you are.

The simple truth is we need to see people we identify with in outdoor spaces so we can imagine ourselves there too. When I first tried highlining, I wanted to know what other women had done before me, because that helped me conceptualize what I could do. It doesn't imply that I think men and women have different levels of capability; it's about a feeling of solidarity and safety, of sisterhood and opportunity. When I stepped into the forefront of the sport, I wanted recognition so the women coming up behind me could easily imagine themselves where I was, or going even further. This same concept is true for all identities, and as our sport continues to grow, we must create space for more women, 2SLGBTQIA+, BIPOC, and disabled participants. It is not enough to simply claim we are inclusive. We have to lift up these individuals, strive for their representation, and show they belong on highlines too. We have to make the path easier for them, and we have to take space and create space.

What I loved about highlining was the way it put me in gaps where usually only birds could fly. The way establishing a new highline was like building a temporary bridge, and every gap became a vision of a line. We weren't aiming for the peaks; we were aiming for the spaces between them. I loved the way highlining was my own, that once I set foot on that line, no one else mattered. I could claim that space and feel completely alone with myself there. The intensity of standing hundreds to thousands of meters off the ground in the void felt like it undressed me to myself, all the thoughts in my head becoming acute and exposed. It instigated some very primal reactions to avoid the exposure, and learning to navigate that and calm my body down amid an outpouring of adrenaline was empowering. If I could control my own mind, I could do anything.

I wasn't constantly contemplating my reality as a woman in a mostly male space. There were numerous highlines and expeditions where I dug my fingers into the soil of the moment, relishing the newness of foods I'd never tasted before, cultures I'd never experienced, and the pure joy of creating a goal and accomplishing it with a team of friends. Highlining was an extremely introspective activity for me. In the same way that very first slackline experience captivated me by bringing my attention to the singularity of a step on a wobbly line, highlining enthralled me. It was a catalyst for self-discovery, as well as a reason to travel to some of the most beautiful places in the world. But knowing that being the best was not enough in a world that valued women for looking and behaving a certain way and fitting the mold that society created for us informed much of my experience of the sport and highlining as a profession. I wish I could say I triumphed against the patriarchy, but most of the sexism I experienced or witnessed over the course of my career created complexes I am still confronting in my own psyche.

We all belong outside, in the sky, on the earth, in the mountains, in the water, wherever you dream. And there is space for all of us, but we must lift each other up and continue to break apart the system that tells us we are not good enough. Highlining changed my life because I let it, but being a woman highliner in a time when there were so few others changed my life even more. Eventually, repeated injuries, burnout, and a lost sense of purpose led me to re-evaluate what highlining meant to me. I had spent years internalizing my accomplishments as the things that gave me value, and fighting for equal representation and recognition of them. But my body was changing, and I couldn't keep going the way I had been. I stopped pushing my limits and breaking records, and eventually other women surpassed them. I had dreamt about that for years – the day that other women would catch up and expand on my triumphs. But all I felt was worthlessness, a profound sense of despair, as everything I had attached to my self-worth slipped away. If I wasn't the best, I had nothing to offer. I'd never been pretty enough, marketable enough, or feminine enough, so without athletic accolades, what the hell was I bringing to the table?

It was sneaky, the way my inner self attached its worthiness to external achievements. It was progressive, and my conscious self would never have known it was happening until I was smacked in the face with an identity crisis and a severe lack of confidence. I did the only thing I knew how to: I pretended I didn't care. I got knee surgery, and the surgeon told me if I continued highlining the way I had been, I would fully destroy my knee. I moved back to my home country and settled in a place with tons of highlining, eager to build a community in one place and figure out who the hell I was. I found a therapist and got a cat and lived in a house and only highlined a little bit, unsure of what it meant to me and why I was doing it anymore.

Slowly, I started to build a sense of self that didn't depend on being the best in order to feel worthy. I reflected on the parts of my highline career I felt the most passionate about – and, funnily enough, none of them were about setting records. It was the Women's Highline Meeting, the facilitating of gathering women, of creating that space and making it happen every year, that felt like my biggest accomplishment. Records were cool, establishing new highlines was great, but the festival was where I shared what I had to give and created more space at the table. I didn't need to be the best in the world to continue doing that, nor did I need to be marketable, tall, skinny, or have straight white teeth or a boob job. I didn't need to endure sexual harassment from famous male highliners or dress more sexy on highlines. And when hikers pass by 40 to 60 exclusively women highlining, not one of them asks, "You do this too?!"

I am still navigating what it means to be a woman in the world, a woman in her mid-30s, a woman who will have children later than what society deems "normal," a woman who chose an unusual path and an unusual career and who is still figuring out what her place is in it now – post-records, post-injuries, and still in the midst of transition. But looking back on that young Faith who was the only woman most of the time, I am so happy that things are changing, that there are more women out there highlining unapologetically, passionately, and with abandon.

So pull up a chair, because there is plenty of room at the table.

Cheering on others at the Women's Highline Meeting in the Czech Republic.

CHAPTER 14

Flying with the Birds: Dancing in the Sky toward My Dreams

By Brenda Gómez Ortiz
TRANSLATED FROM THE SPANISH BY DENISA KRÁSNÁ

I would like to start telling this story, my story, mentioning that this is just one of many stories that begin with a girl full of dreams and the desire to fulfill them. The story of each girl and each dream is unique. Speaking of mine, it began as a girl who dreamed of feeling free, flying, and dancing in the sky. And when I speak of that girl, I refer to the inner child that dwells within every woman, as this story began when I was 24 years old and pursuing my master's studies at university. I was born and raised in México, a country where fulfilling dreams is a privilege for many. Going to university is also a privilege not all women have access to. However, I was fortunate to have the support of my family to attend university. I pursued a degree in biology, and as a biologist, I have understood that not all mammals are born capable of flight. But, throughout my life, I have also learned that with a little luck, discipline, and love we can fulfill our wildest and strangest dreams.

In 2017 I had the opportunity to try slacklining for the first time. Slacklining is an artistic and athletic discipline that allows us to explore our bodily capabilities through exploration and play. It focuses on developing proprioception, body control, to maintain balance. I vividly remember the first time I tried it. It was a sunny day at a festival full of music, yoga, and other physical activities that I attended with my university friends in my city. People from different states of the country and different parts of the world attended this festival. As part of the recreational activities at the festival, a slackline was set up there. The line was just hanging there alone, suspended between two points, set up for anyone who wanted to try and test their balance. The scene reminded me a bit of tightrope walking. Those people I had seen as a child at the circus, walking meters above the ground on surfaces that seemed nothing more than a thread, in perfect balance. The slackline caught my attention, aroused

Bringing yoga poses to new heights at Mineral del Chico. Photo by Francisco Gónzalez.

Finding peace with slackline yoga. Photo by Gabriela Patiño.

my curiosity, so I approached it. I tried to climb and stand on the line, but it was very difficult to control the movement and maintain balance. For a few minutes, I tried. It was totally new to me, very difficult to understand, difficult to control, and it required total focus of the mind and body, working together, requiring presence. I liked it; it was an experience as fun as it was interesting, simple yet complex, challenging. It challenged me to the point that every time I had the opportunity during the festival, I returned to try it, gradually understanding my sensations and controlling my body more and more.

After that first time testing my balance a few centimeters above the ground, I was hooked. The new bodily experience had captivated me to the point that, weeks later, as a birthday gift for my 24th birthday, I bought my first slackline – I needed to try it again. At that time, I was starting to practice yoga, beginning to have an understanding of body awareness. However, something inside me was constantly seeking new ways to help me connect with my body and mind, allowing me to expand my physical and mental limits. It was then, when I got my own slackline, that I could continue practicing in my free time. I achieved small goals. I could already stand on the line, and I even managed to bring some yoga poses onto the moving line. Then I could take a step on it, then another, and over time more steps. I quickly fell in love with this activity, a fun stimulant for the neuromuscular system. I was learning, and I realized that, with practice and discipline, I could improve this body awareness day by day.

But the real progress and a turning point in my life came a couple of months after that first experience when I started practicing slacklining in a community of like-minded enthusiasts. After finishing my undergraduate studies, I moved to México City to pursue a master's degree in science. I was new to the city, didn't have many friends, and didn't know the place well, but I discovered that every Friday a group of people gathered to practice slacklining in the university gardens. The group called itself Tenochtitline, which is a wordplay mixing Tenochtitlán, the name of the city founded by the Aztec empire, our pre-Hispanic ancestors, which nowadays corresponds to México City, and the word "slackline." One day, after finishing my experiments in the lab, I approached this group of people for the first time. I arrived with my slackline at this place known as "The Garden of Eden," and approached these people who gathered to practice, play, and share with the community. Since then, I was adopted by the group, and I didn't miss a single Friday to share and practice with these people so full of enthusiasm to have fun, to explore, and to expand their capacities.

I improved with practice, and the challenges I set for myself on the line became increasingly larger, more complex, longer, but also higher. It was here with my friends from Tenochtitline that I heard about highlining for the first time. Unlike slacklining, this modality is practiced with a safety harness, and the slacklines are suspended meters high, usually between valleys and mountains. Previously, I had seen a picture on the internet that seemed unreal to me at the time: a woman performing yoga poses on a highline many meters above the ground. It seemed wonderful, reflecting calm, harmony, and total freedom. It was then, as I began to learn more about highlining, that everything started to make sense within me. I visualized myself being there like that woman, calm, in the sky, in that place that only birds can reach. I began to wonder if highlining could be the way to reach my longed-for dream of touching the sky, of flying. With this dream in mind, I continued practicing, hoping one day to have the opportunity to try highlining, which at that time was not widely practiced in México. It was only practiced by a few, there was very little highline gear available, and getting your own gear was not economically accessible for most. Simply put, I continued practicing close to the ground, yearning and waiting for my opportunity.

An increasingly common trend in slacklining worldwide is the organization of festivals and gatherings primarily focused on highlining. Participants pay a fee and acquire a ticket that grants them access to highlines set up for a few days in breathtaking locations. However, at that time, there was only one highline festival in México. It took place at the end of the year, so, again, I had to continue practicing close to the ground and wait. After six months of park practices with my friends from Tenochtitline, at the end of that year I finally had the opportunity to attend my first highline festival in the state of Nuevo León. The festival would take place in the famous El Potrero Chico valley, renowned among the climbing community in México and the world. I was very excited to attend along with my friends who were also beginning to practice slacklining; it would be the first time in the heights for some of us. I still remember when I bought my ticket for the festival, my first harness, and my own safety equipment – the excitement was overwhelming. I counted the days until the big day. Six months of training disguised as playing in the university courtyards prepared my wings for my first experience in the heights.

Finally, after longing for it for a long time, I was there, and my turn came to step onto my first highline ever. I entered and found myself suspended on a one-inch-wide (2.5-cm) webbing, with my life tied only to my harness and a safety leash. As I had visualized, I was finally in that place where my greatest dream was coming true, meters above the ground, accompanied by the wind and surrounded by imposing limestone walls. There I was, where only birds can fly. But at the same time it was something new to me, very difficult to understand. Like that first time on the slackline, it required total focus, mind and body working together. It required presence. I remained still, adopted a seated

At a highline festival in Amealco, México. Photo by Samantha Sursock.

position on the line, and stopped to observe. My feet trembled; they were many meters above the ground. I took a pause and stopped to acknowledge my sensations. It was a completely unique and unnatural experience. My body was unfamiliar with that space, and many emotions surfaced: fear of the unknown, nerves, doubt, insecurity. But as my mind flowed in that turbulent sea of emotions, I tried to focus only on my breath, repeating to myself, *breathe, trust, breathe, be thankful, breathe...* At that moment, I managed to understand I was in the sky, fulfilling my greatest dream, and I connected with calmness. Other emotions surfaced: satisfaction, immense gratitude, and enormous happiness. At that moment, I felt completely free, at peace. I fell in love with everything the heights awoke in me.

After that first highline experience, nothing was the same. When I tried to descend and return to normalcy, I was changed. A piece of my heart had remained in the heights. Over the next years, I sought more opportunities to continue practicing and exploring in the heights. With determination, I made progress, gradually calming my mind, overcoming nerves, and focusing my senses to control my body and flow and dance in harmony with the wind, in the sky. Through practice, I began to bring the yoga poses I practiced in the park onto the highlines, learning to stand up and stay balanced. I even started to take one step, two, three, and more. In that journey, in that practice, which built with every experience and every step, I found a space where I simply inhabited my present, where I felt fulfilled...grateful. Without a doubt, I was there. I had found my happy place – the sky. At the same time, I connected and formed bonds with practitioners from different states of the country. I started seeking more highline festivals to attend, both within and outside the country. I also worked hard to gradually acquire my own gear and learn to rig highlines. I was determined to give my best, to do whatever it took to keep practicing whenever I had the chance. I was determined to go further each time, wanting to spend as much time as possible near the sky.

Since then, highline has become a fundamental part of my life, a liberating practice that helps me connect with my body but also with my emotions. When I am highlining, my mind becomes the protagonist, and inhabiting the present becomes mandatory. My physical performance on the line becomes a reflection of my inner self, showing me my multitude of thoughts. Only when I manage to free myself from them and connect with calmness, regardless of the stimuli, do I manage to flow and feel free, connected only with the present and the environment that surrounds me. This practice has become a metaphor in my life. To move forward, one must pause, breathe, trust, let go, even fall, and learn, get back up, and repeat as many times as necessary to achieve a goal. Some scholars and practitioners refer to this sport as a "lifestyle sport," and I would dare to say that it is. Slacklining, and particularly highlining, has captivated me in every sense, and my days revolve around continuing to live this utopia. To continue in this search for connection between my body and my mind, but also to reach the natural environments to which this practice brings me closer. By showing me my vulnerability, it allows me to inhabit nature from a new, loving, humble, and respectful perspective. This practice has led me to create a life story full of adventures, in constant exploration, learning, expansion, and motion.

The practice of this sport has brought many benefits to my life, both physical and mental. It has also brought me a beautiful and diverse community of practitioners, people so different from each other but still sharing common dreams. In this community of highliners, I have found a space where many barriers are broken, regardless of age, gender, language, or place of origin. The body speaks, movement expresses our emotions, and there will always be one, two, or many more people who will make you feel welcome to explore your abilities, to share, and to play. In this community, which grows day by day, I have found a space where I can feel free to be myself. Facing the highline, our fears, our insecurities, but also our greatest capacities, show us who we are. It sensitizes us and shows us transparently, without superficial appearances. In this community, I find a safe space where I feel supported by my friends as I live through my learning process, and unlearning process. In this community, I feel supported by those people with whom I identify in some way, those people who celebrate my achievements as if they are their own, those people with whom we practice the most essential values to function as a team to achieve our goals: respect, unity, friendship. I feel truly fortunate to be part of this community. As a woman in México, just like in many other parts of the world, it is not easy to find these spaces where we can feel free, strong, valued, and respected. This community, while not perfect, is evolving every day, a community willing to learn, listen, empathize, and coexist regardless of differences.

While the majority of practitioners in this discipline are men, every day more women are joining, determined to overcome their fears, doubts, and insecurities, convinced they can achieve anything they set their minds to. These women – each with her own essence, dreams, motivations, and life story – inspire me in many ways. I am grateful to be surrounded by their power and to be able to recognize ourselves in each other. It is important to me to find and create spaces like these, where we can flourish as women, accompany each other, and support each other. I celebrate being part of these spaces where, as women, we inspire each other, not compete, as our culture for many years has fostered competition among women more than unity.

I also celebrate these spaces where the male community welcomes and respects us, although it is not yet perfect. There are still learned micro-aggressions normalized by our society and many paradigms to break. We live in a culture where it is believed that women are not good enough or suitable for extreme activities, mountain sports, or strength training, but in slacklining all those beliefs are shattered. Strong, brave, and determined women are breaking their limits in México and around the world every day. And when I talk about limits, I don't mean records or established boundaries. Slacklining and highlining are very personal practices where limits are individual. They are as far as your personal abilities allow you to go, and going beyond those limits means not competing with others but with yourself to expand your capabilities.

During the seven years I have been practicing this sport, I have seen it evolve and grow exponentially. However, despite

Living my dreams in Patagonia. Photo by Rosendo Casarrubias.

the increasing number of women joining the sport, it remains predominantly practiced by men. What is stopping or preventing women from entering these spaces? What prevents them from inhabiting our natural environments? From overcoming their fears? A recent survey by the International Slackline Association mentioned some things that caught my attention when I read it. For example: "Spending time with friends and meeting new people is slightly more important to women than to men. Accordingly, women are more likely to go slacklining with friends than alone. Men tend to go slacklining more often and also rate their skills and knowledge higher than women."[6] When I read this for the first time, I questioned how true this assertion was and to what extent these numbers are influenced by external factors rather than individual motivation.

While within the slackline and highline community I find a space where values like respect are practiced, and I can feel safe, outside of the slackline bubble the reality for women in my country is very different. External factors impact and hinder us from exploring our full potential. In my experience as a woman practicing outdoor sports, factors such as violence, discrimination, or harassment that we experience daily in my country limit me and many other women from going out to practice alone. These limitations can hinder our individual progress, something men can achieve more easily as they feel safe going out to practice alone in a park or in the mountains until nightfall, knowing they will return home safely that night, and thus they can progress more quickly. For these reasons, it is important to spread awareness and create networks and support groups among women practicing outdoor sports. As long as the reality we live in remains unchanged and makes us vulnerable to danger, we must remain strong and united to explore our capabilities and fulfill our dreams.

My motivations and objectives in my highline practice become clearer every day. It is about creating and inhabiting safe spaces that allow us to grow as individuals, both men and women, within a community. Personally, it's about continuing to flow on the line and in life, in harmony with myself, with my mind and body, and with the surrounding environment. To flow in harmony, aligned with my dreams and with what makes me happy. This practice has been a journey, a channel of self-exploration. A path that, as I walk it, shows me what truly matters is the journey, not the destination. It is about the present – what happens now and what is built around it. From its inception, the practice of slacklining, and later highlining, has been a game of infinite possibilities I never tire of exploring. It's where I can feed my passion for staying in constant motion, expanding my limits, flowing. It's about discovering new ways to play, to fly. I suppose that same search, that same passion that led me to start slacklining and highlining, led me to challenge myself once again with something completely different. In 2021 I began to explore a new way of practicing balance at heights, a form of highlining that challenged me once again, known as highline freestyle, the latest discipline within this sport.

Highline freestyle is a form of highlining also practiced with a safety harness on a suspended slackline at considerable heights. However, this discipline combines explosive movements and acrobatics on the line, requiring great concentration and precision, and demanding both mental and physical strength. This new practice is undoubtedly the most fun I have experienced at heights. Nevertheless, it can sometimes be terrifying, awakening the demons of doubt and insecurity in me. Something I have worked on since I started practicing slackline and highline, and which has not been easy, is achieving a state of calm that allows me to flow, breathe, and stay present without distractions in order to connect my mind with my movements. Some people see highline as an extreme practice, thinking of us as adrenaline junkies, whereas I perceive it more as a practice of calmness, an active meditation where one must learn to avoid distractions, relax, and connect with the present and all our senses to achieve flow. While in recent years I have worked to master a state of calm that allows me to highline, highline freestyle has challenged me again. When I first started this practice, I learned it required something entirely different and new for me: a combination of perfect calmness and explosiveness with decisiveness, all while coordinating my breathing with fast and precise movements. It has required me to trust myself fully, let go, be brave, and believe that, with practice, no matter how slow and long the journey, I can achieve anything I set my mind to, no matter how impossible it may seem at first. This is what highline freestyle has been showing me.

I started highline freestyle as just another physical play, not taking it too seriously, inspired by my male friends who were starting to practice it. It looked like a lot of fun, so I began to play and discovered that highline freestyle fulfills my childhood

Finding joy in highline freestyle. Photo by Antonio Xuitletl Ramirez Sotelo.

dream of dancing in the sky. I started by trying very simple tricks, and then began to combine and flow them into combos for the sheer joy of dancing in the heights! I didn't really worry about the difficulty of my tricks, to instead feel proud of my small but very valued achievements. That's how I landed at my first competition in the heights in 2021, during the pandemic, as some restrictions were starting to ease and people were slowly resuming their activities.

An American athlete, a man whom many of us admire for promoting highline freestyle, called on and encouraged athletes who were starting to practice freestyle to participate in an online competition that allowed participation from anywhere in the world. The requirement was simply to upload a video of yourself performing a freestyle combo to social media. I accompanied one of my best friends, who is also my partner (another story to tell!), to record his video to participate in the competition. We went to a canyon more than three hours' drive from our city, looking for the optimal distance to practice, which is preferably performed on lines between 65 and 75 meters (200–250 feet) in length. At that moment, it never crossed my mind to record a combo of myself for the competition. While I enjoyed myself and felt proud of my small achievements, I didn't have the confidence to participate in an international competition. I had very little experience, and I didn't practice consistently because, in my city, spots to practice highline freestyle were not developed.

That weekend, while we were recording the videos, I also got on the line simply to have fun, to play. My partner recorded a video during my session, and that night when we returned he showed it to me and encouraged me to upload it to social media to participate in the women's category of the competition. It was the deadline day to participate, and he easily convinced me under the argument that I shouldn't take it too seriously, that I had nothing to lose, and that maybe I could win a prize because the number of women participating so far could be counted on one hand. So I uploaded my video and, to my surprise, by the end of the day, we were no longer five; we were 12 women from different parts of the world participating in the competition. This was very different from the men who participated, whose numbers were much larger. Only 12 athletes qualified for the semifinal, and the same rule applied to women. The results came out, and my unplanned combo had placed 12th out of the 12 women who participated. I was in the semifinals!

At this moment, the dynamics changed. It was the first time I had competed. Until then, the only competition I had entered was with myself. But, inspired by the combos and the participation of wonderful, confident, and strong girls from different parts of the world, I decided to commit myself, and this time, give it my best. What I previously took as a game and without much seriousness turned into a commitment to surpass myself and prove to myself I was capable of calming my mind to flow and create something magical, to dance in the sky.

Eager to give my best, I planned a sequence of tricks for the semifinal but faced some serious challenges. The only line near my house was 25 meters (82 feet) long, nothing simple to practice freestyle on. I visualized my sequence on this line, but days later we put all our energy into going back to the canyon where we had initially filmed our combos, where I hoped to perform and record my sequence to compete. To my surprise, this time the place was very windy. We rigged the line, but it was very difficult to find calmness to control my movements in those conditions. I tried, again and again, without managing to control and connect my planned movements. A day passed, and although I asked the stars at night for the wind to ease the next day, it didn't happen. The next day I tried again, over and over, but I couldn't do it. For the first time, the sky, the place where I used to find joy, confidence, and expansion, made me feel sad and defeated. Disappointed, I returned home.

This experience made me start to question whether I really wanted to take my practice, my sacred place, to competitions, to subject myself to the pressure of achieving something in a set time, to face those new and harsh feelings. Additionally, there was only one more week until the deadline to participate, and, economically, it was not viable to travel for over three hours from home to try again. But a part of me still believed I could do it and wanted to achieve it. So, as a Plan B, we went up to the crater of an inactive volcano two hours from our city, where we had previously rigged a small 65-meter (213-foot) line. We rigged our line, and during the weekend I attempted my sequence of movements. This time, it wasn't fun. Trying to calm the demons in my mind, I didn't give up. I tried again and again until I finally managed to execute my sequence of tricks for the semifinal.

Rarely in my years of practice had I been invaded by so many doubts and insecurities: the self-demand to achieve an objective in a very short time, and the fear of failure, of not being able to prove to myself I was capable. But just as rarely had I been overwhelmed by such strong feelings of calmness, gratitude, and immense happiness. I felt empowered, and that day I returned home very proud of myself for facing my fears without fleeing. I had managed to breathe and flow in harmony, invoking my dream to execute that dance in the sky. I achieved a good place and gained much satisfaction in the semifinal round of the competition, competing alongside brave women from all over the world, but many of the rewards behind that effort were yet to come.

When I began practicing this new, and sometimes terrifying, form of highlining, I didn't imagine the impact that overcoming my own fears would have. When I first started practicing freestyle, there were very few women getting involved. But a few warriors around the world were beginning to demonstrate that women could be as strong as men, who until then had been the only ones to achieve most of the tricks at one time. The topic of competitions within adventure sports can awaken our demons of fear of failure, leading to feelings of inadequacy and comparison with other athletes. But it can also lead us to humility, to the loving recognition and acceptance of our own process, to overcoming our limits, and to taking advantage of these moments of motivation and inspiration as a community to give our best and compete against ourselves. Without fear of sharing my process, with its failures and its own pace, an entire community around the world has supported me on this journey, giving me its affection and courage. Overcoming my own limits reminds me not to doubt the superpowers that reside within each of us and to accept failures as one step closer to our destination.

The motivation to continue on this path grows and expands over time. The rewards have been greater than the fears themselves. The satisfaction of living my dreams, and the community that accompanies me, the friends, men and women (more and more women!) with whom I share this passion and who are an eternal source of inspiration. The practice of highline has become a metaphor in my life. It is a path and I am the walker, an eternal apprentice. Moreover, any path is just one among many paths. It doesn't matter which one you take, but don't abandon yourself. Believe in the power of your dreams, believe in the power within you. For this high life, I am grateful for this passion that has led me to expand my limits and meet incredible people. I continue to be enthralled by the infinite possibilities of flying and the natural places where I have been able to dance in the sky. These natural environments, with their calmness and fragility, remind me of my place, with humility, where I can recognize myself as human, fragile, and fleeting, but also very capable of dreaming.

Celebrating competing in highline freestyle. Photo by Mariano Chimés.

CHAPTER 15

Your First Mistake Was to Call Me an Old Lady: Highlining over 60

By Rae Raptor

Slacklife

I am sitting around a campfire on hardpacked sand in the Amazon jungle with a group of new friends to celebrate Pepe's 35th birthday. I don't exactly know what time it is, but it has been dark for a long time. Maybe it's 9 p.m. when Pepe rakes some coals – *brasetas* – from the fire to form a glowing orange bed. He places about ten potatoes directly onto the coals. For about the next hour, Pepe carefully tends to the potatoes, shifting them with sticks, nudging them until they turn over, all the while talking and laughing with everyone in rapid-fire conversational Spanish that my brain is too tired to even try to understand. At last, Pepe maneuvers one charred potato out of the embers and balances it on top of an empty beer can. Dinner! We laugh as Pepe cuts open the potato and passes around pieces for us to eat. *¡Delicioso! ¡Qué rico!* We share pieces of charred baked potato around the fire until all the chunks of all the potatoes are gone. Joel, a yoga and surfing instructor from Lima, Perú, conjures up some vegan cookies and shares them. From his backpack, Fernando, an MMA fighter, pulls out Maricucha – passion fruit schnapps – and passes around shots. People are rolling blunts and sending them around the circle to share. And all the while talking, talking, talking, and laughing and loving life on the sand in the warm embrace of the Amazonian humid air, with a half-moon half visible through diffuse gaps in the clouds, the palm trees, and the leafy jungle trees that are silhouetted against the moonlit sky. It's a perfect night. We are living the dream. And I think to myself, *In what world does a 64-year-old American woman, wife, mother, and retired English professor get to sit around the campfire with a congenial group of beautiful Peruvian* amigas *and* amigos *in their 20s and 30s? In what world does this happen?* Answer: In the world of highlining.

In the area Steve and I developed, the Flintstones, Nevada. Photo by Tom Brown.

First Steps on a Slackline

Sometimes people ask me how I got into slacklining. Well, when I was about 56, my best friend, Eileen, planned to fly into Reno from Fort Collins, Colorado, to visit me. A couple days before her flight, Eileen called to say she tripped on a curb and broke her nose and couldn't come. Her daughter, who was pre-med at the time, warned her, "Mom, you're going to lose your balance as you age." Something about the way Eileen told me this story hit me. And I remember thinking, *Hell, no! Not on my watch!* I began looking around for ways to maintain balance, my hunch being that balance is a use-it-or-lose-it proposition, and that older people start losing their balance when their lives become more sedentary.

I had been meeting my friend Ashley at a rock-climbing gym every week. One week she couldn't make it, but I went anyway since there are some self-belay routes. Whereas normally Ashley and I chatted, on this week, being alone, I happened to notice a short slackline on a rack that had always been there, but that I had never paid attention to. This time, I looked at it. *Hmm, I bet that is good for balance*, I thought. I stepped up onto it. *Yeow*. I couldn't stay on it. I shook, it wobbled, and I came off. Not long after that, my husband, Steve, and I went to a party at another rock-climbing friend's house, and they had a slackline set up in their backyard. Some of the guests played around on the line. I gave it a try and, again, no chance! How could they do it and I couldn't? And how could some of them make it look easy?

In July 2015, for my 57th birthday, Steve gave me a classic Gibbon two-inch ratchet line and we strung it up over our backyard lawn. Thanks to a tip from a friend, I used ski poles at first for stability. I would plant a pole on each side of the slackline, step up, and try to stay up despite the wobbling. I learned that, to keep the line from jiggling, you must step up boldly and not timidly – my first lesson on the necessity of confident, decisive action in slacklining. I learned slowly, but I did learn, first to lift the ski poles for a couple seconds, then to use the ski poles to stand up but, once up, to cast them aside, and then to stand up without ski poles. One day I took a step. And, of course, I learned how to come off the line – again and again and again and again. Learning how to fall off the line without getting hurt was a crucial lesson in being able to progress.

Slacklining grew on me. The challenge of it and the signs of progress were enticing, addicting even. My balance was improving! So cool. I was still an English professor at this time – an all-consuming job – and I found slacklining demanded my complete attention and, as such, was one of the rare times when I didn't think about work. It was refreshing to have a complete escape from the incessant swarm of thoughts that buzzed around in my head like agitated bees. I started calling slacklining "cheap therapy." I began listening to Latin pop music through earbuds while slacking. I felt like I was dancing on the line! My body started to get leaner, and I had to buy a whole new set of smaller pants. I felt great! I felt alive and fit and full of energy. So happy.

I was in love. In my journal, I wrote down 100 things I loved about slacklining. I began requesting a later teaching schedule so I could slack every morning before work. Slacking was the best part of my day. The chemicals that slacklining released in my brain made me feel on top of the world for most of the day. Those were my slackline honeymoon days, when I slacked for the pure fun of it, like a kid. I had no ambitions, really, to get any better. I just wanted to be on a line. When Steve and I went camping or on an outing, I always took a slackline and found places to rig and slack. Progress at this stage was less about striving to improve and more just a natural result of all the time I spent slacklining. Nowadays, I am much better than I was then, but I had more fun then than I do now. It was all so innocent. I wasn't comparing myself to anybody. I wasn't slacklining with anyone. I was just loving slacklining on my own and relishing the sense of well-being it brought me.

For some reason I can't explain, I soon had this sense I should be on Instagram. I don't even know how I knew about Instagram, since I had never used social media. But in 2016 I created an account and made my first post, a photo of my Gibbon slackline slung around an enormous ponderosa pine tree trunk at our campsite at Eagle Lake, California. To me, that picture still conveys the smell of pine needles, the filtered sunlight that came through the trees, and the delight of slacklining there. I was such a novice. The Gibbon ratchet line was the only line I had even heard of. I slacked in tennis shoes. I just played and danced and asked Steve to take pictures of me. I had never been a photo maven before, but now I wanted pictures. I wanted photos to post to Instagram, and I wanted photos to hang in my bedroom in a nursing home someday.

As I started following slackliners on Instagram, I became aware of other webbings, other lengths, yoga slacking, and slackliners around the world. Little by little, I started to have exchanges with other slackliners. I even entered an online yoga slackers competition and won a necklace. I started web surfing for slack-related articles. And that's when I saw a photo of Hayley Ashburn doing the SPLITS (!!!) on a slackline insanely high above the Yosemite Valley floor, with El Cap in the background. My mouth dropped open. My pupils dilated. And that is how highlining got on my radar. Hayley was wearing a climbing harness and was obviously attached to the slackline in some way, so apparently she was safe up there. I could already slackline. I was a decent rock climber. *How hard could it be?* I wondered. I wanted to try it! The photos would be off the charts!

Getting into Highlining

Steve and I wasted no time. My brother has a cabin in the Santa Cruz Mountains of California, overlooking the Pacific Ocean. On his property is a small redwood grove of enormous trees. In 2016, over Valentine's Day weekend, we drove down there to rig a highline. As I look back on that first bold effort, I see we did a lot of things wrong. The first thing we did wrong was rig with a two-inch Gibbon ratchet line. For backup we used a climbing rope taped underneath the slackline. The gap between trees was only about 40 feet (12 m). As any highliner can tell you, that rig was a recipe for a very impactful, harsh fall. But what we did wrong didn't end there. Naively, my plan was to step out onto the

Doing the splits like Hayley. Photo by Steve Glotfelty.

line directly from the tree. What that means, I now know, is that, if I fell, I ran the risk of slamming into the tree trunk. Another thing I don't do today is amp myself up with high-energy music; instead, when highlining, I now put on mellow playlists to calm me down. But on that day, it was Five Finger Death Punch. My whole family and a good friend were down below, waiting to cheer me on and watch the show. I climbed up into the narrow access crotch between two giant redwood trees and managed to get into a position where I could tie the leash to my harness using the doubled figure-eight knot I knew from my climbing days. And then a paralyzing wave of terror hit me. Oh my God. I had not expected it. It was my old Gibbon slackline I knew so well. But the prospect of stepping onto that line with only air below was so unthinkable that I froze. I could not get myself to do it. No way. Not happening.

Regrouping, I asked everyone but Steve to leave. I untied and climbed down from that anchor. I don't remember how we did it, but we managed to get the leash and ring – or maybe we were using a locking carabiner? – to the other anchor, the one where you climbed a tall extension ladder to access. Steve and I thought maybe it would be less intimidating for me to step out from that side, since the fall would be less obstructed by redwood branches. Shaking, I climbed waaaaay up, tied in, and stood on top of the webbing, hugging the tree and contemplating whether to step out. Ugh. It is one thing to write the words, "I was more afraid than I've ever been in my whole life," and another thing to experience the sensation of extreme fear slam you, flooding your synapses with the word "DANGER!!" messing up your breathing and hijacking your body. But somehow there were just enough neurons left in my command-and-control center to do a bit of reasoning. I told myself I was safe. I was attached to the slackline by a tether. The most I could fall was a few feet, and I wouldn't hit the ground. And there was a part of my brain that didn't want all of Steve's rigging efforts to be in vain. I felt I owed it to him to at least try. I don't know how I did it, but I let go of the tree trunk and took one step and instantly fell. I have blocked that fall out of my memory and can't call it up. All I know is I did it, I was alive, and I was done. However, I never for a moment believed I was done for good. Rather, my thoughts were, *I'll be back*. I had so much to learn. It's making me feel good to retell this story, because even though I'm not yet where I want to be in highlining, it reminds me of how far I've come.

If highlining is such a hard nut for me to crack, why do I do it? I'm retired! I don't have to do anything I don't want to do. I have concluded that God gave me this desire. Why else would I have it? I want to gracefully walk long highlines in beautiful places. On a backpacking trip in California's High Sierra, when I was lying in my sleeping bag in my one-person tent waiting out an afternoon thunderstorm, I had a vision of myself confidently standing on a very high highline. My arms were outstretched and up, glorifying God. There were rays of light all around me and coming from me. In my tent, I felt a warm tear roll down my cheek. I recently came across these sentences:

> *God is desperately looking for people who will trust in the dreams He gives to us. There are so few people who are willing to take the inspiration that God breathes into them and hold tenaciously to it until the possibility becomes a reality.*[7]

I chose to trust in my dreams and my ability to overcome any obstacles on the way. The answer to "How hard can it be?" is that it has been very hard for me. Fear is immobilizing. I have been seriously trying to highline for about six years, and although I

Highlining in Box Canyon in Nevada. Photo by Justin Hamot.

can stand up on most lines, I am not yet consistently taking steps. But I am committed to the journey. I'm going to keep chipping away, trying, training, showing up, strategizing, and learning. I don't know why God gave me the desire to highline, but I trust this is what I am supposed to be doing for this chapter of my life and that, if I follow this call, I will discover ways to be a positive force in the world, as was the case when I was a professor.

Community

Steve

I have been very fortunate that Steve actively supports my highline quest. Steve did some slacklining in the early days of the sport, but he has always been primarily into rock climbing. Back in the day, Steve helped establish several climbing areas, he has put up many climbing routes, and he is listed in climbing guidebooks. Back pain from old climbing injuries and back surgery about ten years ago limits what he can do now, but he is still into pioneering new routes, which now take the form of scouting and often bolting new highlines. Together we have established 25 highlines in Nevada. One of these areas, which we call Flintstones, is in a desert canyon of red volcanic cliffs a half hour north of Reno. It now has ten lines, ranging from 20 to 300 meters (65–984 feet), with some longer lines planned.

The Flintstones area is so dry that we are quite aware of environmental impact. The bolts themselves are on top of rock formations and are not visible from below. We spray-painted the bolts the color of the rock, so they blend in. We buried a 50-gallon (190-l), camouflage-painted steel drum in an inconspicuous location between two bushy juniper trees and put a toilet seat on top, so human waste will be confined to that one place. And we have built trails to the major anchor sites to reduce erosion and avoid having random use trails going all over the place. All the highliners I've met pack out their trash, and some pack out other people's trash as well, leaving areas cleaner than when they arrived. Despite our efforts to be eco-friendly, there *will* be an impact if Flintstones gets popular. The parked cars alone will clear spaces and leave tracks. However, it is public land, and just down the road is an established rock-climbing area (that Steve developed more than 30 years ago). In addition, target shooters, hunters, hikers, campers, partiers, and ORVs (off-road recreational vehicles) use the area, so it's mixed-use already.

Steve and I want to continue to develop our sports of rock climbing and highlining in a way that respects the environment and the communities of both humans and nonhumans who inhabit the areas we use.

Xavier

Highlining leads to the most improbable friendships. One of my best highline friends, Xavier, is from Stockton, California, about three hours away from me. He just turned 27 and goes by @tokenslackguy on Instagram, a reference to the days when he was the "token" driver in running drug packages from state to state. Xavier smoked weed every day since junior high school, right up until getting his recent rope-access job that tests his hair for drug use. In his past, Xavier has dealt drugs, smuggled drugs, and taken many drugs often. In contrast, I drink one Bud Light at dinner. Xavier has lived in his van for the past five years, while Steve and I have been entrenched at Scorpion Acres – our house and land – for 30 years, longer than Xavier has been alive. Xavier is an excellent highliner, while I am still learning to take steps. But our friendship is great.

Back in January of 2021, we met at Cosumnes River Gorge to highline, and at that time we agreed to highline together at least once every month for that year. Often hooking up with others, we have gone on many, many fun trips: Taft Point, Elephant Rock, and Tunnel Vision in Yosemite; Sonoma Coast; Stockton canal; GZ canyon ("Ground Zero," where they tested an atom bomb in the 1960s); Thousand Creek Gorge; Lake Alpine; Kirby Cove with its stunning view of San Francisco; Granite Creek Bridge on Highway 1, Oregon, to help rig a 1200-meter (3,937-foot) line; and others. So many adventures! Xavier made a calendar from our photos. When 2022 rolled around, we re-upped, and we haven't missed a month yet. Last weekend, we rigged a new 500-meter (1,640-foot) line, setting a record for Nevada. I've seen X through a couple of girlfriends, and he's seen me through a couple of injuries. I am so grateful for Xavier. He has taught me a tremendous amount, and he believes in me. Books say to surround yourself with people who motivate you – that's Xavier.

Pepe Rivas

Some people call highlines "one-inch wiggly bridges," and it keeps being true for me that highlining has bridged some enormous differences. My favorite example is Pepe Rivas. Pepe is 35, single, speaks Spanish as his first language, and, when I first met him, he lived with his grandfather in Zungarococha, a small village in the Amazon jungle of the Loreto region of Perú in South America. Besides highlining, Pepe loves to talk, and he loves food. I am 66 and have a 28-year-old daughter, English is my first language, and I live with my husband in the high desert outside of Reno, Nevada, USA, North America. I love quiet, and I love to read. There could hardly be two more different people personally, culturally, and geographically. But our shared passion for highlining has become the basis of a friendship that transcends – and is even enriched – by all these differences.

I got involved in the effort of Pepe and his friends to form a nonprofit association called Highlife Perú to promote the sport and work on access issues in the country. I ran a GoFundMe campaign for them from the US, and I've made two trips to Perú, bringing a total of five suitcases of highline gear to them, gear being very difficult to get in Perú. Thanks to Pepe and his friends, I've had some unforgettable experiences highlining and midlining in Perú, from the desolate, tawny, fossil-encrusted cliffs at Cañón de los Perdidos in the Ocucaje Desert in the Ica region, to the green tropical paradise of King Kong in the Amazon jungle, to a magnificent terraced plateau at Ananiso in the Andes, where the highlines are at 14,255 feet (4345 m) of elevation, and we shared the access trail with free-ranging alpacas. These adventures and these friends are highlights of my life and would never have happened without the international community of highliners, my extended slackfamily. Thanks to highlining, and Instagram, I also have highline friends in Venezuela, Brazil,

México, Iran, the Czech Republic, and Australia, with whom I hope to visit and highline someday.

Gender

In pretty much all the sports I have been really into – bicycling and rock climbing being the two biggies – most of my companions in the sport have been men. That doesn't mean women weren't doing the sport, just that my friends in the sport happened to be men, usually boyfriends. I got into bicycling and rock climbing through a boyfriend who was much better than me and who taught me how to do the sport. Although I became fairly good, my boyfriends were always better, especially at the technical aspects, such as bicycle mechanics and lead climbing trad routes. In those sports, at that time in my life, I was content to be a follower and, to an extent, to be taken care of.

Slacklining is different. I got into slacklining on my own. I want to be competent in all aspects of slacklining, including highline rigging. Sometimes I tell Steve to back off and let me rig, even though I'm less efficient than he is. In highlining, when I show up at a rig, rather than standing back and letting the guys do it, I dive in and join the team. I've been fortunate that my good highline friend Xavier trusts me, and we've done many rigs together, just the two of us. He'll show me tricks of the trade (such as installing a weblock upside down if you will be tensioning from above), answer my questions, and check my work, if I ask him, but the assumption is implicit trust. I also have a good highline friend named Sarah who shares rigging with me and has shown me techniques that work for her, such as using a wafer to hold the webbing under tension, freeing up both hands for putting the loose webbing into the weblock. When I invite friends to highline, I generally lead the rig with my own gear.

At a highline gathering, I am not super aware of my gender. There are often natural leaders, and they are typically male, but the rest of us – women and men – seem on par as friends. There are often some expert women and beginner men, just as the reverse is also true. In a sense, we are all on equal footing, because we are all pushing our own boundaries, and many are battling through fear. People get as excited about someone sliding out or standing up for the first time as they do about someone else landing a hard trick for the first time. Yes, I have heard stories from women who feel uncomfortable around a particular man because the man has hit on them. However, no doubt because of my age, I have not experienced sexual overtures myself. I have also heard stories from women who felt their opinions were discounted on a complex rig, but again, I have not experienced that kind of disrespect myself.

At one point in my quest, I began to wonder if I might be hampered by a low testosterone level in comparison with other highliners. In 2019 I had my testosterone level checked. My level is 39 ng/dL. In comparison, for younger men, the average testosterone level is in the range of 650.[8] Higher testosterone levels in men versus women account for greater strength, muscle mass, and bone density, and possibly greater psychological aggressiveness. However, women's strength is perfectly adequate for highlining and, based on the stellar performance of women crushers, women's brain chemistry is not a limiting factor. Furthermore, fixating on testosterone is a negative thought that will get me nowhere. Luckily, most highline teams are mixed-gender, and the heroes and record-holders in the sport are both men and women.

Age

Whereas I don't tend to feel my gender in highlining, I am almost always *keenly* aware of my age. When I show up to a highline gathering, there is literally no one in my age group, *ever*. Well, except maybe spectators. Although there are no demographic survey results for highlining specifically, the 2018 International Slackline Association *Demographics Survey*, drawn from almost 1,200 respondents from 60-plus different countries, reported the vast majority (80.16 percent) of slackliners are in their 20s and 30s. Slackliners 35 and older make up only 11.53 percent (mostly between 35 and 45), while there are zero respondents above the age of 59.[9]

For me, age in highlining is such a complex topic that I'm going to break down my experience of age into three categories: physical, social, and mental.

Imagined Physical Limitations

For the most part, I don't think being in my 60s is a problem physically. I take good care of myself. I exercise, eat well, get adequate sleep, and don't do things that might compromise my health. Whereas many people my age are losing their balance, getting out of shape, and suffering from various illnesses, including depression, thankfully, I am healthy and strong, and my balance is improving. Indeed, slacklining is a fountain of youth. When I am in the backyard slacking, listening to music, I am happy and ageless. I am in flow, feeling great, and loving life. However, I know the processes of aging are relentless, and that, someday, if I don't die first, I will begin losing my strength and abilities. I try to accept this inevitability while remembering to savor every day of health and every day of slacking.

I have had some injuries from slacklining, including a broken collarbone that required surgery and a titanium plate. But I have recovered from the injuries. Fortunately, I have gifted physical therapists that have helped me recover from a series of minor but potentially debilitating aches and pains. My PTs teach me exercises and stretches to deal with the parade of issues I bring to their doors, and my morning exercise routine gets progressively longer as I add each of their prescribed exercises to it.

There are ways my mind sabotages my goals by the way it interprets physical pain. For example, for over a year I've been dealing with some pain in my right groin area. This injury first arose when I did more than 30 leash climbs and line mounts in one highline session – an overuse injury likely. But it has been very slow to heal, probably because I keep using it. A while ago, I began interpreting my groin pain as old age creeping in, maybe arthritis. That idea depressed me and made me feel weak, which compromised how I performed on the line.

My performance coach, Dr. Xuemei Zhong, however, observed

that we inherit socially constructed preconceptions about aging as necessarily entailing decline, and these narratives are all too quick to pop into our head to account for any kind of pain as part of the norm of aging. Xuemei told me such beliefs and imaging are disempowering and prevent us from seeing and experiencing the alternative norm that we can stay strong and pain-free until we die. She also taught me that my body is super intelligent and wants me to achieve my dreams. Sometimes physical discomfort can be a message for course correction or a reminder to pay attention to something I would otherwise ignore.

I had been in a pattern of repeated aborted sit starts, where I'd get into sit start position, lift my body a little bit, and then collapse back down, essentially giving up. Each aborted sit start irritates my groin, and Xuemei invited me to explore what might be the message of my pain. One of the messages we brainstormed was that maybe the pain is teaching me to quit aborting and to fully commit to each sit start. I did not know if it was true or not, but I felt relieved. The new idea that pain had something to teach me that could improve my slacklining felt empowering rather than disempowering. And soon my pain was actually gone, as I was busy paying attention to my Perú trip and other activities. However, whenever I feel fear about not achieving my goal or have doubts about my body and aging, the pain comes back to remind me.

Through this experience, I learned our repeated thoughts, imaging, and narratives of aging and our body make a crucial difference in our performance and healing. Our thoughts lead to emotions, and emotions affect our biology and lead to different performance outcomes. If you want to improve your performance, you must improve your thought process and replace disempowering beliefs with empowering beliefs. Improved thinking also speeds up recovery and healing.

"I belong here too"

Socially, being an old highliner is mostly fantastic. I love it, and I feel extremely lucky to have the opportunity to hang out with and be friends with other highliners. This process was not automatic. At one point, I worked with Cam Nelson, a highliner who was starting a coaching business. When I told him I highlined on my own, Cam suggested it would be good for me to highline with other highliners. I was polite and thanked him for the suggestion, meanwhile thinking to myself, *Oh yeah, like that's gonna happen*. Around this time, I read *The Fear Project*, in which author Jaimal Yogis tells the story of Karen Rogers, a world-record-holding, open-water swimmer, who kept telling herself, "I belong here too. I belong here too," to keep herself swimming after a huge elephant seal rammed into her thigh several times.[10] When I first showed up to a highline meet-up at Emerald Pools in California, I clung to that mantra, "I belong here too." There were about a dozen highliners there, and even though everyone was very nice to me, I felt like an ethnographer in a foreign culture. The Emerald Pools group did not disappoint! These highliners had dyed hair, dreadlocks, pierced bodies, tattoos, checkered sunglasses, and a wardrobe that could have come out of a costume store – or no clothes at all. They engaged in juggling, tree-hugging, and sharing of various psychoactive substances to smoke and ingest. They said things like "sick," "dope," and "I'm down" to mean "good," "cool," and "I'm up for it." They were all in a great mood and were friendly and welcoming to me. But that day. *That* day. I felt utterly out of my element. I felt like I would never belong.

However, as time has gone by, and I've shown up to dozens of highline gatherings and festivals, and even organized a few highline events, I now have the fond feeling, *These are my people*. I have some tattoos of my own and some wild tights. For 28 years I was a university English professor, and one reason I loved my job is I love being around young people that age. Full of energy and fun, daring, freedom, ideas and idealism, dreams, passions, experimentation, optimism, and living in the present. In my experience, most highliners are adults who are kids. They/we are free spirits. They/we love to play and hang out together. They/we do crazy things. Like the time a group of us was hiking back from the Babylon line at Donner Summit in the Sierra Nevada mountain range. We were all talking and laughing so much that we missed the trail and ended up on the freeway shoulder rather than arriving at the rest area where our cars were parked. No worries! No one even mentioned it. Instead, a couple of the guys did arm pumps in the air to every oncoming 18-wheeler, trying to get the truck driver to honk – successfully in most cases, which caused even more merriment. Then, when we arrived at the rest area, as we were waiting for the static-side anchor group to arrive, one of the guys rolled his van door open, turned up some raucous music, and three highliners climbed on top of the van and began exuberantly dancing, rocking the van back and forth. I loved their zest for life (and I almost got up there myself).

My Definition of Success

Once you know how to slackline, highlining is mostly mental. It's a matter of confidence, focus, and overcoming fear. You must believe you can do it. If you don't believe, you won't be able to do it. Your own mind will undermine your efforts and shut your body down. For me, fear on a highline triggers not fight, but flight (automatic whips and catches) and freeze (refusal of my muscles to move). My mind has doubt, and so my brain is not sending clear signals to my muscles. One command says, "stand" or "step," but the louder command says, "DON'T DO IT!" Most highliners, at least initially when they are learning, feel fear. But those who are determined and confident find a way to push through the fear, and eventually the fear lessens. It takes confidence – an "I know I can do it" attitude – to push through fear. I have had a hard time feeling confident. Self-belief is slow to take hold.

Like, really slow. What is difficult for me is I am one of the slowest learners I have ever heard of in highlining. And I don't know why. I'm in shape. I have discipline. I train. I have good places to highline. I try and try and try. But I'm not consistently taking steps yet after six years dedicated to highlining. It can be frustrating, if I let it. I recently went highlining with two guys I first met a couple years ago. At the time we met, I was getting sit starts, and they were not yet able to stand up on a highline.

Now they are both sending lines, standing in exposure, and feeling comfortable on highlines. And I am still struggling to get sit starts and maybe one or two steps. This is so typical. Why? Why? Why? Why am I so slow to learn? Why does fear still prevent me from taking steps? Is it my age? I don't know. But being old, I have to wonder if age has something to do with my blocks. Maybe older people become more cautious and risk-averse than they were in their invincible youth? Maybe I have more deprogramming to do? People kindly remind me everyone is on their own journey, and that you shouldn't compare yourself to others. I get this, but it's not that easy to do when the difference is so blatant.

Highliners define success in various ways. Some define success as a send, while others wear a T-shirt that says, "Fuck sending." Some highliners are attempting to cross ever-longer lines, while others are focusing on freestyle, landing ever more difficult tricks. Understanding the need to stay positive, I have created my own definition of success, which is independent of actual performance results:

Learn
Give effort
Stay positive
Give value to others
Let go and let God

I like this definition because it creates a great day and because it leads to progress over time. However, I must keep reminding myself of this definition, because I tend to revert to interpreting success as external results. As with so much of highlining, staying positive is a process, a work in progress, and a skill to practice.

Flow of Time

It's interesting to me how each vocation teaches us skills. Being a good professor requires initiative, self-discipline, time management, organization, planning, public speaking, energy, and human relations. Being a good highliner requires confidence, calmness, focus, courage, positivity, patience, belief, and trust. Nearly three decades of being a professor sharpened the mental skills required for that job. Now I am in the process of learning highline mental skills. I also need to unlearn or deprogram some of the skills that served me well as a professor but seem incompatible with highline mastery. One of these is my relation to time. As a professor, I wore a watch, and my day was subdivided into timed chunks. I had to get to meetings on time, get to classes on time, end classes on time, have half-hour lunch breaks, meet grant deadlines and writing deadlines, and generally march through the day synchronized to clock time. I became good at it.

But highlining and highliners flow to a more organic sense of time. This difference became apparent to me when I showed up to a Truckee River cleanup day, organized by a slackliner for slackliners. As usual, I arrived punctually. The organizer pulled in about a half hour late, and other people trickled in whenever it suited them. But it all worked. The area got cleaned up, we waterlined, and we had a great day. A watch also dictated my initial approach to highlining. I would literally set a timer for 30 or 45 minutes and stay out on the line until the timer went off. Or, if I was at a festival, I would be very aware of time, not wanting to tie up the line because other people were waiting for their turn. It was like there was a taxi meter ticking in my head, and the longer I stayed out the more uncomfortable I felt. I was also impatient when other people stayed on the line "too long" – my concept. By now, I no longer wear a watch, and I'm often oblivious to time. I get up when it's light. I eat when I'm hungry. I slack for as long or short as I feel like slacking. And I don't expect other slackers to necessarily be "on time." To symbolize this changed relationship to time, which I find liberating and am enjoying, I got a tattoo of a sun on my wrist where the face of my wristwatch used to be.

One mental habit I developed as a professor has proven more difficult to transform than my sense of time. And that is my need for control. As a professor, it really helps to be in control, i.e., to have your act together. As a leader, you chart the direction, steer the ship, and prevent chaos. To a certain extent, you can even control the energy in a classroom. I believe my habit of being in control – or my fear of being out of control – is one of the biggest obstacles I face as a highliner. I'm not overly afraid of heights. And I have learned how to do controlled falls, such as whips and leg catches. But the prospect of a surprise fall scares me, so much so that I intentionally bail rather than taking a step and possibly facing an uncontrolled fall.

Thankfully, I have come to accept I am slow. I'm a slow eater and a slow reader. "Rae Raptor doesn't rush" is one of my mantras. As an academic, my projects took a long time, but they made an impact. And, seriously, what else am I going to do? Go

Enjoying the journey. Photo by Steve Glotfelty.

to senior bingo games? This is what I want to do. There's still time. It could happen. Enjoy the journey.

"Cheryll Legend"

Rather than being bothered by imagined limitations, I decided to create a list of all the reasons why age gives me an *advantage* in highlining. There are some great reasons: I have time, money, a nice house, and a good car. I have developed very healthy habits. My personal life is happy and stable, so I don't have to deal with emotional roller coasters. In Steve, I have a live-in rigging and trip partner and loving support system. I have time to read a lot of books on sports psychology and personal development, and I can afford to hire a performance coach. I have been able to convince myself there is no reason I can't highline, and that I have some good things going for me in this pursuit.

An interesting aspect of being an elder highliner is the impact I have on other people. One day I was exchanging contact info with Jewels, a highliner in her young 20s. When I looked at her cell phone to verify my phone number, I saw the name "Cheryll Legend," and I told her that that was a different Cheryll. But, no, Jewels invents last names for her contacts, and she had put me in her phone as Cheryll Legend. Since then, a few other people have used the same word, and many people have told me I inspire them. Another friend referred to me as an "OG" – it's a compliment, look it up. I've also been called a "badass" and a "stoke factory." Honestly, to me, these recognitions make me feel as good as when I used to win teaching awards. I am not even a good highliner yet, but somehow just my being out there giving effort is enough to inspire people. In fact, many people have gotten personal bests when they are highlining with me.

Another way I sense I may be a good force in the world, at least among highliners, is that I am proof it is still possible to highline when they get up there in years. I've noticed slackliners and highliners cannot imagine themselves ever being old and cannot relate to people who are old, except maybe in the way you would relate to your grandparents. But highliners meet me, and we become friends across the generation gap. So I believe one of my larger roles as a slackliner/highliner is to break down stereotypes of aging and offer a more hopeful and happier alternative to the dominant narratives.

When I was teaching, I screened a lot of literature to potentially assign in my classes. In one novel, I came across a passage that struck a chord, and I've never forgotten it. The narrator recalled reading that the Hindus viewed life in four progressive stages:

20 years a youth
20 years a fighter
20 years as head of a household
20 years in the cultivation of the spirit[11]

At the time, as a professor mom, I was enmeshed in the head-of-a-household phase. From the perspective of that demanding lifestyle, the cultivation-of-the-spirit phase sounded blissfully peaceful and heavenly. I pictured myself sitting in a lotus position under a tree, receiving spiritual insights. I began to look forward to that chapter of my own life.

I could never have predicted that slacklining, which I was not even aware of at the time, would become my vehicle for cultivation of the spirit. But it has. When slacklining, I am in flow. I am at one with the universe. My mind, body, and spirit are in harmony and are connecting with larger energies. Furthermore, to become a highliner requires *spiritual* growth. It is a fascinating and mysterious process. Walking the line has become my spiritual path.

CHAPTER 16

Stepping Forward, Letting Go: Harnessing Courage in Action and Acceptance

By Anna Hanuš Kuchařová

TRANSLATED FROM THE CZECH BY DENISA KRÁSNÁ

Euphoria

Yesterday, for the first time in my life, I stood on a 200-meter (656-foot) highline. And now, half a kilometer of highline stretches out in front of me, shining in the sun. I am definitely not prepared. But how many times in life will I have such a chance? I take a step. The one-inch-wide (2.5-cm) strip pleasantly imprints on the bottom of my feet. The line is much tamer than I expected. I take a step, two, seven. And suddenly a sharp fear passes through me. A chilling feeling I will die. I grab the line with all my strength, as if I were up there completely unsecured. I frantically crawl back to the rock. "Yuck! Yuck, the terror!" As I untie, I realize I feel a little sick. My stomach is swaying and my legs seem not to obey me. I need to get away. Far from this terrifying line. I walk away. The Rectory tower is about 98 feet (30 m) wide and 1,640 feet (500 m) long. I walk slowly to its opposite end. My ears are buzzing. I feel like I just jumped from a great height into the water. As if I broke the surface and descended to the very bottom. My vision is a bit blurry, and I hear an unpleasant gurgling sound in my ears. I don't really calm down until I'm back at the line.

Highlining at Castleton, Utah. Photo by Jan Kamler.

Nobody is highlining. And nobody is getting ready. I watch as the line, like a ribbon, gently floats in the wind. All the way to the other end. To Castleton. The line is so beautiful, and the desert landscape around it is so powerful. Fear and a tremendous desire to traverse this space wrestle within me. I tie back in. I sit on the line. I sway a bit away from the rock. Okay, I know what awaits me now. This line is completely beyond my mental strength. And I know the only way I can stay on the line is in the flow state. I stand up. And in the first step I sink into a state I intimately know. Although I've experienced it before, the beginning is always equally unpleasant. I must put aside everything I am. Shed my individuality. It's like taking off a cloak under which I am completely naked. At that moment, I always feel vulnerable and taste the flavor of death on my tongue. Often, it stops me. I can't surrender to it, and, usually, I fall off the line. It's the only way to end the pressure in my head. But this time that terrifying moment is quite short. And I'm already there. In a state where time does not exist. And where I don't exist as Anna. For now I don't exist so I can become a part of the landscape. It's as if a part of me were the red cliffs, the snow-covered mountains on the horizon, the air, the wind, and even the line. It's a space where no one claims anything, yet, or maybe precisely because of that, there is an inexhaustible amount of energy, love, and peace available to everyone. Including me. I keep walking. For the first time in my life, a fall and the subsequent climbing back onto the line from the leash don't pull me out of the flow state. I don't know how long I have walked, with how many falls. It was the sudden movement of the line in the wind that pulled me out of the flow state. Suddenly, I was back to being Anna. I was about a hundred meters away from the anchor, laughing with joy. And I knew it was time to go back.

I had my first taste of long highlines at the end of 2017. That three-month trip to the States was my honeymoon with Kwjet, my husband. And when I told him about what I experienced, he smiled at me. "Anna, you probably don't want to have kids just yet, do you?" I spent the whole year with the prospect it might be our last childless year. Not thinking my life would end once I had a child, but I knew my priorities and time and financial capabilities would change. And, suddenly, I needed one more year. I wanted to experience more of these big highlines so I could be a calm mom and not feel like I was missing out on something.

How will I make the most of this final year? I want to go back to Castleton! But is it my ego saying that, or is it a genuine desire? Dealing with my ego is tricky; when the main motivation is ego-driven, it always ends up poorly. Either I don't achieve the goal and feel inferior, or I succeed and briefly feel satisfaction, quickly followed by the fear of losing the record-holding position. This was especially the case when highlining was in its beginnings and records were pushed by meters. I was watching my friends attempting to surpass my record and didn't root for them. I went through years of introspection and realized that true joy comes not from ego-driven crosses and sends. When I follow a simple desire without the need for validation, I often see a goal, a dream on the horizon, but the direction is much more significant. Desire is a huge arrow in my inner self with the inscription, "This Way," and when I go in that direction with all I am and have, it always turns out well. Whether I achieve the goal or not, I am left with peace and joy that don't fade even with the passing of years.

The highline in Moab, Utah, leading from the Rectory to Castleton Tower, was first rigged in 2015 by a French-American team, with Theo Sanson sending it and setting the world record at that time. Two years later, a Canadian-American-German-Czech team rigged it again, and Mia Noblet set the women's world record on it. Now it's January 2018, and I want to rig it again in the fall? Normally, I would pause at this bold idea. There are many people in the world better suited for rigging such a project than me. They are better highliners and climbers that can certainly carry more weight than me. But I no longer have time to compare myself to others; I won't get any younger. It is enough to place the challenge that attracts me against my capabilities on the scales. If there is a biological clock ticking within me, it's not in the womb but in the vibrations of long highlines.

Connection

In February I bought about 2,000 feet (600 m) of webbing, and my French friend Chloe Roux-Mollard bought around the same amount. The setup was complete. We began reaching out to various male and female slackliners, but when six girls confirmed their participation, we realized we could turn it into a women-only project. It's not something one often experiences. Highlining is more of a male-dominated sport, or at least it was at that time. I have nothing against highlining with guys and I enjoy rigging with them. However, an all-female team has a slightly different energy. Thanks to Faith Dickey, I had the chance to experience it many times at the Women's Highline Meeting in Ostrov. Luckily, I have never experienced or witnessed any prejudice against female highliners either in France or in the Czech Republic. But in the States I often did. In the best case, it was a surprise I knew the rigging technique. In the worst case, there were comments. "A woman rigged this? I wouldn't trust that."

We refrained from seeking sponsors for this project. The motivation, the entire team coming together – everything was so pure that commercial interests might disrupt it. Each of us covered our own expenses. I wanted someone to film our efforts. "I made enough money to buy the webbing. I can make enough for the filmmaker's flight ticket too." Honza Žůrek, a young Czech filmmaker, was enthusiastic about the project, but he wanted to bring another cameraman with him. When he realized I didn't have funds for the third plane ticket, he bought them from his own pocket. This enthusiasm permeated the whole preparation. Well before our gathering in Moab, Utah, a positive synergy began to flow among us, making every problem easy to solve.

One such problem arose at the end of the summer when we had our webbing cut into pieces. Strong wind tore Chloe's piece of webbing, and thieves that had broken into my car and stolen my electronics cut mine. It was during a time when the first slackliners began walking on connected lines, which the rest of the community watched with considerable unease. Since the early days of slacklining, a single line without connections was regarded as the safest option. Hence, everyone in the community was still approaching connected lines with proper respect and skepticism. It was going to be the main topic at the International Slackline Association's Safety Event that year, so I made sure to squeeze it into my already packed schedule. In the end, Mimi borrowed three pieces of lightweight static lines for backup. The main line also consisted of three pieces, each of them a different length because wind and thieves didn't ask where it would be convenient for us to cut it. Then it was decided. We would be connecting segments on Castleton. It was going to be a new experience for most of us.

And now, after months of intense preparation, planning, and

obtaining permits, we are here, in the free campsite at the base of Castleton. We set the alarm for 4:30 a.m. I'm bundled up in my sleeping bag, breathing the chilly desert air. I should be sleeping, yet the entire plan for tomorrow is unfolding in my mind. It's like choreography. We tested our plan with the girls last week in the Fruit Bowl canyon, which is much easier to access than the towers. The webbing is already connected and packed in four numbered bags. Static ropes, dynamic ropes, anchor material, climbing gear, hauling gear: everything is there. Aurélie and Laure checked the anchor points at the top of the towers a few days ago. Hopefully, everything will work out. Because, if not, people won't be saying we failed. They'll be saying women failed. And that would damn well disappoint me.

In the morning everything is frozen to the bone. I slip into my down jacket, and Aurélie emerges from the darkness. In the beam of her headlamp, her broad smile radiates. "It is gonna be goooood!" she says with such energy and joy that all the tension I felt the previous night melts away. This steel-hearted girl with tender eyes has already made coffee and is distributing it to all of the team members who are still waking up. Laure and Chloe giggle about something, and Camille emerges from her sleeping bag, whispering, "Yay, project!" At five in the morning, we set off. There's nothing but the blue lights of headlamps, the steam of our breath, the tap of trekking poles, and the rustle of girls' voices. By sunrise, we are at the base of the towers. Michelle, Mimi, and Laure start climbing Castleton. Chloe, Camille, and Eva prepare the whole length of the slackline from the base of one tower to another. Aurélie is already climbing the first pitch of Rectory. Louisa and I follow her, climbing just a short distance apart to save time. We reach the fourth and final pitch when the beautiful morning sun rises high above our heads. We throw down the other end of a 395-foot-long (120-m) rope. First, we haul the bag with anchor material. Then we throw the rope down again and start hauling the slackline. On the other tower, the slackline is already up. The line gets stuck on various rock protrusions; it's essential to detect this in time and release the line to avoid abrasion. Last year, there were five of us spreading the line on the ground. Now there are only three girls. The team on the other tower informs us with a walkie-talkie about our progress. Finally, during sunset, we get the other end of the line up and into the weblock. When darkness falls, the temperature drops below freezing and the wind is icy. We spend several more hours pulling up the slackline, but it is still not fully tensioned when we call it a night. On the way down, Aurélie sets up fixed ropes for the next day.

The next morning, we're all properly worn out. But at least some of us have to head up and haul some more things. We want to camp up there for five days, so we need to haul water, food, and equipment – approximately 880 pounds (400 kg). To avoid bothering climbers with bag hauling, we mainly do it after dusk. One girl is at the bottom, securing the load and using a rope to keep the backpack away from the rock to prevent it from getting stuck. Another girl is at the very top, operating a pulley with a brake over which we pull. Instead of one long rope, we have two tied together. At the knot, the rope needs to be taken out of the pulley and reinserted. The third girl is several meters below

The all-women's team at Castleton. Photo by Jan Kamler.

the summit, where there's a great ledge for squatting. The backpacks are lifted by their own weight. The person is attached to the hauling rope, then squats, and the backpack on the other end of the rope moves about 24 inches (60 cm) upwards. One backpack takes about 200 squats.

The first night up brings strong winds and snowfall. We can't hear or see each other at all, so we just estimate what may be needed. These are precisely the moments of discomfort, effort, and fatigue when people are freezing, something isn't working, and it's so easy to accuse others of being incapable. Although I was a bit cold when I wasn't squatting, I actually enjoyed the darkness, harshness, solitude, and at the same time, us being connected with a single rope. At one in the morning, we finish hauling the first six backpacks out of 17 in total.

On the third evening, we all gather at the top with all the backpacks hauled and the highline properly tensioned. We make a small fire from the wood we hauled up and we write down the walking order for the next day. A half-kilometer is a long highline for many of us, so we have three leash rings on the line and a clear resting plan. The first girl will go to Castleton, take a break, wait until another highliner crosses the line and joins her, and then she will walk back to Rectory while her friend rests. On top of Castleton, we already prepared a backpack on the day of tensioning, filled with water, chocolates, a blanket, warm socks, and a down jacket.

It's my turn. I'm a bit nervous. I've never walked such a distance without a fall, not even a third of it. But I came here for something else. I want to experience something powerful with this landscape. Connect with her forever. Leave her a piece of myself and take a piece of her imprinted forever under my skin. It's an exchange where no one loses anything. I stand up and a few steps later I sink into the beloved state of flow. I feel so light. Everything is so gentle and soft. The air caresses me as if it loves me. Something pulls me out of that state halfway through. I try for a little longer to connect individual steps back into a flowy walk, to bring my attention from my mind back down to the core, but I can't do it. I fall. And with me, all expectations fall too. I stand up and walk again. Silently. As if I were a bird gliding through space without flapping its wings. Before I reach the end, I fall again. And then I stand on Castleton.

I am completely silent. I feel centuries-old calmness. I untie. I walk slowly along the edge of the tower, and from below that calmness in me bubbles of joy begin to emerge. I am on this tower for the first time, the one that guided me through the last year of my life. I start to smile. Then giggle. Then laugh out loud. I can't stop it. An avalanche of euphoria. I jump and scream with laughter. Tears flow down my face. I roll on the ground and slap my hands on the cold rock. I laugh so much the girls on the other tower can hear me. My stomach hurts from all that laughter. But every time I try to stop, it makes me laugh even more. The climber who just reached the top slightly doubts my mental health, which doesn't help at all with that laughter. After 20 minutes, I calm down a bit. The walk back is smooth and touching. Like when you meet a good friend after a long time, and you know you now have time to become one person before saying goodbye again for a long time.

Joy in the Moab desert. Photo by Jan Kamler.

Each of the girls on the Castleton team was different, but what connected us were enthusiasm and the ability to appreciate our mutual diversity. It's hard to capture in words the bond that emerged among us without sounding too sweet. We created an atmosphere and space filled with acceptance. It brought out the best in each of us. Courage, strength, and tenderness blossomed from the depths of our beings. Mutual support was the greatest strength of our team.

Each of us gave our best and experienced the best. Mimi Guesdon and Louisa Avenas sent this magical line without a fall. But we all rappelled down, satisfied. The line, all the girls, and all the ropes were safely on the ground. Darkness surrounded us, and the stars seemed to reach out to us. I grabbed my backpack and took a head start. I was exhausted. My knees hurt with every step, even though I leaned on my poles. The subsequent week was immersed in the wave of euphoria we carried from the Rectory. The girls recovered in two days. I, on the other hand, was unable to exert any effort until the end of the trip. Even after returning from the States, it took almost a whole year for my strength to fully recover. I wasn't surprised. I had invested a lot in this project throughout the preceding year. But I came back enriched beyond measure.

Pause

I stopped highlining at the beginning of the second month of pregnancy. It surprised me that I stopped so early, but I just felt that way. If I had felt differently, I would have continued until childbirth. Every pregnancy is unique. Every mom is different, but they all deserve respect and trust that they are doing their best. I experienced nine divine months. My senses seemed to become more sensitive. I realized how much life pulses around us unnoticed. I heard new sounds, smelled new scents. It was as if my organs were rejoicing. And for that tiny, fragile human inside me, I felt so much love that my heart would burst with sorrow if I lost him.

The labor lasted for three nights and two days. Despite all the support and love I received from all sides, I felt desperate at the end. This body, which had accomplished so much, was unable to do the most natural thing. I had one night between deciding on a cesarean section and the operation itself. In those hours, I moved from a feeling of failure to acceptance. I entered the operating room with a smile. And my scar is a memory of that wonderful day when we saw our son for the first time.

I will never forget the mixture of immense love, breathtaking gratitude, and brutal physical pain that accompanied the first days after childbirth. They said I would be fine in a few days. But I wasn't. I spent a full month in bed. Kwjet didn't go to work and took care of our son and me. Then his parents took care of me for another two weeks, while my parents were taking care of my grandmothers during the COVID pandemic. In the blink of an eye, I went from being a woman capable of anything to being incapable of the most basic tasks. I was so exhausted I didn't have the energy to feel shame in asking for help.

It slowly got better. There were some days when I felt fairly good, but there were many more when I lay on the floor in a messy apartment and didn't have the strength to get up. Once a week Kwjet had to come home from work because taking care of the baby was beyond my capabilities at that moment. My whole body hurt, every movement cost me so much strength. Neither Western nor Eastern medicine found the cause, nor a solution. I tried various diets, herbs, and vitamins. I underwent countless examinations.

On top of everything, I had diastasis, a separation of the abdominal muscles. I did special therapeutic exercises every day. But for the first nine months they yielded no results, except for some relief in my back pain. Amid the love for my son, Kwjet, family, and friends who tried to support us, I often felt powerlessness, anger, and sadness. I am a person of change. When I have a problem, I solve it. But gradually I realized I couldn't pin my hopes on the day when I would feel better. That, in doing so, I would be depriving myself of all the good that could happen on the days when I felt bad. I've experienced it so many times already. Joy doesn't wait at the end of the road; it rolls throughout its length. You just need to notice it. The only sensible thing is to accept what is now. But, damn, how do you do that? There were moments when I could see the beauty of the world, even in my helplessness. And then there were moments when self-pity was accompanied by anger at myself. That I was wallowing in my own mess. I may have been exhausted, but I have a healthy child with a big smile on his face, a husband who loves me, and so much support from all sides.

I desperately wanted to pull myself together, at least in my spirit if not physically. It didn't happen instantly. It was a

Becoming a mom. Photo by Pavlína Martin.

Returning to highlining. Photo by Dan Černoch.

process and continues to be so. Acceptance requires the same courage and perseverance as setting and achieving a goal. It just all happens beneath the surface. Invisibly. When I find that point of release where everything is okay, even my exhaustion, I feel at ease, and it feels like it will last a lifetime. Sometimes it lasts for a few hours. Sometimes even a few days, occasionally even weeks. It's like being on the highline. When I sink into the flow, it feels like it will never end. Yet, in the next moment, I find myself once again struggling to regain balance.

In the second year after giving birth, I didn't feel such profound fatigue anymore, but my immunity and regenerative ability seemed to be impaired. I caught anything that flew around, and it took me a month to recover from such benign illnesses as the common cold. Altogether, I was sick for five months of the year. I continued to search for the causes and solutions to my weakness. Regular visits to the doctor, physiotherapist, psychotherapist, and healers. I think my condition didn't have a single cause; it was many small causes combined. None of them could have led to this by itself. And similarly complex will be the solution. Many small changes, assistance, and support will hopefully come together at some point.

In the third year, I managed to heal my diastasis, and for the first time I began to feel my energy coming back from somewhere deep within. Then I was sick again for several months. But for the first time since getting pregnant, I could again highline without the fear of falling. I have returned to the lines quite weak and fragile. But the lines don't care. Their calm vibrations are here for everyone. I know I can't rush my body. That, on the lines and in life, I must take slow steps and stop whenever I feel the need to rest. Maybe I'll never be as physically strong as before. But I don't regret it. I know I gave the best of myself. That I used every opportunity to the last drop. I wouldn't have spent my youth any better. And I intend to experience middle age the same way. Boldly, fully, offering the world the best I have inside of me and letting myself be surprised by the best it has for me. If my life followed the dreams I had in my 20s, I would have missed a lot. Reality has far exceeded my imagination.

I'm still drawn to the heights. Because of everything. The movement. The people. Even the moments when walking is born from fear and trembling steps. When I encounter the landscape in my human smallness and she breathes on me with her eternity. She embraces me with an invisible force and remains in me as a gentle calmness.

CHAPTER 17

One-Fall Sender: Learning from the Fear of Success

By Denisa Krásná

Alpine Highlines

When my friend Lukáš mentioned he wanted to rig an alpine highline on the famous Tre Cime di Lavadero in the Italian Dolomites, my heart started racing. "Is there any chance Peňa and I could quite possibly join you?" I asked him cautiously, and the few seconds I waited for an answer felt like an eternity.

Highlining captivated me when I first heard Danny Menšík (one of the most recognized highlining pioneers) talk about his alpine highline projects at an outdoor festival in my hometown. With a sparkle in his eyes, he was describing and showing us pictures of highlines that, like threads, connected high towers of the Italian Dolomites, French Alps, and Slovakian High Tatras. I'd never seen anything so aesthetic, so close to my idea of perfect artwork I had no idea existed. I left the festival soon after Danny's talk, as I could no longer focus. When I came home, I watched all the highline videos I could find, especially the ones from the mountains.

At that point, I had no idea that one day I would become a highliner myself – as someone who had practiced sports all my life, knowing how much effort and training most activities necessitate, I simply assumed these people had been doing it since their childhood and it was too late for me to even dream about dancing on the line like them. Regardless, I was mesmerized by the moving images I was seeing and instantly became what I call a highline aficionado – someone who doesn't practice highlining but appreciates it for its artful aesthetics. Two years later, when I was taking my first steps on a slackline, those images of alpine highlines were my secret fuel. I was already a climber and an avid hiker before I took up slacklining, so I dreamed about rigging and walking an alpine highline one day.

But when Lukáš mentioned his plans to me, I was still in the very

Highlining at Taft Point in Yosemite National Park. Photo by Alena Rainsberry.

On my first alpine highline in the Italian Dolomites. Photo by Jarda Adam.

beginnings of my highlining journey. Wasn't it too audacious to even ask if I could join him? Maybe. But Lukáš said yes and agreed that my climbing and highlining buddy Peňa and I could join the already quite numerous team. But there was a catch. Lukáš only had one free weekend so the weather had to be good. I forced myself not to watch the forecast every hour. It was raining a lot in the Dolomites that week, and I was coming to terms with the fact I would probably have to wait a little longer for my first alpine highline. "The weather looks good for Saturday! Let's get ready and leave tomorrow," said Lukáš after checking several weather apps. From that point on, I could no longer curb my excitement. And when we were distributing the gear in the parking lot the evening before our rig, it seemed like nothing could stop us anymore. But just one hour later, the sound of thunder dispelled this illusion.

"Are you sure neither of you want to sleep in the car instead of me?" shouted Halfi into the man-made cave/tunnel Italian soldiers had dug during the First World War that we were using as a shelter for the night. We thanked Halfi for the offer but stayed in the tunnel. As the thunderstorm intensified, we moved a little bit deeper and I started to worry we'd have to abort our highline mission the next day because the rock would be too wet to climb on.

We got up at four in the morning and ate breakfast in the fog that had engulfed the valley after the overnight rain. Luckily, the forecast looked favorable, so we decided to set off on our adventure. We chose the normal route to climb Cima Piccola as the fastest way to get to the top, loaded with highline gear. We free soloed the first four pitches, which saved us a lot of time, and then quickly free climbed to the top of the 1,148-foot (350-m) route. We reached the highline anchors around nine o'clock in the morning and, still in a thick fog, we rigged the 53-meter (174-foot) highline called Elysium. It had been exactly ten years since Reinhard Kleindl and the late local highliner, Armin Holzer, rigged it there for the very first time.

We could still barely see the other end of the line when it was time to walk. The atmosphere was unique in the thick fog, but walking the line was hard. Lucky for me, the fog started to clear just as I was sitting on the line, preparing for my first steps on the dream alpine highline. I was not afraid of the deep abyss below me, and, to my surprise, I was not afraid of failure either. Free of any pressure, I stood up and took my first steps 984 feet (300 m) above the ground, on the top of one of the most beautiful rock towers in the world. I just wanted to enjoy the line, and I was succeeding. On my second attempt, I crossed it with only one fall, which was a great personal success for me at that time, only four months after I had stood on my first highline ever.

That first alpine highline was just as magical as I had imagined. Kačka, another Czech female highliner, was also on the team. That very day, she and I started planning another alpine highline – this time in the Slovakian High Tatras. We rigged it one month later in a group of four – two men and two women highliners. It was yet another beautiful weekend that marked the end of my first highline season. I continued training hard over the winter in order to be ready for more adventures in the mountains. I set my heart and focus on alpine highlines.

Risk and Fear Management

My second highline season was just starting when, on a warm spring day, I just finished an exhausting highline rig in an abandoned quarry close to the place where I grew up. I wasn't in the right headspace that day. Overwhelmed with work responsibilities and many exciting highline projects to organize, I was irritable and quite neurotic. Slacklining usually helps me to calm down and slow down. But I was leading a highline rig that day, assisted only by two newbies for whom I was responsible. There was nobody else who could check the anchors, so I made sure my backup system was not only highly efficient but also a bit excessive that day – "rather safe than sorry" was my mantra. When I finally finished the last touches, it was already quite late so, without taking a break, I went on the line.

I took out my Rollex and slid down to the place where it was safe to stand up – far enough from the rock so I couldn't hit my head if I took the leash fall. When I was in a sitting position on the line, I removed the Rollex and prepared to stand up. I tried to consciously focus on my breathing to calm down after the tiring rig. As a routine, I looked down to check my figure-eight knot before standing up. *Wait, what? Where's my knot? Where's the leash?!* Surprisingly, I was not paralyzed by fear but remained perfectly calm upon the realization I had forgotten to tie in. I was just sitting there, on a one-inch-wide (2.5-cm) piece of webbing, above a rocky abyss, without any protection whatsoever. That day I was grateful for Mia Noblet's advice to always check the knot before standing up. It saved my life.

Highlining in my home country, the Czech Republic.
Photo by @krasyjiznichcech.

I don't know if it was my neurosis that day that caused this major mistake that could have easily been fatal. Forgetting to tie in is the number one cause of death in highlining, but I never understood how it was possible for any highliner to go on the line without the leash (unless it was on purpose, to practice free soloing). I could have been the next victim of this stupid and completely avoidable mistake. Had my relationship to risk so significantly altered over the past year?

I have never felt that fear other highliners describe. That fear that overwhelms most highliners when they sit on the line and imagine standing up. It's completely natural to be scared, the human brain is not conditioned to accept a situation in which we are so close to flying like birds. Many highliners take weeks, others take months, and some take years to adjust to this new sensation. Most give up before they do. My lack of fear facilitated my quick initial progress, as I could spend hours on the line, taking one fall after another.

My friends maintain I must be a psychopath to not be scared. I attribute my boldness to rationality. It's not that I'm not afraid of anything – I am. Very much so. When there's an objective risk of getting hurt, I panic. I freeze on a climb when it's clear I'm too far above the last piece of (good) protection and any misstep could end up in a bad fall. And I'm too scared to lead on the infamously unprotected Czech sandstone. It doesn't matter that the climb is far below my abilities – I still can't chase away the thought I could slip, even on easy terrain. But in highlining, when I trust the rigging team and the gear, there are objectively very few risks. I just need to tie in.

Fear of Success

While I may excel at fear management, I fail at self-confidence. In fact, one of my buddies started calling me a "one-fall sender." He even came up with an abbreviation for my style of highlining – "DS," which stands for "Denisa Send," i.e., crossing a highline with one fall. It doesn't matter if the line is 50 meters (165 feet) long or 140 meters (460 feet) long – I struggle to avoid the one low-confidence fall, especially when I'm trying for a new personal record.

My low self-esteem probably stems from my involvement in competitive sports in my childhood through to my adolescent years. I played badminton starting when I was about 7 years old and, due to my quick initial progress, I was soon among the best 30 domestic players in my category. But there was a bitter price to pay for being in the top group. The tournament draw was always the same – me against the best player, who ended up winning many championships in a row and had a splendid career. If she missed a tournament, I played the second-best player. I had to motivate myself by setting achievable goals – "let's try to score three points this time." I learned how to lose, but I forgot how to win.

When I started walking in the sky (during the COVID-19 pandemic in 2021), there were only a handful of women highliners in my country. Anna Hanuš Kuchařová paved the way for Czech women slackliners, with Tereza Panochová soon following in her steps. Both Anna and Tereza were part of the first wave of slackliners and experienced firsthand the quick evolution

Sunset sessions at Trosky Castle in the Czech Republic. Photo by Jiří Krásný.

of the sport. When I entered the world of slacklining, both of these women provided a great deal of inspiration for my own journey, even before I got to know them personally. But Tereza had moved to France, and Anna had recently become a mom, so there was an urgent need for more female representation in the sport. Fortunately, parks and slackline gatherings have become increasingly frequented by women slackliners, and while there were some eager women attempting to get into highlining, they eventually prioritized longlining for various reasons, from time constraints to physical or mental barriers.

But soon after my highline debut I overheard rumors about two women who were becoming more and more confident on highlines: Kačka and Silva. When I first met Kačka, I was learning how to take my first steps on the highline, while Kačka had just sent a 55-meter (180-foot) highline that marked an important moment for Czech highlining, which hadn't seen much progress among women in years. Finally, there was a new promising woman in the community. While female highliner Mia Noblet held the world record at the time, at nearly two kilometers (1.2 miles), the Czech female record was just above 100 meters (328 feet). Why such a great difference? Lack of representation and role models is my guess.

Meeting Kačka motivated me to work hard toward my goals. She showed me it was possible for a woman to highline just as well as men, and progress quickly if one is determined. And since Kačka was also relatively new to the sport, she was able to relate to my initial struggles and give me helpful advice and encouragement. Silva, the second up-and-coming female highliner, was just as inspirational. Her journey is different from mine: slacklining for several years, she became a very skilled and confident slackliner before taking up highlining. Despite initial mental barriers, Silva gradually overcame her fears and her persistence paid off. Free from the worries that had stood in her way, Silva flew like a bird on a 172-meter (564-foot) highline from the moment she stepped on it to its other end. Silva sent a very hard highline in September 2022, and thus established the new Czech female highline record.

Meanwhile, I was pushing my own highlining limits, unaware of Silva's own accomplishment. Our personal successes couldn't have been more aligned. On the same day, and at roughly the same time, I crossed a 150-meter (492-foot) highline "DS" style. This happened one and a half years after I'd embarked on this turbulent but exciting flight. Despite it being a great personal success, I felt like I had failed. "You really fucked that one up, you know that, right? Could have been a new female record," commented my highline buddy, but with warm empathy in his voice. He knew all about my mental struggles, and I was grateful for his attempts to drive me to the performance we both knew I was capable of. When I later found out about Silva's send, I was relieved and happy but also amused and moved by our alignment. Who knows? Perhaps we somehow motivated and supported each other as we both walked in the sky, seemingly unaware of the other one. While I was still grateful for my fast initial progress, I was slowly getting irritated with my one-fall crosses. Little did I know my fear of success was one day going to define my whole highlining experience.

But not just yet.

Connection

My second highlining season was just starting and, despite my near-sends, my expectations were still fairly low. I wasn't chasing any records. I was just focused on improving my style, finding beautiful spots, and having fun. After the pandemic restrictions lifted, I traveled to Vancouver, British Columbia, for a postponed research stay at the University of British Columbia. I chose this province in Canada for my research before I started highlining, so it was just a lucky coincidence my work destination turned out to be one of the biggest highlining hubs in the world! I couldn't wait to meet the local community and dreamed of highlining on the Stawamus Chief, near Squamish, British Columbia.

I settled into a productive routine in my first two weeks in Vancouver. I was working on an academic article for most of the day, with only short interruptions for quick stretching, jogging, or slackline sessions. Simultaneously navigating the two worlds of academia and outdoor adventure can be frustrating at times, but generally the two complement each other in unexpected ways. I strongly believe balance is the core ingredient in life, and while slacklining *literally* brings in balance, outdoor sports in general balance the time one spends working. Academia facilitates my access to the outdoors, and my outdoor activities boost my academic performance – it's a win-win.

Tosha became my first and best friend in Vancouver. A mutual friend from Oregon whom I never met in person introduced us. I matched him on a vegan dating app and he knew Tosha from a vegan festival she organized. Despite not knowing any of us very well, he rightly assumed we might get along, not only because of our passion for animals and veganism but also because we were both enthusiastic slackers. He couldn't have been more right.

Tosha and I first met in a park on a warm sunny day that begged for a slackline session. We stayed outside until sunset, the first of many we ended up watching together. That evening marked the beginning of a beautiful friendship, as well as the start of an approaching highline season in the Pacific Northwest. The timing was perfect. I was almost done with my article and eager to incorporate more balance into my Canadian life. Tosha was just as stoked to highline more regularly, and so we started rigging together several times per week. Our training spot was just a few minutes' drive from our houses (conveniently, Tosha lived just two blocks away from me).

The 70-meter (230-foot) highline was hidden in a lush rainforest, full of ferns and moss, where only majestic bald eagles occasionally interrupted our sessions. We trained hard and motivated each other to perform better. Sometimes we focused merely on highlining and quietly waited for our turn in the shade of majestic tall old-growth trees. Other times, we split our attention between highlining and arts and crafts, painting and knitting. And every time we shared some delicious vegan food.

As I was getting ready for one of our regular highline sessions in the rainforest, Tosha messaged me: "Hey, I know we already have plans, but would you prefer to go highlining to the Lighthouse today?" She explained there was a chance to spot the Northern Lights that night. Aurora in Vancouver?! Of course, I was in! But not just for the Northern Lights – I'd wanted to visit this famous lighthouse spot for a while. It was here where Tosha first used the term "girl power rig" to refer to our projects. This highline was slightly more challenging to rig than our training line in the rainforest, as we had to get the tag line across the ocean without a drone and past several trees and bushes on a rather steep cliffside. Regardless, we overcame all obstacles and prepared the line for walking in just over an hour. I was excited to walk above the ocean, listening to its soothing sound while watching the sunset.

Without any expectations, I started walking and felt absolutely no resistance from the line. It felt almost like walking on the ground. In no time I was approaching the other end. The pervasive thought that I couldn't possibly succeed on my first try entered my mind, but I managed to chase it away and do a few last nervous steps before I sat down. I turned around and saw Tosha jumping up and down with a camera: "Wohoo, ONSIGHT, yeeeah!" I had just interrupted my one-fall streak and onsighted a highline for the first time. For the time being, this onsight was a great confidence boost. It showed me it was possible to control my mind.

We didn't see the Northern Lights, but the night was still magical. Surrounded by new human and animal friends, with two beautiful highline bridges across the ocean, I didn't need anything else. Tosha showed me more highline spots in the next few weeks. We often drove to Squamish and spent the whole day or the whole weekend on the nearby lines, connected to our beautiful surroundings. Some highliners recall experiences from the line that involve interspecies interactions, be it with beetles or spiders that also use the line as a bridge, or with birds that want to become part of the playful act. Such encounters are intensified by the highliners' complete presence and heightened attention. Highliners, especially when walking really long lines, are also more aware of sounds that surround them, such as chirping birds, buzzing bees, or running water in a nearby stream. These aural experiences also deepen the highliners' connection with nature, even if merely subconsciously.

One of my most profound experiences of interspecies connection and interaction happened on one of the midlines Tosha showed me, in a place called Seal Cove, on the Traditional Territory of the Squamish Nation. As we were spending the whole day on and around the line, we got to appreciate the spectacular surroundings whose local, other-than-human inhabitants got used to our presence. Local sea lions and seals became especially interested in the midline that was rigged above the ocean and over time engaged in a playful game with me as I was walking and bouncing on the line while they were interacting with me from below, seemingly having as much fun as I did. The most magical moment came when I spotted a whale not too far from me. While this was not my first (nor second or third) encounter with a whale, catching a glimpse of this magnificent animal directly from the highline was somehow more transformative and meaningful.

My departure was fast approaching and I didn't want to leave without rigging a highline on the iconic Stawamus Chief. Squamish wouldn't be the same place without the Chief, which overlooks the valley and the ever-growing city from a height of 2,303 feet

Highlining above Seal Cove, in the Traditional Territory of the Squamish Nation. Photo by Megan Hansen.

(702 m). Called Siám' Smánit by the local Indigenous Peoples, the Chief is one of the largest granite monoliths in North America and its walls attract climbers from all over the world. In the end, we were hiking up the Chief in a large group. Another highliner and a group of aerial silkers decided to rig the same highline as us that very day: "The more people, the better slacklife!"

We decided to rig a 70-meter (229-foot) highline called Heaven, one of the most exposed lines on the Chief. As I was looking into the 984-foot-deep (300-m) void below me, I checked the knot on my harness at least four times before I stood up. But I wasn't afraid. I only felt a pleasant adrenaline rush, which noticeably quickened my breathing after the first few steps – I was unable to calm it down and I fell. I felt both relief and great joy. The exposure was surreal and my brain was in a kind of weird euphoria because it didn't know how to deal with the space. It was one of my most beautiful walks until then. The walk also marked one year since I stood on my first highline. I can't imagine a better-celebrated anniversary. I also felt a strong connection with every single person with whom I spent the day. And I can't even remember most of their names! That's what slacklife is all about. The connections we make. With people, with other animals, with the environment that surrounds us, and with ourselves. I left Canada with great inner peace. I no longer cared if I was a one-fall sender. Not then and not for the rest of my second season. But that was about to change. One year later, when I came back to North America, I was living a very different highline story.

Second Trip to the Dolomites

After my first alpine highline the previous year, I decided to plan my very own trip to the Dolomites. It was getting cold and dark, but September was still a good month to go and finish the season on a high note. We ended up going in a small group of four: me, Peňa, our good friend Vojta, and Pavel, a badass highliner and excellent climber who, on the brink of 60, brought important wisdom to the team. I had ambitious plans for this ten-day trip, to put it mildly. I chose the most aesthetic highlines up to 100 meters (328 feet) that I knew of. The rest of the team was happy to follow my directions and let me organize the whole trip. We had rigged three highlines in three different locations, climbed five rock towers to get to the anchors, got soaked while

Highlining on the Stawamus Chief in Squamish, British Columbia. Photo by Alena Rainsberry.

rigging when a strong rainstorm came, and were already feeling pretty exhausted, both physically and mentally, when we set out for our final, most ambitious highline rig. We decided to repeat an alpine highline that our friends, led by Lukáš, had established about two years before.

"Bear in mind that Dolomites are just a big pile of loose rocks." The words of my friend's parents resonated in my mind as Peňa and I faced one rock avalanche after another while climbing on a rarely climbed mountain. In contrast to many of our previous climbs in high mountains, we didn't get lost this time. But this little victory was no consolation in the face of the many other challenges we encountered. Except for the last two pitches, we free soloed the whole tower and had to be extra careful about what we stepped on or held on to. I was starting to get really nervous when a huge boulder fell off the rock right next to me, but we kept scrambling up a gully that felt particularly hostile. Nearing the final few pitches, Peňa said out loud what had been on both of our minds for the past two hours: "Any idea how we're going to get back down?"

The last straw was a sketchy unprotected traverse. When we finally reached the highline anchors after the six-hour-long approach, we had little mental strength left. Rigging a highline – the reason we were there – was the last thing on our minds then. But Pavel and Vojta had been waiting for us on the opposite tower for hours now, full of energy and enthusiasm to rig. Well, kind of. Pavel was fairly tired from the previous days, and Vojta was chilling in the sun after a short, uneventful climb to the top of a regularly climbed tower. Nevertheless, they were both ready to finish what we had started. Peňa and I, on the other hand/side, were discussing our options.

"I think we should maybe just try and get down right away. It's going to be dark in four hours. It'd be really foolish to rig right now." Normally, I'd try to persuade Peňa to rig. Wind, fog, snow, exhaustion...nothing ever seemed like an obstacle we couldn't overcome. But I truly couldn't imagine our descent this time, as it was clear we wouldn't be able to rappel the whole way through the crumbly terrain. We called Vojta and explained the situation to him. Even though we were separated by several hundred feet of space, I could see the disappointment in his movements and hear it in his voice. He didn't push us but suggested a very quick session – we'd each get one try, 10–15 minutes on the line. And Pavel was feeling tired, so he'd just help us with the rigging.

The plan sounded good to me, but Peňa was looking for an assurance that we were not making a terrible mistake. We texted a friend who helped to establish this line, asking him for advice on how to get down. His response only exacerbated our anxiety: "Honestly, a helicopter would be your best bet." *Great, just what we thought.* "We can't lose any more time if we're doing this," retorted Peňa as I started unpacking the anchor ropes. It was our most efficient rig until then. We were fast, precise, and we didn't even bicker during the process. We rigged two lines that day, the other one being a signal line with big orange windbags, those that are used at airports or near highways. The line we were rigging was in an airspace that normally registers heavy helicopter traffic. We notified local services and fortunately didn't see a single helicopter that day. At least one less worry to occupy our minds.

Both lines were rigged in just over half an hour, which was quite possibly our record time. The anchor Peňa and I built was also among the best ones either of us had ever made. Everything went smoothly and I hoped it was a sign we were going to be fine. Vojta crossed the line first and sent it on the way back. He said he was too afraid to fall so he didn't. It's incredible how differently our minds work. Peňa was pretty vocal on the line, so I assumed he had to fight because it was hard. As it turned out, he was also just too scared to fall – the chasm underneath was incomprehensibly deep and terrifying.

When it was my turn, I realized I didn't care at all about the highline. The only thing on my mind was the descent. I was trying to mentally prepare for the worst in order to be able to fully concentrate and minimize not only the risks but also my emotional responses that would only make the descent more dangerous. I was sitting on a beautiful highline, surrounded by magnificent mountains, seeing distant alpine meadows and valleys in all directions, but I wasn't really present. "I'll just take two or three falls and will go back. Be ready to derig right away!" I shouted at Peňa and Vojta.

I was still buried in my thoughts when I stood up and took a few steps. I kept walking and soon I found my way to the present moment. I was walking with ease and couldn't comprehend it. *How come it's suddenly so effortless?* The first fall didn't come until I was in the middle and, if I had fought harder, I probably could have avoided it. But I didn't feel like it. I loved the feeling of ease; I didn't want to fight that day. Not on the line, I had to save the energy for later. I stood up again and flew to the other end where I saw sparks of joy in Pavel's eyes while he was capturing my walk on his camera. "Are you sure you don't want to go?" I would have given up my time on the line so he could try it too. But Pavel was sharing the moment with us in a different manner that day. Connected to his surroundings and observing the art he had co-created, he was just as much part of the whole experience as the rest of us were. The real accomplishment was the creation of this temporary artwork anyway.

I only took a short break at the other end before I stood up to walk back. I was still prepared to quickly "rollex" back to the anchor after two more falls. But I only fell one more time and got back within 15 minutes, which felt much longer because I

Back to the Dolomites. Photo by Vojtěch Fejta.

cherished every second of it as soon as I became fully present. Under the stress and fear for my life, I was able to relax and truly enjoy the experience more than any other time before. The highline also helped me to de-stress and prepare for the grueling descent. It took us about two hours to get down and out of the most dangerous zone before it got dark. We rappelled as much as possible and survived a near miss of a large boulder that got loose above me when the rope hit it. But we only left behind two pieces of our own gear that will hopefully help whoever decides to climb this tower in the future. That evening, when we reunited with Vojta and Pavel, we celebrated life. We also celebrated the connection among us, and our connection with the environment we had felt intensely in the past week. The successful highline project was just icing on the cake. But very nice, indeed.

Discovering Flow

When I came back home and the adrenaline and enthusiasm slowly wore off, I felt a bit lost. The trip was amazing overall, but I was tired, both physically and mentally. I knew I needed a break from the stress of planning and rigging alpine highlines, but I also craved that feeling of full concentration and happiness I had experienced above the mountaintops. Was I becoming an adrenaline junkie? Confused and slightly depressed, I jumped at the opportunity to join a team that set out to rig a 250-meter (820-foot) highline amid autumnal nature in Súľov, Slovakia. I left for the long weekend hoping to get some distraction from my intrusive thoughts. What I experienced, however, was beyond my wildest dreams. I came back home with a newfound energy and zest for highlining.

We started as a small team of five, which meant carrying fairly heavy backpacks on a steep uphill trail for about an hour. We scouted and built the anchors in the evening and prepared the tagline for the next day. We were finishing the last touches in the dark, carefully dancing on the rock edges, enjoying the serene night scene, when we heard an excited scream from the other side. Our phone rang: "Did you guys see that? There was a huge meteor falling above you!" We thought they were exaggerating the size, but the next day the media was full of articles about a large meteor falling in Slovakia.

The next morning, the valley was shrouded in beautiful fog, giving it a wholly new appearance. I was getting more and more excited to see how our line would temporarily alter the landscape in a nonintrusive way. And I was even more curious to see the valley from the bird's perspective. Standa, our leader and the visionary of this project, kept encouraging me to think big. He was convinced I could cross the line from anchor to anchor with minimum falls. I won't lie. Being naturally ambitious, I was already thinking about how beautiful it would be to step on the rock tower on the other side after having walked over the valley on a 0.07-inch-wide (1.9-mm) bridge.

But when I was sitting on the extra-thin, high-tech, ultra-light Dyneemite webbing for the first time, looking into the distance, the opposite anchor suddenly looked miles away. *I can never walk all this way...and back!* I made a promise to myself that I'd turn around as soon as I felt tired. I stood up and took the first step. The line was perfectly calm. I took a few more steps and suddenly I felt like I was flying. My first fall came after a fairly long distance and I started believing I could walk all the way to the other side. But by the time I was about two-thirds of the way across, I was getting increasingly thirsty in the still-strong autumnal sun. Intrusive thoughts interrupted my peaceful walk as they sent anxious vibes into the line, which responded accordingly. I slowed down and was afraid of taking any abrupt steps. Suddenly, the anchor was not getting closer. I realized I either had to walk steadily again or turn around. I refused to give up without even trying, so I took a deep breath and let go. I reached the anchor soon and took a big sip of the water we had stashed there while rigging. After a short break, I walked back. It wasn't easy, as I was starting to feel tired, both physically and mentally, but I was still enjoying every step.

That weekend, I felt like I discovered a whole new universe. I'd never walked so effortlessly on a line before. Don't get me wrong. I like the challenge of hard lines; it's fun in a different way. But when I'm walking a long distance, I love that I can save a small portion of my focus for the gorgeous surroundings. And not having to fight for every step also means entering the flow state more easily. In Slovakia, I experienced it for the first time. And I was hooked.

But that weekend was also significant because Peňa and I decided to plan a big highlining and rock climbing trip to North America. We would leave in January, in about three months. About time to start looking for a van!

American Highlife Blues

Our trip started in Hawai'i in January, where I went for a research trip. Peňa joined me one month later, and we rigged our first highline, which we named Paka'a. In Hawaiian mythology, Paka'a is the god of the wind. To say that it was windy that day is an understatement. But, compared to the gusts of previous days, we were in luck. We found the spot by accident on a hike. We weren't even looking for highline spots. Hawai'i was just way too windy to rig at that time a year (the big wave surfing tournament, the Eddie Aikau Big Wave Invitational, was held at Waimea Bay just a few days before). Still, this perfect little valley with a view of O'ahu's highest peak was too tempting to pass up. And so we came back and rigged the 170-meter (557-foot) beauty. In order to walk, I had to force myself to be patient. Really patient. I was getting swept off even just sitting on the line, so I almost gave up the idea of a walk. I still enjoyed the view of, and from, the line, so I didn't regret rigging it. As I was holding on to the line tightly, I soon noticed the gusts were coming in waves. I waited for the perfect moment of relative calmness and walked. I crossed the line there and back, even though I sometimes had to sit down and be patient again. That day, I really connected with the wind, eventually learning how to walk with it.

Even though I didn't realize it at the time, 170 meters (557 feet) was a length that defined the trip and my most significant (highline) development. In contrast to Paka'a, in popularity but not in length, our next highline was quite likely one of the most often walked in the world: the highline in the famous Fruit Bowl in the Moab desert. We rigged it on my birthday and highlined over the next two days. Maybe it was the Fruit Bowl energy lingering from all the slackliners who had walked here before me that motivated me to my best results ever. I felt like I made a significant breakthrough, crossing the line multiple times, with only two to four falls each try. And I had lots of fun while I was flowing in the space, thinking of Faith Dickey and other women highliners who had left their marks in Moab. I was recharged and positively motivated to become a "marathon highliner." Ever since that line in Slovakia, I yearned to walk longer and longer distances.

Over the next three months, we dedicated most of our time to rock climbing, but we also rigged shorter, but very scenic, highlines in most places we climbed. I was highlining with ease, onsighting two highlines in Sedona, Arizona (60 m/196 feet and

30 m/98 feet), crossing two dreamy highlines in Zion (90 m/295 feet and 150 m/492 feet), and sending my first 100-meter (328-foot) highline in Joshua Tree, rigged between the Cyclops Rock tower and the Peewee tower, for all the tourists to watch. It was here I realized I still hadn't overcome my fear of success. The line was perfect for me. I flew on it as if nothing could stop me, not even the bee chasing me all the way to the other side. But then I felt it again. That intrusive thought/doubt that spreads through my whole body like a spasm and doesn't leave until I'm hanging below the line. What finally helped me overcome the pressure was visualizing an even more fear/excitement-inducing goal of mine. I was thinking of climbing El Capitan in Yosemite National Park, and that got me to the anchor.

That evening, I wrote in my highline diary: "It felt easy from my very first try but I still kept falling for no good reason a few meters from the end. Once I finally sent it, I didn't fall again and sent the line multiple times, easy as that." That day, I had the luxury of time and could thus afford several attempts. But I knew I wouldn't always have that luxury. Plus, the longer the lines, the fewer the number of attempts I'd have in me. So, while I was celebrating my personal success, I still had my many one-fall sends lurking over me, like the bee who chased me all the way back to the main anchor and made me run into a dark cave where I free solo down-climbed to hide. But there's no hiding from bees or from our fears. Eventually, I had to come out of the cave and surrender. The bee didn't leave, but she didn't sting me either. As I accepted her presence, we became friends. Maybe she was there to teach me a lesson. Don't fight it, but surrender, accept, and connect.

We spent the next month adventuring in Yosemite in a climbing and slacklining community full of stoke and life. There's no place on Earth more historically and spiritually meaningful for a slackliner than Yosemite, the birthplace of this sport. We rigged four beautiful lines, from 40 meters (131 feet) to 270 meters (886 feet) in length. Like proper pilgrims, we set our hearts on rigging the famous Lost Arrow Spire. The fact that Scott Balcom decided to rig the very first highline right here, in 1985, is beyond any highliner's understanding. This place is so exposed and windy that it still represents a true physical and mental challenge for any experienced highliner. The rigging itself is very technical and includes climbing, abseiling, and creating anchors in very uncomfortable vertical positions more than a thousand meters above the ground. The long and steep approach itself was no walk in the park either, especially not this year, when Yosemite registered the most snowfall in history, which was just melting and turning the meadows of the valley into lakes. On our way back in the middle of the night, we waded ankle-deep in water that had flooded the steep trail while getting soaked from all the rain coming from the roaring Yosemite Falls. All in all, Yosemite provided me with a break from constantly thinking about pushing my highlining limits. I was appreciating other, in many ways more meaningful, aspects of the sport. From getting better at rigging more sophisticated anchors to deepening connection with this special place and all the wonderful people in it.

It was hard to leave Yosemite Valley. As our friend and big wall climber Ryan Sheridan says, "It sucks you in like a black hole and doesn't let you go." He's lived in Yosemite for almost a decade now. We were slowly heading to Canada, but not before visiting Cheryll aka Rae Raptor. In the depths of the Nevada desert, we rigged a 175-meter (574-foot) highline Cheryll established with her husband. It was a fun day with the Nevada crew, and I had no ambitions whatsoever. There was a storm coming later in the afternoon, so I just planned to enjoy my one walk and take drone videos of others. All that changed, however, when I walked past the midpoint without falling. I remembered the Joshua Tree bee and was determined to fight my fear of success. I just knew I had it in me to send this line. And then I fell. Not far from the anchor. I tried to stay positive and use my anger as fuel. I still had the walk back. I wasn't feeling tired at all and a small breeze was providing the best possible conditions for highlining. Knowing there was nothing to stop me except for my own mind only exacerbated my frustration as I fell, about two-thirds in again.

That day, Cheryll became my heroine. This amazing woman gave up her session just to give me another chance at sending. And not just that. She pretended to go for her session only to rollex the full length of the line there and back to untwist it for me and thus increase my chances of sending it. "It's my favorite workout!" shouted Cheryll back at me when I protested and tried to make her come back. "She's crazy...and determined like you," retorted Peňa, who maintains Cheryll and I are the same person in two different bodies. I take that as a huge compliment. I didn't send, but I was closer than any other time because I heard Cheryll's encouraging words. She walked with me below the line as far as I could hear her and kept telling me to keep going. When I fell, very close to the anchor, Cheryll started to clap and shouted excitedly, "That was an excellent attempt! You got much farther than the last time!" She was right. Yet I felt broken.

I never imagined I'd become obsessed with sending. But at this point sending became personal – it surpassed highlining. It mattered to me because I wanted to win the internal battle in my brain. I realized how much I hated not being in control of my own mind. I realized I wanted to learn how to be calm and how to keep my thoughts in check. After witnessing how my mind was throwing me off the line that day, Hugo, a visiting highliner from Perú, wisely stated, "I think you should talk to someone." Many people around me naturally told me to celebrate my one-fall crosses as great successes. In their view, I was "too ambitious" and "not humble enough," wanting to send these lines after only two years of highlining. But this went beyond comparing my journey to those of others. I just wanted to accomplish what I knew I was capable of. But, more importantly, highlining made my inner anxieties visible and it was a catalyst to start addressing them.

After that day in Nevada, I felt very vulnerable. I finally admitted to myself that my falls were rooted somewhere else, but I didn't have a clue how to uncover these roots, let alone how to fix them. While I knew I needed to talk to a therapist about my lifelong anxiety, I also believed highlining could provide a tool for curbing it. If I succeeded in learning how to control my mind on a highline, maybe I would learn how to relax my mind in other situations too. Maybe highlining could be a fun means to a more important end. Could it even be a remedy for my anxiety? I liked that thought. Peňa showed his support by buying me a self-help book by Jen Sincero titled *You Are a Badass: How to Stop Doubting Your Greatness and Start Living an Awesome Life*. He didn't know how else to help because he truly didn't understand my struggles. Self-doubt is not something he experiences, certainly not on the line. Challenges motivate him to even greater performances, and his mantra – "Come on, you're Peňa" – makes him an excellent sender. And so I turned to Cheryll, who became my mental coach with whom I consulted on all the different mental techniques I could try on the line.

But I had to wait longer than I thought before I could test them all on my next send attempt. Not long after Nevada, we rigged a 215-meter (705-foot) beauty leading from Smith Rock's Monkey Face in Oregon, but our last highline in the States was even windier than our first one in Hawai'i. It was also a very challenging rig and derig for just two people, involving lots of climbing, rappelling, jumaring, and creating elaborate systems, all while getting swept by the wind. I somehow managed to make a full cross (no idea how I did that), but I refused to walk back, exhausted both physically and mentally from the wind. Peňa rollexed back from the middle, feeling dizzy after multiple falls and deciding a cross was not worth the effort. He tried again the next day with the same outcome – the wind was just too strong. Pierce, one of the local highliners, managed a beautiful cross, fighting off not only the strong wind but also peregrine falcons that decided to tandem with him as he walked! Derigging the line was a true challenge and took us six hours. The last straw was when one of our ropes got stuck and we had to come back the next day and climb the tower again in an even stronger wind. I ended up with a muscle fever that evening, with Peňa having to take care of me. Another great lesson learned in our wonderful outdoor classroom. It was time to take a rest.

Breaking Records in Canada

Fast-forward one and a half months: I was standing on a 170-meter (557-foot) highline in the Cheakamus ("Chek") Canyon, back in Squamish. My fateful length. This time I knew I had time and I intended to use it. We wanted to leave this line up for at least one week, maybe more. I'd give it my all, but I promised I wouldn't mentally punish myself for falling. And so my attempts commenced. I usually had two per day. But I preferred to think of them as sessions. George, my friend and one of the local highliners whose personal record stands at 1200 meters (3,937 feet), encouraged me by saying we must train our brain to get used to the pressure and be able to withstand it. Literally. It made sense, so I started to see my one-falls, which were closer and closer to the anchor, as progress, not failure. I remembered Cheryll's positive "Good, you got closer than last time." And so, one day, I finally reached the anchor. With the pressure off, I added a full ma'am (i.e., a send in both directions). From that day on, I sent the line regularly every day.

One morning I decided to try a blindfold session for the first time ever. I had avoided it until then because I always thought it would be a shame not to see the beautiful surroundings. I also didn't want to get disoriented and nauseous when falling into a dark space head first. But to my great surprise, I didn't fall much.

In fact, I didn't find the line much harder to walk when I couldn't use my vision to balance on the tiny piece of webbing. My other senses seemed to manage to do the job just fine, which was a very transcendental experience. While it's still hard to comprehend for me, I was somehow "seeing" my feet with my other senses. And I got into the flow state much faster. Addicted to the feeling, I crossed the full length of the line with my blindfold on with only about five falls. Most of these happened when I realized I was actually blindfolded, which I kept forgetting quite quickly after entering the flow state.

One morning one of my friends and I decided to go for a session on two parallel 235-meter (770-foot) highlines the community kept up for most of the summer. What a wonderful training opportunity! I was happy and fulfilled after having sent the 170 meters (557 feet), so I gave myself a sending break. I was just having fun. But when I realized the anchor was getting closer and I still hadn't fallen, the thought of sending naturally crossed my mind. This time, however, I didn't shake. I felt the adrenaline/excitement run through my body, but it didn't paralyze me like it usually does. On the contrary, it empowered me. I didn't stop but instead channeled my inner Peňa and, like him, started trusting I could do it. Maybe it was ego that got me to the anchor, or maybe it was just the healthy self-esteem I had gained after having accomplished my long-term goal just a few days before. Or maybe it was just good energy and a positive attitude. But when I stepped on the ground, I couldn't believe it. I had also just broken the Czech female record that Kačka and Silva held at 220 meters (721 feet). Who would have thought just a week ago that I could be a record breaker? I didn't care about the new record, but it was symbolic of the journey I'd undertaken. I was ecstatic for the rest of the day.

One evening George suggested rigging an 880-meter (2,887-foot) highline that he and his buddies established last year. We joined forces, and our segments of Dyneemite, and in a team of about ten people we set out to rig a half-mile-long highline. The entire mission was jeopardized right at the beginning when a drone with fishing line barely made it over the canyon. The battery was too low, but luckily the drone emergency landed directly on the anchor rock. The rest of the long day went smoothly, and by ten in the evening the highline was rigged. The next day our week of sessioning started. The most crucial factor on such long lines is the weather. Favorable breeze gently leaning into the line from one side contributes to its stabilization, making the walk noticeably easier. On the other hand, strong gusts of wind significantly complicate the stroll.

My first session was more like a walk through hell than a journey to an altered state of consciousness. Strong gusty wind was throwing me off, and the anchor didn't seem to be getting any closer. When, for the umpteenth time, a strong gust threw me off about 300 meters (984 feet) from the end, I couldn't distinguish what was reality and what were delusions. *Is it even windy? Why do I feel like I'm floating at sea? Maybe I have heatstroke?* As if on cue, Björn, one of the local highliners, cheered me on through the walkie-talkie: "Denisa, you are killing it in the crazy wind! Good job!" His words encouraged me, and somehow I managed to fight through the last hundreds of meters. The highline was twisting like a snake, and the backup loops were extending over the main line in all directions. The next day I was incapable of doing anything. I was just sitting and staring into space, trying to understand how much my mind had played tricks on me the previous day.

Before my next session, I was nervous the entire day. I had doubts about my ability to deal with the vast open space and remain calm. Moreover, the wind had shifted, blowing smoke from nearby forest fires. The surrounding nature looked apocalyptic, mountains had disappeared and the sky had turned red. Amid all the gray smoke, our white highline sparkled, its end invisible. I was a bit afraid of inhaling smoke and losing consciousness. In a harness, I wouldn't have survived unconsciousness for long, and it would have been difficult for someone to reach me in time. However, once I decided to go for it, I pushed away the dark thoughts and focused entirely on the walk. This time the remaining distance didn't intimidate me. I concentrated only on each successive hundred-meter segment. And I was doing great! After just under two hours I reached the other end of the highline, with five falls. I didn't feel tired, and it felt as if no time had passed at all.

In the following days, I reduced the number of falls to just two and began to hope for a send. Crazy? Perhaps. But although it would have been a big leap, I felt I had a chance. The whole team supported me, and we cheered each other on. However, both our mental and physical strength were dwindling. Additionally, luck wasn't on our side regarding the conditions. It was either too smoky from the wildfires, too gusty, or too humid with no wind at all. On my best attempt I fell after half a kilometer, and at that moment I accepted I'd have to wait a while longer for a send of such a monster line. "Don't be greedy," my dad wrote to me, and my mom wisely added, "Slow down and enjoy it." She was right. I didn't enjoy this fall-free but nervous, tired, and cautious half-kilometer at all. I took a break and decided to enjoy my last session and find the flow. However, as I sat by the anchor on the last day, watching the highline being tossed to all sides by a strong gusty wind, I couldn't shake the memory of the first day. *Was it going to be hell again?*

Three times within the first hundred meters, I turned around. "Give it a try, you'll see that you might be surprised at how it turns out in the end," said George over the walkie-talkie. With a long breath in and a long breath out, I took his words to heart and started to make my way to the other side where the crew was hanging out, playing the guitar and celebrating slacklife. In the meantime, I was drowning in self-pity. The first half of my walk was the anticipated hell. I tried to walk quickly, but strong gusts unexpectedly threw me off, and I found myself hanging in the leash again and again. On the verge of mental exhaustion, I gave up and remembered George's simple advice: "Just run." I don't remember the next few hundred meters. I ran through them in a flow, feeling invincible. The wind was still blowing, but it no longer bothered me. All the hardships were worth it. I found the perfect flow.

Home Sweet Home

I woke up in my car from a dream in which I onsighted a highline I was about to session that day. *Can I onsight what would be my personal record?* I ate my breakfast and walked over to the line. It was the end of September and I was still getting used to being back home in the Czech Republic. This weekend was meant to be a welcome highline gathering for Peňa and me. The whole community rigged seven highlines, ranging from 30 meters (98 feet) to 350 meters (1,148 feet). The longest one was a Frankenline assembled from many different kinds of webbing. An experiment that failed badly, as barely anyone was able to walk it. That's why I had my heart set on the 280 meters (919 feet), rigged on the same webbing as the 880-meter (2,887-foot) line in Canada. I wanted to use the momentum and send this line now when I was well trained and the distance still seemed short in comparison to the length I had just sessioned. There was no wind that morning and the air was heavy. It was hot and humid as rain was coming later that day. But I was fresh and determined. I felt streams of sweat on my body after just a few meters. Leaving the shirt on was a bad idea. My leash got stuck on each of the three connections, so I had to take a step back to get across. Surprisingly, that didn't shake me and I stayed focused until the very last short segment, rigged on a slightly harder piece of webbing than the preceding 250 meters (820 feet). Only a month ago, knowing the hardest part was in front of me would have thrown me off. But I stayed strong and remembered the dream from the previous night. *You'd already sent this, remember?* And so I walked to the anchor tree, onsighting a 280-meter (919-foot) line and setting my new personal record and a new Czech female record for the second time. And I felt strong doing it.

As Cheryll put it, I'd been on a "send train" since Squamish. But I still remember well the long mental struggle and frustration from many one-fall crosses that preceded it. I like the train metaphor because it implies movement and change. Most of us get on and off trains and that's okay. No matter how much you love trains, who would like to be on a never-ending train journey? Sometimes it's equally fun to look at other trains passing by and take a break from the constant movement. But for a long time I was on a train that kept stopping just before reaching its desired destination. The journey was still fun, but it was also frustrating to never arrive where I wanted to. Metaphors aside, I trusted the time would come and that I just needed to "train" my brain more than the muscles in my body that support me when I balance high in the sky. And, after many one-fall crosses of highlines, I knew I had the physical ability to send. My brain finally responded to all that training and I started sending more and more easily. I don't expect to be on this send train forever, but I hope that, with training, I will now be able to hop back on it more easily. And not because I think sending is the most important part of highlining or climbing (hell, no!), but because I believe training our brains and being in control of our emotions can be beneficial in other aspects of life as well. Not to mention the fun in facing our fears and taking on new challenges. In the end, it is the fun, the flow, and the connections that make this journey special.

So hop on, it's a hell of a ride!

CHAPTER 18

Like a Regular Mom, Just Cooler: On the Line, Fear and Flow Have No Gender

By Dorothea Hamilton

The feelings of fear and flow are both crucial to the highlining experience. Throughout my highlining journey, I've observed that how we are taught to overcome fear or embrace flow differs greatly depending on the gender of the highliner. How many times have I asked women passing by if they wanted to try walking our permanently rigged midline? "No, I might fall" is the most common answer. *Yes, you are right. You will fall.* It often seems more accepted to not try than to try, fall, and stand up again. It seems more common for men to be encouraged to try something even if they feel fear or are likely to fall.

On the other hand we find flow – the state of mind where you forget about time and space and only exist. It is a state much aspired to in highlining (and other sports), even though in the beginning it is usually only achieved for short moments. The flow state is also often associated with male athletes in mainstream adventure sports media. And, dishearteningly, mothers are rarely mentioned in the flow context. They are either meant to find flow in their care responsibilities or not at all – they are not expected to need or work toward it. The truth is, in order to find these flow moments in outdoor sports, you need a lot of practice. Specifically for highlining, you need time to scout locations, rig the highline, wait for your turn, and practice. After putting in countless hours, you may overcome fear and finally experience flow. The first steps are necessary to achieve this state. But in order for this to be possible for women with children, someone else needs to take on caregiving responsibilities. Only then will a mother be able to put in the required time to overcome her fear and experience flow.

At the time I started highlining as a single mom of three kids, I was amazed that a woman – Mia Noblet – held the world record at the time. My male friends repeatedly referred to this fact when they claimed there was no need to focus on the question of why there were so few female highliners in the community. I thought about that a lot. Yes, undoubtedly there are and have always

Highlining in my home country, Germany. Photo by Michael Streuber.

been some exceptional world-record female highliners like Mia Noblet and Faith Dickey, and in freestyle Delaney Lyman and Salomé Cholet. But it didn't answer the question of why there are almost no women at my mid-range, nonprofessional level of highlining while you find men of all levels in the highlining community. Even more absent – where are the moms?

Ever since I first felt the fear of taking steps on a highline, I have felt how gender plays a role in this sport. In fact, slacklining and later highlining are how I initially got interested in feminist literature. Suddenly, and more clearly than ever, I was confronted with the differences of having a female body and female socialization. Perhaps I was acutely aware of this difference from the beginning, because my first highline experience was at the Girls Only Slackline Festival (now called the Women's Highline Meeting), organized by Faith Dickey in the Czech Republic. Or maybe because later, when our local meetup group, The Highline Force, started to form, I was the only woman. Maybe because I was the sole woman, I found it hard to see myself as an equal athlete to the men.

I made progress in highlining rapidly. I had been slacklining intensively before having my first child, so keeping my balance proved to not be much of a challenge. But the height and the length of a highline, as well as learning the technical aspects involved in rigging, definitely were. Reflecting back, I've wondered many times why I stuck with highlining. As a beginner, I had many reasons to quit. I went through rough personal times, I often didn't even enjoy being on the line, and I didn't always feel like part of the group.

Even in overcoming my fear of falling – which persisted for a rather long time – I felt my gender shaped my highlining experience. As I was the only woman in my group, I felt pressure to not be the only person who was too scared to stand up. But I found I couldn't handle as many leash falls, physically or mentally, as "the guys." It was only much later when I was highlining with other female beginners that I noticed that many female bodies seemed to have a harder time than male bodies when climbing the leash back to the line after a fall. Generally, the percentage of body fat on women is higher and situated at inconvenient positions – the hips and legs – and upper body muscle strength tends to be lower – maybe due to biology or stereotyped use of bodies. This anatomical difference does impact the ease of leash climbing, which almost entirely relies on upper body strength.

But apart from the physical aspects, I realized I had to learn a whole new form of communication. Not only did I need to know several different weblocks by name, but I also found that communication in larger all-male groups functioned in a way I was not socialized to participate in. In all-male groups, acknowledgement and appreciation seem to work differently. The way of determining who goes on the line next works differently. I actively had to learn to say, "I am going first." If I had waited for an invitation to take my turn – as I had learned in all-women's groups – I wouldn't have been able to get on the line at all because I had to leave early to pick up my kids. But most highliners aren't used to factoring in parenting responsibilities. Perhaps understandably so, as there simply aren't that many highlining moms. Not yet. I also had to learn that I could take as much time

Taking a leash fall.

Hanging out with my oldest son, Joshua. Photo by Maik Dobbermann.

on the line as I needed, even if my skill level was not as advanced. No one expected me to shorten my session just because of my level. This was just a self-imposed construct I had to learn to dismantle. And, yes, I had to watch a lot of YouTube videos (mostly made by men) that explain setups, techniques, and other useful tips after I put my children to bed so I could participate in their discussions.

There was a moment in my journey where I almost quit. It wasn't after a person in the park where we practiced had underestimated my skills, or when I fell off a super difficult line and hurt my arm. It was when I felt that being the only woman in the group was altering my ability to be myself. I came to understand that, as the only woman, you would not change a group's dynamic but would instead have to adapt to it. I became harsh on myself. I used as many technical terms as I could. I refused to show pain when I got hurt. I would never talk of my kids, in order to become "one of them." And all of that happened without any of them noticing the effort I made when they were just "highlining." I felt I had to learn an entirely new form of communication, like a new language. I observed how they spoke, how to interrupt, whose rigging technique was accepted as the "right" one. I spent my entire weekends on and next to lines from dawn until dusk and many nights thinking about highlining and freestyle tricks. I neglected the necessary recovery, even though I was exhausted between kids, work, and cleaning the house. Regardless of this effort, I was the least of the most dedicated. I was the last one to own gear, the last one to send a line, and the last to rig my own highline. I always felt like the little sister – although I was considerably older than the rest of the group – who was taken along out of obligation.

But my male friends without families had no housework to take care of. No school lunches to prepare and no children's birthdays to plan. No clothes to wash and no groceries to shop for. No need to earn enough money to feed a family of four. Most nights I would fall to sleep exhausted next to my kids after a long day of paid and unpaid labor. My family obligations added to a weekend of highlining meant I had no days to rest my body. My brain was filled with under-recognized daily housework, almost always done by women, especially moms. I was comparing myself, and my highlining, to men who were around 12 years younger than me, and who had no additional chores. I pushed myself to the limit to achieve their level. I ultimately failed, to no surprise. My energy level was not the same as theirs, and I found my ambition to improve also decreased because my self-esteem depended on more than my skill level.

After becoming confident with midlines, it took a long time to see the first woman on a highline. The ratio of women to men for highlining in Germany is especially low. The gender gap is one of the largest in the world if you take into account the distance records at the time (male: 2000 meters/6,561 feet; female: no official record, unofficial 200 meters/656 feet). When I first saw Carmen Schillingmann freestyling, I noticed I had never in real life seen a female body making any of those movements – showing it was actually possible. This might sound silly because obviously you do not need a penis to do a rocket mount. But I was affected more than I had expected to be, as I realized how much the lack of representation and visual examples had limited my understanding of highlining.

I was inspired to practice harder – I experienced flow moments in the first lines I sent but at the same time felt frustration about my rate of progress. I could not travel to distant locations to practice on higher lines. I was simply lacking the resources to invest enough energy to pursue a few fleeting moments of joy. No matter how powerful these moments felt, they did not pay the bills. And there was still the matter of finding child care. It can be easier and more socially acceptable for men to have the energy and time to invest in their leisure activities. They either are not fathers, or the responsibility of taking care of the children while they practice their sport falls onto the mother in a way that is often not reciprocated.

On the days I was able to highline, I could only participate in either rigging or derigging, as my time was too short to contribute to both. Surrounded by many people with fewer obligations, the sense of time is different. There is no need for them to "hurry up," while my time is always limited and constantly ticking away in my mind. I must use my time efficiently. This means I cannot stand around for several hours to create the perfect anchor. This difference creates a gap between me and my community. I experienced this carefree attitude toward time only once, years ago, on a two-week highline trip without the kids. All the other times I've been to festivals, I would overestimate my strength, go on as many lines as quickly as possible, and finish exhausted.

And then there is the other thing about exclusion in highlining. Most highliners usually go with a small crew in order to assure enough time on the line. Because a woman rigs most lines with her male buddies, she will undoubtedly be asked if she is either one of their girlfriends or if there is a possibility she might become one. As a mother, and with no desire to start a relationship with anyone from my sport, I was out of that game. And thus out of many midline projects.

Once I was invited to another place and I answered that I had some of my kids with me. No one asked me to come anyway and volunteered to watch the kids while I was on the line. I did not go.

Circumstances somewhat changed when our local highline group established a perma-rig. Suddenly, I could go by myself. I was not dependent on being asked or coordinating with other people's schedules. I could go for an hour or two and not need an entire free day. This was a game changer. I got into the flow state

Highlining while pregnant in the local woods. Photo by Alex.

more regularly. The feeling when your brain shuts up and all you know is your focus. Unfortunately, as you become confident with a certain line, that state diminishes and you start thinking about lunchboxes. Walking the same distance on the same line becomes natural. In order to feel that moment of flow again, you have to either walk longer lines – which is rarely possible – or start doing "something else" on the line.

For me, that something became highline freestyle – a subdiscipline of the sport that requires a lot of dedication. It is the ultimate feeling of flow when you bounce on a line, but in order to progress or even maintain your level you need many hours a week. The fear of falling disappears as falling becomes part of the game of bouncing up and down on the line, yet you become more susceptible to accidents. Sometimes it's just a hard leash fall, and sometimes you come down from the line bleeding. There are few women at a high level of highline freestyle. I aspired to be one of them before realizing it was not realistic for me to dedicate as much time to freestyle as I would need.

One time, I was invited to a freestyle competition and my children came along to watch. Even though I got into the second round, I did not perform at the level of the other participants. "Mom, why don't you ever do cool stuff on the line?" my son asked me afterwards. I wanted to say, *Well, my dear, because I spend my time taking care of you and feeding you and have way less time than all of these guys here.* But I didn't.

Things took another turn when I decided to have another child, as I had wanted my entire life. But because highlining occupied much of my brain, I questioned the decision to bring another life to this earth. While searching for pros and cons, I found mainly cons, but still, as I have also heard from many other women, there is that persistent desire to give life to another human being. Despite all the changes that would occur, and even though it would set me back considerably in highlining, I listened to my body and my heart.

My partner and I made that decision knowing I would highline as long as my body would permit. There is very little knowledge regarding how long a woman can highline while pregnant. So I decided to create updates of my highlining and pregnancy journey on Instagram and YouTube, with the goal of visibilizing it to others. It is a story told the other way round because I have been recording myself losing the progress I had made. I watch my videos and see how I've lost strength, skills, and have increasingly more weight to carry. Yet I also show it's technically possible to highline throughout the first two trimesters. I'm curious how long it will take (if ever) for me to regain my previous skills and the physical strength necessary to highline again.

So what about mothers in the flow state on a highline? Is it possible? Of course. But higher levels of highlining where you can achieve a flow state are currently still part of a very white-, male-, heterosexual-, no-family-dominated sport. There is no child care at festivals, no preference line for parents, and few people who would say, "Yeah, I'll take your child while you go on the line." For the future I hope to inspire more women and moms to stick to a sport like highlining, even with the understanding they may never become "the best." But to do it as a way to take time for themselves, search for that flow state of mind, and show their kids that moms do other things besides lunchboxes and house cleaning.

Two years later, some things have changed, but others have not. My youngest son is now a year old and accompanies us to highlining. We mostly highline close to our house – with the exception of a highline in the Peruvian desert – so most lines are not that spectacular. My son plays at the anchor with the other highliners while my partner or I highline. It somewhat increased the "teams" closeness to have mutual responsibility for a baby. He sits in the baby carrier while we rig, which becomes difficult during rain and snow. How long will he want to come along? I don't know. My older kids don't really like highlining. Physically, I am at the same level as before the pregnancy, but I am now approaching my 40s. So I have started to put more effort into rigging and organizing – for example, helping to organize an event to set up a German female highline record. Things are going in a positive direction. Yet I do hope for more openness from the community to be aware of the needs of those who care for others.

CHAPTER 19

Trailblazing the Sky: Mia Noblet's Art of Extending Highline Possibilities

By Denisa Krásná

She was born with a passion for outdoor adventures, so Mia's love for the mountains became evident early in her life. At the age of 8, a poster of Dean Potter balancing on a highline sparked something deep within her. It was then that she first learned about highlining. However, it wasn't until another 12 years later that she tried slacklining herself.

Growing up, Mia embraced the mountains in all their glory – skiing down slopes, hiking through challenging trails, and camping under starlit skies. Being homeschooled provided her with the flexibility to immerse herself in these outdoor pursuits. This unique lifestyle not only shaped her education but also instilled in her a deep appreciation for the wonders of the outdoors.

Despite the freedom her homeschooling offered, Mia's path diverged when she embarked on a career in figure skating and short track speed skating. For eight years, the icy arenas and rigorous training schedules drew her away from natural landscapes. However, this deviation didn't dampen her spirit. Instead, it added a new layer to her journey, setting the stage for a remarkable return to the outdoors in the years to come.

She started figure skating in Nelson, British Columbia, at the age of 11. By the time she turned 16, Mia had moved to Vancouver to further pursue the sport. It was here that her dedication to training and remarkable physical abilities caught the eye of her new coach. Recognizing her potential, she suggested Mia try her hand at short track speed skating. Due to her background in figure skating, Mia progressed quickly. Yet she also felt the pull of the mountains calling her back.

In 2015, at the age of 20, Mia started slacklining, and it proved to be a pivotal moment in her life. That year marked the end of her skating career and the commencement of a new chapter filled with slacklining adventures. Mia's ultimate aspiration was to venture into highlining, but she didn't know any highliners. Without the guidance of a mentor, Mia took matters into her own hands. She used instructional online videos

Highlining at Sapphire Lakes in Kokanee Glacier Provincial Park, British Columbia, in her home country, Canada. Photo by Just Linder.

Highlining in the French Alps. Photo by Daniel Laruelle.

to learn the basic skills. But soon Mia discovered there were people highlining in her area who knew the ins and outs of the activity – how to rig highlines and where the best spots were. It was only after connecting with the vibrant and passionate highlining community in Squamish, British Columbia, that she immersed herself in the world of highlining, around the end of July 2015.

The summer of 2015 marked Mia's first slackline trip to Europe. In Switzerland, she attended Bern City Slack, a longline festival, and TransAlp for waterlining. "Tom, what setup should I get?" Mia inquired of Thomas Buckingham, the then vice president of the International Slackline Association. "If you're serious about training, go for a 200 m Core," he advised. Mia followed his advice, and it's likely this recommendation is what fueled her rapid progression. To this day, she owns and rigs this objectively difficult webbing that only the best slackliners master. Mia's anticipation peaked for the highline at Monte Piana in the Italian Dolomites. It became evident to her that she was fully committed.

Upon her return to Canada, the winter season was setting in – a period typically seen as hibernation for most highliners in British Columbia. It was the time to stow away slacklines and embrace the slopes for skiing until the arrival of the next spring. However, Mia harbored a determination to push her limits. Throughout the winter, she diligently practiced, engaging in longlining sessions on her new Core.

As the new season approached, Mia found herself physically prepared, yet mentally she faced a formidable adversary – fear. It had a way of gripping her, paralyzing any attempt to move forward on a highline. Often she would summon the courage to stand up only to find herself immobilized, prompting her to retreat from the line. The battle between her physical readiness and the mental barriers posed by fear became a defining challenge for Mia. It was a test of resilience and determination as she grappled with the psychological hurdles that impeded her progress on the highline.

Every August, highliners from all corners of the world meet in Squamish to highline on the magnificent Stawamus Chief. During the gathering, slackliners seek respite from the summer heat by the lakes, where they practice on waterlines that are often considered objectively more challenging than highlines. It's not just the visual illusion caused by the water playing tricks on the slackliner's mind, making it incredibly challenging to resist swaying with the waves forming on the water. It's also technically more difficult to walk.

During that summer, Mia chose to stay in Canada for the Chief gathering and joined world-class slackliners by the lake in the days leading up to the festival. She watched as even the most skilled slackliners found themselves taking plunges into the water. That's why Mia's accomplishment really stood out – she managed to send the waterline without taking a single fall, defying the common struggles faced by the best of the best. Within a year of wholeheartedly dedicating herself to slacklining, Mia was becoming a prominent figure in British Columbia's slacklife community. And, in the days to come, she would catch the attention of slackliners worldwide.

However, on the first day of the Chief gathering, fear continued to grip Mia, paralyzing her movement. Some of her friends teased her, playfully suggesting she should abandon slacklining and pursue a career as a highline photographer because she was incapable of moving from her spot. This taunting stirred a fire within her, transforming her frustration into determination. "I'll show you what I'm capable of!" she declared, channeling that irritation as fuel.

Determined to confront her fear, Mia assigned herself the challenge of intentionally falling off the line, recognizing that overwhelming fear hindered that initial step. She was tempted to try a 130-meter (427-foot) highline at the edge of the canyon. However, she chose to ease into it, starting with a 90-meter (295-foot) line. She stood up and took that first step. She then managed to slowly walk approximately halfway before succumbing to a fall, her mind grappling with the intense sensations. Too overwhelmed to continue, she returned to the anchor and rested her mind. The following day, with renewed resolve, Mia returned and stepped onto the line.

She was surprised at how comfortable she felt on the line, so she just kept walking. Slowly and cautiously. After each step, she waited until the line beneath her feet quieted down completely. She fell 30 meters (98 feet) before the end. If she had made those last meters, it would have been a new women's world record. On her way back, she decided that if she couldn't take a leash fall unintentionally, she would do it consciously. At the midpoint, she turned into exposure and stood there until she fell. And again and again. She walked the rest of the line with a newfound sense of freedom and ease she had never felt on a highline before.

One week later, Mia and the SlacklifeBC team prepared for a trip to northern British Columbia, along with world-class German slackliners Friedrich Kühne and Lukas Irmler, to rig three highlines at Hunlen Falls. From the outset, the 222-meter (728-foot) highline they rigged captured Mia's attention. Despite the daunting 1,312-foot-deep (400-m) chasm below, this time her desire to highline surpassed her fear. She wasn't looking at the end of the line. Her attention was solely on each individual step, the tension in the line. She moved incredibly slowly. As she approached the end, she had been on the line for a good two hours. She was starting to sense fatigue throughout her entire body and eagerly anticipated the end. Yet Mia kept reminding herself, *This isn't the end. You can still go. You're still here.* Because, when she starts something, she likes to see it through to the end. Approaching the anchor, Mia didn't feel any stress or pressure, in contrast to the experiences of many other slackliners. Despite fatigue, she remained fully relaxed: "The concept of time and the mental challenges at the line's end disappear during the walk. I'm not aware of reality until I'm sat down at the anchor, off the line. This lack of struggle at the line's end is pivotal in my mindset." And just like that, she sent the line, establishing a new women's world record.

The highline at Hunlen Falls marked a turning point for Mia. It was also just the beginning of her remarkable journey into the record books. She was glad she set the record at 222 meters (728 feet) and not at the Chief the week before: "It would have been a record by just a few meters. It's much better to push a record by 80, 100, or 500 meters." But records don't matter much to Mia: "I'm interested in my abilities, what I can learn, and how much I can improve." One year after Hunlen Falls, in 2017, Mia shattered her own record in Moab, Utah, walking an awe-inspiring 493-meter (1,617-foot) line between the Castleton and Rectory towers, suspended approximately 395 feet (120 m) above the ground. The following year, in Cânion do Espraiado, Brazil, she pushed the boundaries once again, breaking her own record with a breathtaking 614-meter (2,015-foot) highline, soaring 1,476 feet (450 m) above the ground.

In those first years of her highlining career, Mia still walked pretty cautiously to avoid line wobbles as she continued to grapple with occasional fear. While she was slowly gaining confidence, others around her seemed more convinced of her abilities than she was. Contrary to the common belief that self-confidence precedes external validation, Mia's journey was somewhat reversed. The support around her bolstered her confidence, making her believe more in her abilities over time. She became known in the slacklining world for her extraordinary physical endurance.

Mia vividly recalls one of her earliest experiences on a highline. It was the longest nylon line rigged back then, with Spencer Seabrooke, Alex Schulz, and Anthony Boulay. Mia struggled with the forward and backward movement of the stretchy nylon line, so she walked out slowly, trying to adapt. As fatigue set in, she eventually decided to turn back. It was close to the end of the day, and upon her return, Alex and Anthony told her she had been walking in one direction for three hours. "I'll never forget their expressions," she says. In her perception, it felt like only ten minutes had passed. Alex, known for his fast walking, covered the same distance in just over 20 minutes. Back then, Mia became aware of her ability to assess her strengths and ensure her safety on the line, albeit at the cost of losing a clear sense of the passing time, an important skill for walking long highlines, a discipline in which Mia now excels.

The excitement for big highlines grew organically as Mia relished the experience of walking longer and longer lines. The prospect of attempting something unprecedented added an extra layer of thrill, although breaking records was never the primary goal. The experience of walking a long highline introduces a different dimension to the sensation of walking. In an alpine setting, the lines tend to be shorter, resulting in shorter walking distances. Consequently, the mind doesn't establish the same deep connection with the body, often described as the flow state or being in the zone. The mission encompasses everything from leaving the car, train, bus, or bike to the completion of the entire project. Highlining ceases to be just about the line itself. In the case of longer lines, the rigging and the whole process is, of course, very complex, but the walking is a significant part of the experience because it takes a much longer time.

Mia also reflects on the flow state that is much easier to achieve on big lines:

> *There's a unique aspect where the concept of time seems to fade away. You're not dwelling on the future or the past; instead, there's a heightened awareness of the present moment. It's not like you consciously think about specific things; rather, you're attuned to your body's signals, like the feeling of tired shoulders or mental cues for safety. There's still that connectedness to reality – checking in on your well-being and observing how conditions may be changing – but at the same time, nothing really exists besides what you're doing. This sense of being completely absorbed in the present is a significant factor that contributes to my enjoyment of walking long highlines.*

In August 2018, Mia walked the magical length of one kilometer on a beautiful highline in northern Norway: "I vividly recall setting a goal of walking one kilometer, and achieving that was a milestone for me." She thought she was going to take a break from long lines for a while; it was the end of summer after all. But only one week later, she was balancing in the Québécois sky on a 1.9-kilometer-long (1.1-mile) highline over a decommissioned mine in Asbestos (now Val-des-Sources), Québec. The highline became the new world record that Mia, alongside five male slackliners, set in September. This feat not only broke a world record for highlining but also placed her in a league of her own, transcending gender distinctions in the sport.

Mia sent the highline on her second attempt. However, she found her first walk a lot more rewarding. Facing challenging weather conditions, she was forced to fight and, despite falling 150 meters (492 feet) from the end, she learned a lot more from this walk. On the other hand, her send was not remarkable in any way: "I remember it not being nearly as satisfying as the first walk, yet nobody will ever talk about it unless I do." That day, she began to recognize the human tendency to always seek more, driven by societal expectations. Over time, she has learned the importance of stepping back, taking a break, and re-evaluating personal desires, detaching from external pressures. While society tends to value records and clear achievements, Mia has come to appreciate the value of pausing and reassessing goals for personal fulfillment.

One year later, the team reconvened in Asbestos, aiming to raise its own record to two kilometers (1.2 miles). As if history were repeating itself, Mia faced unexpected wind on her first attempt, just like the previous year. Mia described her first walk as one of her most unforgettable highlining experiences ever. Initially, conditions were favorable, but they quickly turned gusty, causing the line to sway 50 feet (15 m) from side to side. Known for her steady walking, she found herself on one leg, teetering on the edge in the first 150 meters (492 feet), narrowly avoiding a fall. The realization struck her: she still had a long way to go. Fatigue set in around the 200–300-m (650–985-foot) mark, and thoughts of turning back crossed her mind. Despite contemplating catching and sitting down again at 500 meters (1,640 feet) to ease the relentless struggle, Mia couldn't give up. The fighting spirit to stay upright persisted in her. This internal struggle continued for a couple hundred meters, an uncommon challenge for her. Eventually, the turbulent conditions subsided completely, allowing her to find her rhythm and rest her arms. Not only did she cross the line but she also sent it during that session.

Upon reaching the anchor, Mia was unable to lift her arm, exhausted to the point where she needed assistance from her other arm. This walk remained etched in her memory as one of the most satisfying experiences as she succeeded in the face of a substantial and rewarding challenge. In the end, only Mia and Lukas Irmler sent the line without falls. Most highliners who were present had higher expectations, but many overestimated their abilities. Interestingly, those who accurately predicted their times on the line were also the ones who approached the challenge with a healthy dose of respect, even fear. And rightly so – big lines can be dangerous.

As Mia reflects, there is a common misconception surrounding big lines, often perceived as "easy" by those who have never walked such monumental distances. This viewpoint overlooks the difficulty of maintaining the right mental state and efficiency throughout the entire journey – something that becomes increasingly challenging with every additional segment. This process also involves being prepared for difficult sections and unpredictable weather conditions. The true challenge lies in sustaining the right mindset, sometimes for hours, as the journey on these lines is about endurance, not just the difficulty of individual steps. The ultimate goal is not to make the line so difficult that only one person can walk it after numerous attempts but to experience walking while maintaining a mental state that is both alert and relaxed, allowing for efficient movement. Mia sums it up this way: "It's an experience that might be challenging to grasp unless you've lived it."

While exploring the boundaries of highlining remains vital to Mia, it certainly isn't her sole focus. Highlining, being a lifestyle sport, encompasses various dimensions, with one of its most enriching aspects being travel – an element Mia fully embraces. Between May 2017 and December 2018, Mia traveled to China five times. The Chinese government paid her and a team of slackliners to rig highlines. During her trip to Tianmen Mountain near Zhangjiajie city, Mia learned she is capable of walking in high heels – maybe not on solid ground, but definitely on the highline. At Wanfo Lake, in Lu'an, China, she helped rig the world's longest waterline, at 675 meters (2,215 feet). On this trip Mia learned she doesn't let societal standards get in the way of her enjoyment of the line. She realized this when she fell 50 meters (164 feet) from the end of the waterline, which would have been a new world record for her. She says, "Despite not achieving that specific goal, I considered it a success because it provided me with a novel experience that I enjoyed. Our society often applauds those who set goals, win races, or break records, framing these as benchmarks for success. This relentless pursuit of doing better, achieving more, and being faster seems deeply ingrained in our society." Understanding the fine line between wanting success and not letting it become a hindrance is a crucial aspect of Mia's highlining journey.

In October 2019, Mia was invited to join a team of French slackliners on an expedition to Tunisia. The goal was to introduce slacklining, climbing, and other outdoor pursuits to the country. Her team engaged in setting up highlines, demonstrating rigging techniques, and providing necessary gear. Among the ten slackliners who traveled from Europe, only two were men. Their presence seemed to resonate profoundly with the local community and festival attendees eager to experience highlining. Interestingly, a majority of those who tried it were women. The team's gender composition introduced a fresh perspective on the sport to the local community, framing highlining as an activity suitable for women. This dynamic underscores the significance of representation in influencing and diversifying participation in outdoor sports.

When Mia started highlining, the gender disparity within the sport was striking. In Canada, where highline projects often involve demanding hiking and efficient rigging, Mia acknowledges that the physical challenges might have deterred some women, especially those unfamiliar with the strenuous demands of carrying a heavy backpack. Her personal background, growing up with two brothers, proved advantageous. Being accustomed to strapping on a heavy backpack and ascending swiftly, she found herself well prepared for the physical rigors. Still, there were significantly fewer women entering the world of highlining compared to men.

A paid gig in Tianmen Mountain National Park, China.

This landscape has undergone significant evolution over the years. As time progresses, the sport is becoming more inclusive, particularly evident at European slackline festivals where the numbers of women on the lines are often the same as men. "This transformative shift is a positive and dynamic change," Mia says. The gender dynamic in highlining now varies significantly based on the location: "In Nelson, where I now live, there aren't many highliners, and I often introduce the activity to new people. In these cases, there's generally a good mix of both women and men." In Europe, the highlining community includes an increasing number of strong and enthusiastic women. Whether it's freestyle projects, carrying hefty backpacks, or engaging in

alpine pursuits, Mia noticed there's a diverse range of interests among women highliners these days. Yet it's still not uncommon for Mia to find herself as the only woman on a particular project: "My perspective remains focused on the shared enjoyment of highlining rather than gender distinctions. As long as everyone is having a good time, gender composition becomes a secondary consideration."

However, there is a noticeably different dynamic in all-women teams. A notable experience for Mia was attending the Women's Highline Meeting, organized by Faith Dickey in the Czech Republic. The festival primarily caters to beginners with shorter lines and no freestyle rigs, but due to its location among sandstone towers, it offers a unique environment. When Mia attended, the atmosphere was notably calm, with no stress about line time and a relaxed approach to sharing the space. Mia says, "I think this tranquility could either be attributed to the fact it was an all-women event, fostering a supportive and understanding energy, or to the fact that most women there were beginners, so still a bit scared and needing more time to get ready." Be that as it may, she is grateful for the experience: "It was intriguing to observe and be part of an environment that felt so different, in a way more cooperative and communicative in its approach."

Another interesting experience came when Mia decided to accept an invitation to participate in the filming of a Discovery Channel documentary. *Pushing the Line* came out in 2021 and in six episodes follows highliners and base jumpers as they adventure in the Moab desert and Colorado. Instead of capturing the essence of slacklife, it makes it into a reality show, focusing on interpersonal and romantic drama, with the main premise being about setting record lines. Mia recalls that she deliberated for some time before deciding to be a part of it because she was apprehensive about the direction it might take: "Despite concerns, I ultimately decided not to care about people's perceptions and gave it a try." The process was exhausting as the producers tried to steer the narrative in a certain direction. As is to be expected when filming a show like this, there was little privacy: "We were mic'd up from the moment we left our tents until we returned, making it quite intensive. I'd pull the plug on the mic to have a private conversation with friends."

It was a clash of two vastly different worlds. In the desert, if you need to pee, you go behind a bush. However, Mia remembers that some producers, particularly a lady accustomed to home design reality shows, had never peed in anything other than a flushable toilet. The collaboration was a collision of extremes, leading to friction and a learning curve on how to work together. The producers' objective was clear: to create something that sells. Unfortunately, what sells often involves setting records, drama, and elements Mia personally doesn't find appealing. The push was toward that narrative, and she consistently tried to steer it back to the essence of slacklife – the enjoyment, safety, and personal satisfaction. "Success, to me, is not just about breaking records. It's about relishing the journey, learning, and being safe. I emphasized this perspective, recognizing that my attitude toward records might be different, having walked many."

Highlining in Shenxianju, China. Photo by Anthony Boulay.

The challenge was finding a balance between what the producers believed would sell and what the slackliners valued.

In the end, the show turned out better than Mia expected, although she believes the series could have presented a more authentic portrayal without fabricated elements. At some point, Mia realized that, despite pulls toward certain directions – partying, creating false drama – she had to let go. “People will edit how they want. I stayed true to myself, aiming to contribute positively to the sport, regardless of how it’s portrayed.” Some of the producers were supportive, while others were the opposite. Nonetheless, Mia remembers that some crew members were genuinely inspired. Until this day, she still receives occasional messages from a producer who made positive lifestyle changes after spending that month with them, opting for a healthier diet and making improvements in his life. Mia says, “These small, positive impacts matter the most to me, irrespective of what happens or doesn’t happen in the larger context.”

Mia believes positive change often stems from doing what you love. Regardless of the outdoor activity you pursue, a genuine love for it usually instills respect for the outdoors. The little things we do that are environmentally more respectful can capture other people’s attention and inspire them. Mia asserts, “The key is to minimize environmental impact where possible, such as picking up garbage and being mindful of consumption. Respecting the outdoors doesn’t mean completely avoiding activities that burn fossil fuels. It’s about being a conscious consumer and making choices that align with your values. For instance, if you choose to fly, make the most of your trip and spend a longer duration to balance the impact. Focusing on experiences over material possessions and minimizing single-use items are all steps in the right direction.”

Accepting that we are consumers and doing our best to reduce our impact is a practical approach. “The key is to strike a balance and acknowledge that perfection may be elusive.” In the end, enjoying the outdoors, prioritizing experiences, and minimizing unnecessary consumption all contribute positively. As an example, Mia recalls a highline that she recently rigged with climbers who were relatively new to highlining. They were around 22–23 years old and brought friends with varying experience levels. Despite most of these young people being more inclined toward parties and drinking, the outdoor experience had a transformative effect. “After a day of active outdoor activities, they found themselves opting for yoga, stretching, sauna, healthy meals, and early bedtimes.” Engaging in outdoor activities tends to lead to a healthier lifestyle, disrupting unhealthy cycles like excessive drinking, late-night partying, or staying home playing video games. It’s a testament to the positive impact that outdoor activities can have on one’s overall well-being.

So what motivates Mia these days? As she says, “There are always new goals that emerge. It’s no longer about extending the maximum time spent on the line. Instead, it’s about choosing which lines I genuinely want to walk.” August 2022 witnessed another historic moment when Mia broke the world record again, alongside seven other highliners, sending an astonishing 2.7-kilometer-long (1.7-mile) line in France. This time, she wasn’t the only woman to achieve this. Tania Monier from France also

Mia Noblet on Tianmen Mountain, China.

joined the ranks of the world's elite and forged a friendship with Mia. The two of them could be seen crossing a 500-meter (1,640-foot) highline in tandem shortly after breaking the world record together.

While Mia maintains the desire to undertake more of these substantial projects, she acknowledges the time constraints, recognizing they might not materialize even once a year, potentially extending to once every couple of years due to the significant commitment they demand. To push her boundaries, Mia has decided to explore highline freestyle. She sees this challenge as a catalyst for personal growth: "Exploring different styles and embracing opportunities to learn, even when they don't perfectly align with your preferences, is what makes you stronger, in my opinion." This attitude reflects her continuous commitment to self-improvement and embracing diverse aspects of the highlining world.

As Mia continues to push her limits and explore new frontiers in highlining, her story illuminates the indomitable spirit that thrives in the face of challenges. Her story embodies a profound connection with nature, a dedication to personal growth, and a passion for sharing the joy of outdoor adventures. Mia's influence reaches far beyond the highline, inspiring individuals to embrace challenges, forge connections, and find fulfillment in the exhilarating pursuit of their passions. In her footsteps, the highlining community witnesses not just a record breaker but also a trailblazer shaping the narrative of what's possible in the world of outdoor sports.

Denisa and Alena in Yosemite. Photo by Jamie Sayegh.

AFTERWORD

In the River

I'm flowing on the Snoqualmie River in Washington in Alena's extra kayak. I've always been apprehensive about water. I experienced its power firsthand as a child when big ocean waves kept me underwater for longer than is tolerable for anyone, let alone a 10-year-old. My back was bruised from the sandy bottom I kept hitting, wave after wave, and so was my relationship with water. But now I had been fairly easily persuaded to go whitewater kayaking because I was with Alena, whom I trust with my life. Plus, we had just decided to create *Flow* together. And if we were to write a book featuring kayaking, I had to taste what it's like to be on the river. "Just look at it as field research," says Alena when she detects my nervousness as we hit the first rapids. "Right, this is for *Flow*." I feel a sense of responsibility but also excitement as my adrenaline rises.

We're on the river with Eric, too, which means I'm with two experienced kayakers who are ready to help me if needed. But both Alena and Eric are a little concerned about the high level of water in the river. It flows fast and looks scary. We go through the first two rapids, and I manage to stay upright. Despite this, I'm unable to let go of my fear and anxiety. The current is fast, and I don't want to experience what it's like to be whisked downstream. Perhaps unconsciously then, I manage to park my boat between two big boulders right before a big drop in the middle of the rapid. "Okay, that's it." Terrified, I climb on the big boulder. Here, I feel safe. As a climber, I'm in my element here. Unfortunately, there is no slackline I could cross from here to the riverbank. Eventually, I make peace with the fact the only way out is through the rapids in front. So I let Eric help me unstick the boat and follow him exactly where he tells me to paddle. "We just got past a hole! You made it through the worst part!" *A hole? But they said there are no holes here, just waves.* As he finishes the sentence, I panic and flip for no good reason. Luckily, we are at the end of the rapid and in a safe eddy.

After the flip, I'm unable to regain my focus. I'm unable to stay present and just flow. I already anticipate the worst and have zero self-confidence. All I can think about is how I'll be drowning in the fast current. With this mindset, I enter the longest raging rapid and flip immediately. I'm underwater, briefly above, then under again. I don't know where my boat is, but I'm still holding on to the paddle. I'm being tossed around and the fast current is taking me downstream where all the large boulders are. *Am I going to hit them?* I didn't, but I'm suddenly unable to breathe. *What is happening? Where is Alena?* I honestly think I'm going to die, so I turn to Alena for help. She is right there, next to me, telling me it's going to be fine. She is focused, navigating both the rapid and her drowning friend. I can't take a breath, but I still trust her. If she says I'll be okay, there's no reason to think I won't. Except for my inability to catch a breath. And the fact this swim is seemingly never-ending. After what feels like eternity, Alena makes me hold on to her boat and takes me to shore.

I regain my breath after about a minute. Eric tells me it was the combination of shock and cold water that caused me to be unable to breathe. He adds that it happens to kayakers all the time. *Wow.* Back there, I couldn't imagine ever wanting to kayak again. But, as an academic, I know one experience is not representative. I need a bigger sample. And so I went to the river with Alena one more time. When there was less water and the rapids were not that scary. This time, I didn't flip. And I had fun. Alena and I connected with each other and with the environment around us like many other times before. But this time, instead of in the mountains, it was on the river.

In the Sky

I'm about to use Denisa's Rollex to slide my way out on the highline, far enough away from the cliff where the line is anchored. Using the technique she taught me in the park, I swing my leg up then down in order to gain enough momentum to shakily roll myself from under the line to be on top of it. The wind from thousands of feet below rushes up at me, making my stomach lurch. I'm sitting on a one-inch-wide (2.5-cm) piece of webbing, connected with a harness and leash to the highline but surrounded completely by nothing. My brain knows I will be safe if (when) I fall off the line, but my body is convinced I'm one inch from falling to my death.

We were at Taft Point in Yosemite National Park after hiking six hours from the base of the valley because the road to the Taft Point trailhead was closed for construction. So Denisa and I, along with our friend Jamie, hiked backpacks filled with webbing, gear, and camping supplies up 3,500 feet (1066 m) of elevation to rig this highline. As climbers, Jamie and I knew the basics about building anchors, but Denisa took the lead with rigging the highline. As the single highliner among us, she was the only one with enough knowledge to truly know if the rig was safe. She had to trust her rigging skills with her life as she took her first steps on it, suspended in the sky across the valley from the iconic El Capitan. I held my breath as she stood up, took the first steps, and sat back down. She seemed scared to fall, something I didn't sense often from her. I felt my adrenaline rise when she decided to take her first leash fall to truly test the rigging.

But now it was my turn. In my years of climbing, I always felt my lack of fear of heights was a gift, often feeling pure ecstasy and ease at the edge of cliffs. But sitting on the line at Taft Point, I felt my mortality in every micro-movement. I shifted the line under my butt, slowly bringing one foot to the line, then the other. I knew I was supposed to try to stand up, but I felt all my survival instincts screaming at me to stay seated, to grab the line with my hands, and crawl back to land.

I couldn't understand. I trusted the gear that would catch me, and I knew Denisa had already walked the line. If it held her weight, it would hold mine too. But the thought of dangling from the line several thousand feet up from the ground paralyzed me. I tried to breathe through it, hearing shouts of encouragement from Denisa and Jamie on the cliff. "Just try to stand up!" I inhaled one last desperate breath and shifted my weight forward, pushing down on the stretchy line beneath my feet. As I fell, I grabbed the line, not quite taking a full fall, but I was satisfied.

We had rigged the line in the late evening, and I watched Denisa walk, illuminated by the sunset's red and orange light, while Jamie and I cooked dinner. That night, after watching Earth's shadow briefly obscure the moon, we slept under the stars. The next morning, I awoke before the others. Wrapped in my sleeping bag, I watched the first rays of morning light spread across the infamous Dawn Wall of El Capitan. I didn't go back on the highline again that morning but captured plenty of magic from my sunrise vigil, revering the beauty of the valley, the friends, and the adventure.

Flow

We met on Mount Seymour in British Columbia in 2017. We were both members of the hiking club at Western Washington University where we studied, Denisa as an international exchange student. It was February, and the mountain was covered in layers of beautiful powder snow. As we made our way to the top, we started chatting. "Wait, you're Czech? I want to move to Prague!" said Alena enthusiastically. "Do you think it's a good idea?" she inquired. "I think it's a terrific idea! I'm no patriot, but I think Prague is one of the most beautiful cities in the world! And it's very international too." That response sealed Alena's decision and set the foundations for *Flow*.

When Alena moved to Prague a year later, we reconnected and our friendship deepened with every outing to the outdoors. On our first venture to the mountains in Slovakia, we survived an unexpected blizzard in the mountain pass. Snow reminded us of our first meeting at Seymour in Canada, and since then we've been adventure buddies. Alena wasn't a kayaker yet, and Denisa wasn't a highliner. But we were both enthusiastic hikers and climbers, and these two passions created a special bond between us. When Alena moved back to the States, we simply exchanged our playground from European rocks and mountains for American crags.

When the idea for *Flow* was born in Yosemite Valley, we knew it was a journey we were destined to embark on together. Feeling the urgency of this new path, we began reaching out to potential *Flow* authors soon after taking our initial steps toward our goal. We felt recharged with every new response from women who were enthusiastic to share their personal stories with the world. Their words further forged the path we walked to create *Flow*.

As we worked together, we were constantly reminded it's not the summit that matters but the journey we have undertaken together, and the new connections that were created along the way. *Flow* has revealed the many connections between the seemingly unrelated sports of whitewater kayaking, climbing, and highlining that can all function as bridges across difference. Through communication with our authors, we have planted the seeds of new friendships we hope will only bloom over the summer when we plan to meet in Squamish, British Columbia. The spontaneous idea to invite our authors to get together in Canada has been met with so much excitement that it has ignited a spark for more collaborative projects to come. We are now planning more events where our authors can come together in different geographical locations so we can further solidify these transcultural networks of solidarity and friendship among women from across different adventure sports.

Despite their diverse backgrounds and interests, *Flow*'s authors have a lot in common, especially their passion for pushing their limits, embracing the unknown, and establishing strong connections with the environment and their communities. It is their determination in pursuing their own paths and overcoming obstacles that unites them, and it is this spirit that resonates with all of us. So, whether you are an adventurer yourself or prefer to stick to reading about adventures, we hope this book has touched your heart and inspired you to pursue your own passions and dreams, whatever they may be, to break down barriers and to continue following your desired path. Cherish every step you take, as it is the journey that matters and will lead you to flow.

GLOSSARY

General

2SLGBTQIA+: Acronym used to represent Two-Spirit, lesbian, gay, bisexual, transgender, queer, intersex, asexual, and additional people who identify as belonging to sexual- and gender-diverse communities. The "2S" at the beginning recognizes Two-Spirit Indigenous Peoples as the first of the 2SLGBTQIA+ communities.

beta: Information or advice from others about how to navigate a specific obstacle, whether it's a river's features, hazards, or optimal routes, or a climbing route's sequence of moves, location of holds, or any other specific techniques and strategies that may be helpful.

BIPOC: Acronym used to represent Black, Indigenous, and people of color intended to center the experiences of, and demonstrate solidarity between, communities of color that have been marginalized and minoritized. It is important to note the acronym does not resonate with everyone it was meant to embrace.

flow: A state of optimal experience and enjoyment characterized by complete absorption and focus in an activity, often associated with high performance and satisfaction.

line: The intended path through an obstacle. In this context, a path through rapids, up a rock face, or across a chasm.

stoke: Extreme excitement for something.

Rivers: Whitewater Kayaking

boof: A kayaking technique where the paddler lifts the bow of the kayak with a paddle stroke at the edge of a vertical feature.

brace: A technique used to stabilize the kayak by placing the paddle blade on the water's surface to provide support.

charge: To paddle determinedly toward a rapid or feature.

class I–V: Rapids classified based on their difficulty, starting with class I, which describes moving flatwater, through to class V, which describes the most dangerous, advanced whitewater.

cockpit: The opening in a kayak where the paddler sits.

confluence: The point where two rivers or streams meet.

creeking: A style of whitewater kayaking focused on navigating steep, technical rivers with tight channels and frequent drops.

crux: The most difficult part of a rapid or section of a river or climbing route. Where the moves are typically the most challenging and require the most strength, technique, or problem-solving skills.

downriver freestyle: Refers to performing tricks and maneuvers while navigating downriver on moving water.

eddy: A calm area of water behind an obstruction, often used by kayakers to rest or regroup.

eddy line: The boundary between the fast-moving current of the river and the slower-moving water in an eddy.

ferry: A maneuver used by kayakers to cross the river diagonally, paddling at an angle to the current to reach the desired destination without being swept downstream.

flow: The volume of water passing through a river or rapid, usually measured in cubic feet per second (cfs).

freestyle: Freestyle kayaking involves performing various tricks and maneuvers on moving water, typically in a river or whitewater feature.

gate: A pair of poles suspended over the water that kayakers must navigate around during slalom racing.

hole (hydraulic): A powerful feature in a river caused by water flowing over obstacles, often creating turbulence and potential hazards for kayakers.

horizon line: The point where the river drops out of sight, indicating the presence of a significant drop or rapid.

hucking: The act of kayaking over a big drop or waterfall, sometimes used to imply recklessness.

paddle stroke: Techniques used by kayakers to propel and maneuver their kayaks, including forward stroke, sweep stroke, and draw stroke.

peel out: A maneuver where a kayaker leaves an eddy to enter the main current of the river.

playboating: A style of whitewater kayaking focused on performing tricks and maneuvers in dynamic river features such as waves, holes, and eddy lines.

portage: Carrying a kayak overland to bypass a dangerous section of river.

practice laps: Repeated runs down a section of river for the purpose of training and improving skills.

put-in: The starting point of a kayaking trip where paddlers enter the water.

putting on: The process of committing to running a river by entering the water.

rapid: A section of a river where the water flows more swiftly, often characterized by turbulent, aerated water and obstacles such as rocks and drops.

recirculating hole: A hydraulic feature in a river where water flows back upstream, forming a circular motion.

rodeo hole: A large hydraulic feature often used for playboating or freestyle kayaking.

roll: A kayaking skill used to quickly right a capsized kayak by using the paddle and body motion to initiate a controlled rotation back to an upright position.

running shuttle: The process of driving back up to the top of a river section.

safety kayaker: A kayaker who is there to provide assistance in case of emergencies.

scouting: The process of inspecting a rapid or section of river from shore, or by climbing to higher ground to assess its features and determine the best route through.

self-support: A kayaking trip where paddlers carry all their gear and supplies in their kayaks without external support.

slalom: A competitive whitewater kayaking event where paddlers navigate a series of gates suspended over a river, testing their precision, agility, and speed while racing against the clock.

sprayskirt: A waterproof covering worn by kayakers to seal the cockpit of the kayak, preventing water from entering.

start ramp: A structure or platform used as the starting point for a race.

stern: The back end of the kayak, opposite the bow.

swim: To intentionally or unintentionally exit the kayak, typically after capsizing.

take-out: The ending point of a river trip where paddlers exit the water.

throw bag: A rescue device consisting of a bag with a length of rope inside, used by kayakers to throw to someone in the water to assist in a rescue.

tributaries: Smaller rivers or streams that flow into a larger river.

whirlpools: Circular currents of water caused by turbulence, often found in eddies or behind obstacles.

whitewater: Water that appears white due to its turbulence and aeration.

Rock: Climbing

acclimatization: The process of adjusting to high altitudes by gradually exposing oneself to reduced oxygen levels.

alpine trad climbing: Traditional climbing in alpine environments, which adds complexity due to factors such as long approaches, remote locations, multi-day ascents, and variable weather conditions.

anchor: A fixed point to which a climber attaches a rope for protection against falls, often created at the end of a climb.

ascent: The act of climbing or moving upward, typically toward the summit of a mountain or rock face.

base camp: A temporary campsite set up at the foot of a mountain or near the starting point of a climb.

belaying: Managing the rope to protect the climber in case of a fall, typically done by a partner on the ground or at an anchor, using a special belay device.

bolting: The process of installing bolts into rock faces or other surfaces to create anchor or protection points for climbing routes or highlines. Bolts are typically drilled into the rock and secured with glue or resin.

bouldering: Climbing short, challenging routes (typically without ropes) close to the ground, usually on large boulders or low rock faces.

cam: Short for camming device, a type of climbing protection device that expands when placed in a crack to provide secure anchor points.

carabiner: A metal loop with a spring-loaded gate used for connecting components of a climbing or highlining system.

chimney: A vertical or near-vertical crack or gap in a rock formation that a climber can ascend using opposing pressure with the hands, feet, or back.

climbing gym: An indoor facility equipped with artificial climbing walls, holds, and safety equipment for climbers to practice and train in a controlled environment.

climbing hold: An artificial or natural feature on a climbing wall or rock face that provides grip for the climber's hands and feet. Holds come in various shapes and sizes, including jugs, crimps, slopers, and pockets.

climbing shoes: Specialized footwear designed for rock climbing, featuring sticky rubber soles and a snug fit to provide traction and support on the rock.

crack climbing: A technique used in rock climbing where climbers ascend cracks or fissures in rock faces by wedging their hands, feet, or other body parts into the crack for support and progression.

crag: Outdoor rock climbing locations with natural rock formations suitable for climbing.

crampons: Metal spikes or traction devices worn on boots to provide mobility on icy or snowy surfaces, commonly used in ice climbing and mountaineering.

crevasse: A deep crack or fissure in a glacier or ice field, often posing a hazard to climbers.

crimp: A small, sharp hold on a rock face that requires the climber to grip with their fingertips.

descent: The process of coming down from a high elevation, typically after completing a climbing route or highline, often involving rappelling or hiking down.

dry tooling: A climbing technique where climbers use ice tools to ascend rock faces or mixed terrain without the presence of ice.

dynamic move: A climbing move that requires the climber to make a quick and explosive motion, often involving jumping or lunging between holds.

first ascent: The initial successful climb of a route or mountain by a climbing team, establishing a new line or path for future climbers.

fixed protection: Permanent anchors or bolts placed in the rock by climbers or route developers to protect climbs. These fixed pieces are often used in sport climbing and some trad climbing routes.

friction steps: Smaller footholds on a rock face that require the climber to rely on friction rather than actual holds.

gear placement: Placing protective devices (e.g., cams, nuts, hexes) securely into cracks or other features in the rock to protect against falls.

grade: A numerical or alphabetical rating system used to indicate the difficulty of a climbing route, considering factors such as technical difficulty, exposure, and length.

highball: A bouldering route that is particularly tall or has a high risk of injury in the event of a fall.

ice axe: A specialized tool used in ice climbing and mountaineering, typically consisting of a sharp pick on one end and a curved adze or hammer on the other. Used for cutting steps, self-arresting in the event of a fall, or anchoring oneself to the ice.

ice climbing: Climbing on ice formations such as frozen waterfalls, glaciers, or ice-covered rock faces, using specialized equipment such as ice axes and crampons.

ice tool: A specialized tool used in ice climbing, typically consisting of a pick and an adze or hammer, designed to provide grip and stability on ice.

lead climbing: Climbing a route from the bottom while attaching the rope to protection (either bolts or traditional gear) as one ascends. Lead climbers must also clip into protection to prevent long falls.

mixed climbing: A style of climbing that combines elements of ice climbing and rock climbing, often involving climbing on both ice and rock surfaces.

mountaineering: The activity of climbing mountains, often involving technical skills such as rock climbing, ice climbing, and glacier travel.

multipitch climbing: Climbing routes that are longer than a single rope length, requiring climbers to belay each other at intermediate anchors along the route.

no-fall zone: A section of a climbing route where falling is not an option due to the severity of consequences, such as injury or death.

pitch: A section of a climbing route between two belay points or anchors.

quickdraw: A piece of equipment consisting of two carabiners connected by a short, sewn loop of webbing, used to connect the rope to bolts or other protection.

Sky: Highlining

aerial silking: A form of aerial acrobatics involving the use of long fabric strips suspended from a height for performers to climb, wrap, and suspend themselves from.

anchor: A fixed point, typically a sturdy rock, tree, bolt, or other secure structure, to which the highline is attached.

backup (line): A secondary safety line used to prevent catastrophic failure in case the main line fails.

Core (slackline webbing): A type of high-performance slackline webbing known for its strength and low stretch, typically used by advanced slackliners for longlines and highlines.

derigging: The process of taking down and disassembling a highline after use.

dynamic rope: A type of rope designed to stretch under load, commonly used in highlining and climbing for safety purposes.

Dyneema/Dyneemite webbing: A brand of ultra-high-molecular-weight polyethylene fiber known for its strength and durability. Dyneemite webbing refers to a type of slackline webbing made from Dyneema fibers.

Frankenline: A highline assembled from various types or pieces of webbing, often as an experimental setup.

free solo: Climbing or highlining without the use of a harness and rope or safety leash, relying solely on one's skill and abilities.

freestyle: A style of highlining that focuses on performing tricks, flips, and other acrobatic maneuvers on the slackline.

harness: A safety device worn by highliners, climbers, and rope-access workers to secure themselves to the line.

highline: A type of slackline setup at considerable height, typically spanning across a gap like a canyon or between cliffs or trees.

highline gear: Equipment specifically designed for highlining, including harnesses, safety leashes, and tensioning systems.

leash: A safety line attached to a highliner's harness to prevent falling to the ground in case of a slip.

leash falls: Occurrences in highlining when a participant falls from the line but is caught by a safety leash attached to them.

leash ring: A metal ring attached to a highline or slackline used for attaching a safety leash to prevent falls.

midline: A highline set at a lower height, typically closer to the ground, often used for practice or training purposes.

onsight: In highlining or climbing, refers to successfully completing a route or line on the first attempt without any prior knowledge or practice.

perma-rig: A permanent rigging setup for a highline, allowing for easier access and more frequent practice sessions without the need for extensive setup each time.

personal record: The best performance or achievement by an individual in a particular activity, often measured in terms of distance, time, or difficulty.

proprioception: The sense of the relative position of one's own body parts and the strength and effort being employed in movement.

ratchet line: A type of slackline tightened using a ratcheting mechanism, commonly used for beginner and short-distance setups.

rigging: The process of setting up and securing the slackline, including attaching it to anchors and tensioning the line properly.

Rollex: A specialized line-locking device designed for use in slacklining and highlining. It is used in tensioning the slackline while also facilitating sliding on the line when hanging below it in the harness.

send: Refers to successfully completing a highline crossing without falling.

session: A period of time dedicated to practicing or attempting a particular highline, often consisting of multiple attempts or crossings.

sit start: A technique for starting a highline from a sitting position, often used to minimize the risk of falling during initial attempts.

slackline: A length of flat webbing tensioned between two anchor points used for balance training.

tagline: A paracord or other thin rope used to assist in setting up the highlines by pulling the webbing across a gap.

tether: A short length of rope or webbing used to connect a highliner to the slackline or leash.

wafer: A small, flat device used to hold tension on the slackline or highline while rigging, allowing for easier adjustments.

webbing: The material used for slacklines and highlines, usually made of nylon or polyester.

weblock: A device used to tension and secure the slackline or highline, providing a safe anchor point.

NOTES

1 Julie Rak, *False Summit: Gender in Mountaineering Nonfiction* (McGill-Queen's University Press, 2021), 6.

2 Brené Brown, *Daring Greatly: How the Courage to Be Vulnerable Transforms the Way We Live, Love, Parent, and Lead* (Avery, 2015), 32.

3 René Daumal, *Mount Analogue: A Novel of Symbolically Authentic Non-Euclidean Adventures in Mountain Climbing, trans. Roger Shattuck* (Exact Change, 2019).

4 The worldwide standard for measuring highline *lengths* is the metric system, so metric measurements will appear first for these, followed by the imperial conversion.

5 Sarah Gmeiner and Philipp Gesing, *ISA: Demographics Survey*, International Slackline Association, 2022, data.slacklineinternational.org/publications/demographics-survey/.

6 Sarah Gmeiner and Philipp Gesing, *ISA: Demographics Survey*, International Slackline Association, 2022, data.slacklineinternational.org/publications/demographics-survey/.

7 Alan Cohen, *The Dragon Doesn't Live Here Anymore: Living Fully, Loving Freely* (Fawcett, 1981), 140.

8 "Men's Health Questions Answered: What Is Low Testosterone?" Department of Surgery, Washington University School of Medicine in St. Louis, June 11, 2020, surgery.wustl.edu/mens-health-low-testosterone/.

9 Sarah Gmeiner and Philipp Gesing, *ISA: Demographics Survey*, International Slackline Association, 2022, 2, data.slacklineinternational.org/publications/demographics-survey/.

10 Jaimal Yogis, *The Fear Project: What Our Most Primal Emotion Taught Me about Survival, Success, Surfing...and Love* (Rodale Books, 2013), 150.

11 David Guterson, *East of the Mountains* (Bloomsbury, 1999), 138; my paraphrase and formatting.

WORKS CITED

Brown, Brené. *Daring Greatly: How the Courage to Be Vulnerable Transforms the Way We Live, Love, Parent, and Lead.* Avery, 2015.

Cohen, Alan. *The Dragon Doesn't Live Here Anymore: Living Fully, Loving Freely.* Fawcett, 1981.

Daumal, René. *Mount Analogue: A Novel of Symbolically Authentic Non-Euclidean Adventures in Mountain Climbing. Translated by Roger Shattuck.* Exact Change, 2019.

Gmeiner, Sarah, and Philipp Gesing. *ISA: Demographics Survey*. International Slackline Association, 2022. data.slacklineinternational.org/publications/demographics-survey/.

Guterson, David. *East of the Mountains.* Bloomsbury, 1999.

"Men's Health Questions Answered: What Is Low Testosterone?" Department of Surgery, Washington University School of Medicine in St. Louis, June 11, 2020. surgery.wustl.edu/mens-health-low-testosterone/.

Rak, Julie. *False Summit: Gender in Mountaineering Nonfiction.* McGill-Queen's University Press, 2021.

Yogis, Jaimal. *The Fear Project: What Our Most Primal Emotion Taught Me about Survival, Success, Surfing...and Love*. Rodale Books, 2013.

Denisa Krásná, Tenerife, Spain. Photo by Pena Vychodil.

WERNER

CONTRIBUTORS

Part I: Rivers

Maddie Kimmel (United States)

Maddie Kimmel comes from a family of whitewater kayakers and was introduced to the sport during summers with her family in the Ottawa Valley. After a nomadic early childhood, she and her family settled down in the Washington, DC, area where she started training slalom at the age of 9. In 2019 she was a member of the US National Canoe Slalom Team and competed in the world championships in Kraków, Poland. Eventually, she transitioned into the creeking side of the sport and her passion for going fast has only grown since then. She has twice won the Great Falls Race, qualified for the final at the North Fork Championship at 16, and competed in the Little White Salmon Race in 2023. She was also the first woman to land a Cobra Flip and was voted Grom of the Year by Whitewater Awards in 2022. However, the accomplishment she is most proud of is authoring the Zero Excuses Policy, the first in the sport to formalize and advocate for equal pay, recognition, and representation for women in whitewater. She is a self-proclaimed nerd whose overnighter essential is a book. Currently, she lives in Seattle where she is pursuing an environmental engineering degree at the University of Washington. She is still trying to figure out what she wants to do with this one life but hopes it is something that makes this planet slightly better and more just than when she found it.

Rafa on the Misahuallí River. Photo by Luigi Castilloni.

Naina Adhikari (India)

Naina Adhikari is leading the charge for female kayakers in India. Growing up in Nainital, a small town in the Himalayan foothills, she moved away from home as a teenager to be able to practice kayaking. On the mighty Ganga River, she honed her skills with passion and determination. After a fortuitous reach out to an American kayaker, she traveled to Chile to paddle in a crew of all women, changing her perspective on kayaking and ultimately the trajectory of her life. She competed in Germany at the Canoe Slalom World Championships in 2022 and won the Best Indian Female Paddler Award at the Ganga Kayak Festival in 2023. She is currently living in her home country with a mission to get more women on the water. Stepping into a leadership role, she founded the Ganga Girls, with the mission of creating a space for women to train, instruct, and empower each other on the river. She is proud to be an instructor with the Ganga Girls, which has already begun leading all-female expeditions, and Nari Nauka, the first Indian all-women guide course.

Darcy Gaechter (United States)

Darcy Gaechter is the first and only woman to kayak the Amazon River from source to sea. She has participated in whitewater kayaking races throughout the world and has led kayaking expeditions in 18 different countries. She owns her own adventure kayaking business called Small World Adventures and has been a kayak adventure travel guide for two decades. She is also a long-time volunteer for the Ecuadorian Rivers Institute. She is the author of the adventure memoir *Amazon Woman: Facing Fears, Chasing Dreams, and a Quest to Kayak the World's Largest River from Source to Sea* that chronicles both her life and her trip down the Amazon River. She is also a co-author of *The Kayaker's Guide to Ecuador* and an author of numerous articles about whitewater kayaking, the guiding business, and river conservation. She has long been a groundbreaker for women pushing the limits in whitewater kayaking and other outdoor pursuits. Leading by example as to what women can accomplish in a predominately male sport, she has inspired other women athletes to push themselves to achieve extraordinary things.

Jenny Vasquez (United States)

Jenny (Jennifer) Vasquez is an American Colombian whitewater kayaker. She is a first-generation American whose parents emigrated from Colombia. She recently closed a chapter of her life by graduating from Appalachian State University in 2022 with degrees in political science and Spanish. With a fierce desire to explore life outside of the southeastern US, and improve her whitewater skills, she moved to the town of White Salmon, the heart of Pacific Northwest whitewater. She worked as a guide where she quickly became proficient at whitewater rafting and kayaking. She loves the joy and challenge of combining whitewater kayaking techniques with acrobatic maneuvers and tricks in her slicey boat, along with running difficult whitewater. She is often on the local rivers before sunrise or finishing a lap at sunset. She plans on combining her passion for whitewater with her connection to her Colombian roots by exploring the local whitewater on the rivers of Colombia in the winter of 2024.

Alena Rainsberry (United States)

Alena Rainsberry is a queer American kayaker who wants to explore rivers all around the world. Introduced to whitewater kayaking four years ago, she quickly fell in love with the joys and challenges of the sport and has been dedicated to improving her river running skills ever since. Before long, she found herself navigating rapids from the Ecuadorian jungle to the Indian Himalayas. She previously traveled and worked for multiple years as an English teacher in the Czech Republic (where she became friends with Denisa!). She thrives in immersing herself in diverse cultural environments and has a knack for making friends and community wherever she goes. She is a passionate advocate for increasing representation, getting women into the outdoors, and encouraging people to experience new skills. She is from the Pacific Northwest, where she currently lives and kayaks.

Rafaela Sánchez Castillo (Ecuador)

Rafaela (Rafa) Sánchez Castillo is a rising star from the province of Pastaza in Ecuador. She began her kayaking at just 11 years old, finding both peace and exhilaration in the sport. With the help of her coaches and friends, she has learned how to overcome fear and obstacles as she navigates the jungle rivers of her home country. She is passionate about being a steward for the environment, consistently removing litter from the water, and is an advocate against the illegal mining that is destroying her local rivers. She has her sights set on ambitious goals and trains hard to improve her skills. She has also started competing, participating in the slalom Cosanga Race in 2023 and is a two-time national kayak champion. When she is kayaking, she revels in the joy of new friendships formed on the rivers and the natural beauty of her jungle home.

Part II: Rock

Janel Lynn Rieger-Chávez (United States)

Janel Lynn Rieger-Chávez is a rock, ice, and alpine climber with eight years of experience. She is of the Otomi Tribe in the Nahua Nation. She grew up in the Midwest and works as an engineering and programming teacher and climbing guide. While she has only been ice and alpine climbing for two years of her climbing experience, she has climbed some big mountains, including Tacoma (Rainier), Wilson, and Koma Kulshan (Baker). She loves long days in the mountains, creating spaces for BIPOC climbers, and outdoor education. In the summer of 2022, she led nine BIPOC climbers from the Midwest up Koma Kulshan. She spent the preceding winter teaching the group technical mountaineering skills like crevasse rescue and snow travel to properly prepare everyone. When not climbing and teaching, she loves to hang out with her two cats, bird watching, and watching sci-fi TV shows while eating ice cream.

Kavitha Mohan (India)

Kavitha Mohan is a passionate climber hailing from Kerala, India, whose journey to self-discovery has taken her from the bustling streets of New Delhi to the majestic heights of the Himalayas. Born into a progressive family that valued education and independence, she found solace in nature from a young age, exploring the lush forests and sun-kissed meadows of her homeland. After earning a degree in chemical engineering and embarking on a career in the corporate world, she found herself grappling with the pressures of a toxic work environment and the societal expectations placed upon women in their 30s in India. Determined to forge her own path, she made the bold decision to leave her job and pursue her passion for climbing, despite facing skepticism and judgment from those around her. Today, she continues to pursue her passion for climbing with unwavering dedication, seeking out new challenges and adventures both on the rocks and in life. Through her journey, she hopes to inspire other women to break free from societal constraints and embrace their true selves, one climb at a time.

Marianna Tarczyńska (Poland)

Marianna Tarczyńska is a professional climber, mountaineer, photographer, and author. Supported by big brands such as La Sportiva, Petzl, and Deuter, she is a professional athlete with worldwide outreach, motivating real change for women in adventure sports. Originally from Poland, she has been based in Ecuador for more than five years, working as a professional mountain guide. She is the founder of the Ropes of Freedom project (Cordada Libertad) that is looking for gender liberation in adventure sports like mountaineering. Through the project, she wants to redefine the values necessary to climb mountains. Up until now, she has led several women's teams climbing the most important peaks in Ecuador, including Iliniza Sur, Antisana, Cayambe, Cotopaxi, and Chimborazo. You can find her both on glaciers in the Andes and climbing hard routes on the rock.

Sydney Pham (United States)

Sydney Pham is a queer Vietnamese American rock climber and mountaineer born and raised in Washington state. Her love affair with the natural world started from a young age as she grew up surrounded by the beautiful, lush, mountainous scenery of the Pacific Northwest. She now enjoys long, challenging days climbing in the mountains and pushing her limits. While she enjoys many forms of climbing, her absolute favorite is alpine climbing due to the remote exploration and the physical and mental demands. She is currently a graduate student at the University of Utah studying nurse anesthesia. When she's not studying or climbing, she enjoys sewing custom gear and bags.

Anna Šebestíková (Czech Republic)

Anna Šebestíková was born in Prague and grew up in České Budějovice in the south of the Czech Republic. She is a versatile climber with a strong passion for mountaineering and Czech sandstone climbing. Her climbing journey spans various disciplines, from sports routes and traditional climbing to mixed and ice climbing. Some of her proudest ascents include Crackistan and Bloody Mary, both in Nangma Valley, Pakistan, and the first repetition of Dionýsos on Les Petites Jorasses in Chamonix, France. Besides her big wall ascents in the mountains, she values her off-width ascents in Adršpach, in the Czech Republic. By climbing Turkey Crack in Cadarese, Italy, she also became the first Czech woman to climb a trad route graded 8a. She is currently studying for a master's degree in data engineering in chemistry in order to be able to work from anywhere in the future. Apart from climbing, she enjoys skiing, cycling, and baking cakes, which she eagerly shares with friends. An avid enthusiast of good beer and music across all genres, she finds joy in these simple pleasures. Known for her stubbornness and penchant for doing things her own way, she approaches challenges with determination and resilience. She dreams of climbing beautiful crack routes all around the world, in Utah, Yosemite, and the mountains of Patagonia.

Sofia Tapia (México)

Sofia Tapia is an avid climber and co-founder of a project aimed at developing new climbing zones in Chiapas, México. She and her husband have now opened over 200 routes across various climbing zones in Chiapas. As an Indigenous woman climber in southern México, she has become a leader in the outdoor community and an inspiration to many other women whom she introduced to the world of outdoor adventure. For her, climbing has become a new way of understanding her existence and a personal challenge for self-improvement. It has helped her find motivation in life and achieve harmony between her body, mind, and spirit. With her partner, she has founded Vertigo Rock Climbing, a company that offers climbing courses and day tours. She guides and teaches beginners in rock climbing, and has recently opened a bouldering gym where she teaches classes to children, young adults, and adults, and slowly creates a community of climbers in her home state of Chiapas.

Part III: Sky

Faith Dickey (United States)

Faith Dickey is an American slackliner renowned as one of the world's first professional slackliners. Throughout her impressive career, she has achieved several remarkable milestones, including becoming the first woman to free solo highline and matching men's world records in the sport. Notably, she set multiple records for the longest highline walks, including a groundbreaking 96-meter (315-foot) highline send in the Czech Republic in 2012, where she also organizes the annual Women's Highline Meeting. She has crossed highlines in stunning locations such as the French and Swiss Alps and the Todra Gorge in Morocco. Beyond her highline achievements, she is a passionate advocate for gender equality in extreme sports. Through her guiding company, she actively inspires and encourages more women to participate in the sport. She has been featured in numerous documentaries, television shows, and publications, sharing her love for slacklining with a wider audience. She currently resides in Moab, Utah, with her partner and their cat.

Brenda Gómez Ortiz (México)

Brenda Gómez Ortiz is a Mexican highliner who believes in making dreams a reality. She has been practicing slacklining for over seven years, with a particular passion for highlining. She also started practicing highline freestyle, a subdiscipline of highlining still dominated by men. Slacklining has given her a world of opportunities where she has learned that, with dedication, practice, and discipline, even the wildest dreams can come true, including walking and dancing in the sky. Her love for constant movement and exploring new ways to play drew her to this discipline. She focuses on making her practice fun by experimenting with new body postures on the line, combining elements of yoga and acrobatics. As a biologist, she is always curious to discover herself and the world around her. Highlining has allowed her to connect with her body and mind, as well as the natural world, enabling her to discover incredible new places from a new perspective. Her community of fellow slackliners has been another motivation for her to continue developing her skills.

Rae Raptor aka Cheryll Glotfelty (United States)

At 66, Rae Raptor is quite likely the world's oldest highliner. As Cheryll Glotfelty, at the University of Nevada, Reno, she became the nation's first Professor of Literature and Environment. She enjoyed a 28-year career before retiring in 2018 to start a new chapter of life. Glotfelty published six books as an academic, including *The Ecocriticism Reader: Landmarks in Literary Ecology*, *The Bioregional Imagination: Literature, Ecology, and Place*, and, most recently, *Peter Goin and the Photography of Environmental Change: Visual Literacy and Altered Landscapes*. As Rae Raptor, she is currently writing a new book about her highline journey entitled *Step by Step: Come Alive at Any Age*.

Anna Hanuš Kuchařová (Czech Republic)

Anna Hanuš Kuchařová discovered the world of slacklining while studying architecture in times when slacklining was still a very marginal activity. She became the first Czech female highliner to gain worldwide recognition as a holder of a series of highlining records, including the European women's highline length record and being the first highliner to spend 24 hours on the line without a break. More importantly, she began to organize international highlining expeditions in areas that were waiting for their first highline projects. Many of these expeditions are documented on film and have been streamed at outdoor festivals all around the world, such as Jan Žůrek's 2020 film, *Connection*. Her passion for highlining soon outgrew her zest for architecture, and since both required her full attention, she decided to become a professional slackliner. She became one of the first women in the world to make slacklining her profession when she founded the Slackline Academy through which she started offering exhibitions, lectures, and slackline courses for the general public. She wrote her own book (in Czech), married her husband on a highline in the world's first highline wedding, and became media-famous in her country. She has decided to use her public voice to break stereotypes about women in adventure sports and beyond, most recently by documenting the physical and mental challenges she's had to tackle since she gave birth to her firstborn son two years ago. After a long recovery, she is now returning to highlining, ready to bring her new life experiences into her sport and continue to inspire others to pursue their dreams.

Denisa Krásná (Czech Republic)

Denisa Krásná is a Czech highliner and climber with ambitions as lofty as her lines in the sky. After making remarkable progress in her first year of slacklining, she started taking her webbing to new heights and rigging lines reaching hundreds of meters in length, thousands of feet in the air, in places such as Yosemite, the Dolomites, the Stawamus Chief, the Czech sandstone towers, the Bavarian Alps, Tenerife, and others. She aims to walk long lines in high, beautiful airscapes all over the world, particularly in the mountains where she can combine her passion for highlining, climbing, alpinism, hiking, and simply appreciating the beauty of the mountainous landscape from new perspectives. When she's not on the line, she is a dedicated scholar. Her main areas of expertise are Indigenous studies, critical animal and vegan studies, environmental humanities, and ecofeminism.

Dorothea Hamilton (Germany)

"Like a regular mom, just cooler," Dorothea Hamilton is a record-breaking highliner, geographer, and the mother of four kids, who is constantly breaking gender barriers in adventure sports. Her Instagram handle, Highlining_mom, reflects her mission to inspire and motivate women to follow their passions and to challenge the conventional notion that motherhood necessitates sacrificing one's own interests. Through her social media platforms, she has been able to document her journey as a highliner and mother of four, encouraging other women to see that motherhood need not be an obstacle to pursuing one's dreams. She recently gave birth to her fourth child. Yet, even when she was pregnant, she continued to pursue her passion for highlining, documenting her training and adventures on social media until the very late stages of her pregnancy. Despite the challenges of pregnancy and motherhood, she refused to let go of her love for highlining and continued to push herself to new heights, both physically and mentally. Her ability to continue training and documenting her journey while pregnant is an inspiration to other women. By showing it is possible to balance motherhood and adventure, she is paving the way for a more inclusive and empowering culture in adventure sports.

Mia Noblet (Canada)

Mia Noblet, born with an innate love for the mountains, has emerged as a trailblazing figure in the world of highlining. Her journey into highlining began in 2015, marked by a fearless pursuit of new challenges and records. Renowned for her exceptional endurance and physical and mental strength, she has shattered world records and is currently one of the world-record holders after she sent a 2.7-kilometer-long (1.7-mile) highline in France. With a pioneering spirit and a commitment to pushing the boundaries of the sport, she continues to inspire and empower enthusiasts worldwide, leaving an indelible mark on the world of highlining.

We would like to take this opportunity to acknowledge the Traditional Territories upon which we live and work. In Calgary, Alberta, we acknowledge the Niitsítapi (Blackfoot) and the people of the Treaty 7 region in Southern Alberta, which includes the Siksika, the Piikuni, the Kainai, the Tsuut'ina, and the Stoney Nakoda First Nations, including Chiniki, Bearpaw, and Wesley First Nations. The City of Calgary is also home to Métis Nation of Alberta, Region III. In Victoria, British Columbia, we acknowledge the Traditional Territories of the Lkwungen (Esquimalt, and Songhees), Malahat, Pacheedaht, Scia'new, T'Sou-ke and W̱SÁNEĆ (Pauquachin, Tsartlip, Tsawout, Tseycum) peoples.